Resilient Destinations and Tourism

Sustainability is one of the most important issues currently facing the tourism sector. Recently, the role of resilience thinking has been highlighted in sustainable development discussions as an alternative perspective. This book approaches these concepts as interwoven processes and looks at change through a socio-ecological lens.

Instead of seeing resilience and sustainability as alternative approaches, *Resilient Destinations and Tourism* argues that resilience should be understood as a fundamental part of sustainable tourism thinking for destination systems, and calls for better governance in implementation and management. Improving governance is the key issue in sustainable tourism development. The chapters in this edited collection focus on resilient destinations from a governance perspective, in which tourism resilience is contextualized as an integral part of pathway creation in the process of moving towards sustainable tourism. The contributions to the book represent a range of theoretical and empirical approaches with a wide international scope. *Resilient Destinations and Tourism* calls for rethinking the meaning of sustainable development in tourism and looks at how sustainability and resilience could be integrated.

This book will appeal to a wide range of research disciplines and students whose modules focus on the relationship between tourism and sustainability planning, governance, the environment, and hazards and disasters.

Jarkko Saarinen is a Professor of Geography at the University of Oulu, Finland, and Distinguished Visiting Professor (Sustainability Management) at the University of Johannesburg, South Africa.

Alison M. Gill is a Professor Emerita in the Department of Geography and School of Resource and Environmental Management at Simon Fraser University, Vancouver, Canada.

Contemporary Geographies of Leisure, Tourism and Mobility
Series Editor: C. Michael Hall
Professor at the Department of Management, College of Business and Economics, University of Canterbury, Christchurch, New Zealand

The aim of this series is to explore and communicate the intersections and relationships between leisure, tourism and human mobility within the social sciences.

It will incorporate both traditional and new perspectives on leisure and tourism from contemporary geography, e.g. notions of identity, representation and culture, while also providing for perspectives from cognate areas such as anthropology, cultural studies, gastronomy and food studies, marketing, policy studies and political economy, regional and urban planning, and sociology, within the development of an integrated field of leisure and tourism studies.

Also, increasingly, tourism and leisure are regarded as steps in a continuum of human mobility. Inclusion of mobility in the series offers the prospect to examine the relationship between tourism and migration, the sojourner, educational travel, and second home and retirement travel phenomena.

The series comprises two strands:

Routledge Studies in Contemporary Geographies of Leisure, Tourism and Mobility is a forum for innovative new research intended for research students and academics, and the titles will be available in hardback only.

Contemporary Geographies of Leisure, Tourism and Mobility aims to address the needs of students and academics, and the titles will be published in hardback and paperback. Titles include:

Co-Creating Tourism Research
Towards Collaborative Ways of Knowing
Edited by Carina Ren, Gunnar Thór Jóhannesson and René van der Duim

Resilient Destinations and Tourism
Governance Strategies in the Transition towards Sustainability in Tourism
Edited by Jarkko Saarinen and Alison M. Gill

For more information about this series, please visit: www.routledge.com/ Contemporary-Geographies-of-Leisure-Tourism-and-Mobility/book-series/SE0522

Resilient Destinations and Tourism

Governance Strategies in the Transition towards Sustainability in Tourism

Edited by Jarkko Saarinen and Alison M. Gill

Routledge
Taylor & Francis Group

LONDON AND NEW YORK

First published 2019
by Routledge
2 Park Square, Milton Park, Abingdon, Oxon OX14 4RN

and by Routledge
52 Vanderbilt Avenue, New York, NY 10017

First issued in paperback 2020

Routledge is an imprint of the Taylor & Francis Group, an informa business

British Library Cataloguing-in-Publication Data
A catalogue record for this book is available from the British Library

Library of Congress Cataloging-in-Publication Data
A catalog record has been requested for this book

ISBN 13: 978-0-367-58216-6 (pbk)
ISBN 13: 978-1-138-06177-4 (hbk)

Typeset in Times New Roman
by Wearset Ltd, Boldon, Tyne and Wear

Contents

Figures

Tables

Contributors

Susanne Becken is Director of the Griffith Institute for Tourism and a Professor of Sustainable Tourism at Griffith University, Australia. Susanne has led a broad range of large-scale government-funded research projects and consultancy work in Asia-Pacific and for global organizations such as the UNWTO, UNEP, UNISDR and UNESCO. Susanne has widely published on sustainable tourism, climate change, resource use, tourist behavior, environmental policy, and risk management.

Patrick Brouder is a Researcher at Vancouver Island University as well as a Senior Research Fellow at the University of Johannesburg. He serves on the editorial board of *Tourism Geographies* and on the steering committee of the International Polar Tourism Research Network. His research interests are tourism and economic geography.

Bishnu Devkota graduated with a Master's in Tourism Policy and Planning from the Department of Geography, University of Waterloo, Canada. He currently works with Toronto Community Housing Corporation. His research interests are the impacts of development on local communities, tourism, and disasters.

Dianne Dredge is a Visiting Professor in the Department of Service Management and Service Studies, Lund University, Sweden. Her research focuses on tourism as an agent of change from macro to micro contexts wherein she employs story-telling, policy ethnographies, policy network analysis, and social learning approaches. Dianne is currently Chair of the Tourism Education Futures Initiative (TEFI) and a member of the International Academy for the Study of Tourism.

Alison M. Gill is a Professor Emerita in the Department of Geography and School of Resource and Environmental Management at Simon Fraser University in Vancouver, Canada. Alison has published extensively in the area of mountain resort communities with a focus on issues of sustainability and the politics of place. Her recent research focuses on path creation and aspects of governance in tourism destinations through the lens of evolutionary economic geography.

Peter Groote is Associate Professor in the Faculty of Spatial Sciences, University of Groningen, the Netherlands. He holds a PhD in Economics (1995). A common thread in his research cross-cuts the fields of heritage studies, place meanings, and tourism.

Tina Haisch is Head of the Centre of Excellence for Innovation, Development of Regions and Competitiveness at the University of Applied Sciences and Arts, Northwestern Switzerland. She holds a PhD in Economic Geography and a Master's in Geography, Economics, and Business Administration. Her area of expertise is in local and regional economic development with a particular focus on the dynamics of innovation, value creation processes, creativity and tolerance, and resilience and sustainability. Her articles in the field of economic geography and urban planning appear in scientific journals.

C. Michael Hall is a Professor at the University of Canterbury, New Zealand. He is also a Docent in the Department of Geography, University of Oulu, Finland, and a Visiting Professor in the School of Business and Economics, Linnaeus University, Kalmar, Sweden. He is a co-editor of *Current Issues in Tourism*. He has published widely on tourism, regional development, food and wine, and environmental change.

Kevin Hannam is a Professor and currently Dean of the Faculty of International Tourism at City University Macau and a Research Fellow at the University of Johannesburg. He is a founding co-editor of the journals *Mobilities* and *Applied Mobilities* (Routledge) and has published over 100 research articles and book chapters. He has a PhD in Geography from the University of Portsmouth and is a Fellow of the Royal Geographical Society (FRGS).

Jasper Heslinga obtained his PhD at the Department of Cultural Geography in the Faculty of Spatial Sciences, University of Groningen, the Netherlands and currently works for the European Tourism Futures Institute (part of NHL Stenden University). He is interested in tourism planning, nature-based tourism, landscape management, multi-level governance, institutions, stakeholder analysis, historical content analysis, and policy analysis.

Api Movono is a recent PhD graduate (Griffith University, Australia) and Lecturer at the School of Tourism and Hospitality Management, University of the South Pacific, Suva, Fiji. His research is focused on indigenous communities that are involved in tourism and examines issues related to vulnerabilities, resilience livelihoods, and change in society.

Johanna Nalau is a Postdoctoral Research Fellow with Griffith Climate Change Response Program (GCCRP) and Griffith Institute for Tourism (GIFT), specializing in climate change adaptation policy-making and decision-making processes. Her research focuses on understanding how policy-makers and decision-makers deal with some of the central assumptions related to climate change adaptation and the array of factors and processes that drive and constrain climate change adaptation, including constraints emerging from adaptation science and theory.

Sanjay K. Nepal is a Professor in the Department of Geography and Environmental Management at the University of Waterloo, Canada. His areas of interest include environmental and social complexities in local interactions with parks and protected area agencies and ecological and cultural change associated with tourism development.

Jarkko Saarinen is a Professor of Geography at the University of Oulu, Finland, and Distinguished Visiting Professor (Sustainability Management) at the University of Johannesburg, South Africa. His research interests include tourism and development, sustainability in tourism, tourism and climate change adaptation, tourism–community relations, and wilderness studies. He is editor of *Tourism Geographies*. His recent publications include co-edited books: *Borderless Worlds for Whom? Ethics, Moralities and Mobilities* (2019), *Tourism Planning and Development* (2018), and *Political Ecology and Tourism* (2016).

Sayaka Sakuma is a PhD candidate in the Department of Geography and Environment at the University of Hawai'i at Mānoa, Honolulu, USA. Her dissertation research focuses on homestay tourism and nature conservation initiatives in the northern part of Okinawa Island. She conducted ethnographic research as a Center for Japanese Studies Fellow from 2016 to 2018.

Frank Vanclay has been a Professor and Head of the Department of Cultural Geography in the Faculty of Spatial Sciences, University of Groningen, the Netherlands, since July 2010. He is transdisciplinary as well as transcontinental in his perspective. Originally from Australia, he specializes in the following areas: social impact assessment (SIA); social understandings of place; social aspects of environmental management; and natural resource management.

Sarah Wongkee is a recent graduate from Simon Fraser University, Canada with a Master's in Resource Management where her research focused on the factors of resilience and vulnerability in a resort municipality's retail sector. She is currently a Policy Analyst at Natural Resources Canada in Vancouver.

Part I

Introduction

1 Introduction

Placing resilience in the sustainability frame

Jarkko Saarinen and Alison M. Gill

Introduction

Sustainability and resilience are complex ideas and their relationship can be conceptualized and applied in multiple ways. This book approaches these concepts as interwoven processes that work with change in socio-ecological system contexts. Although there are some key differences between the concepts, for example, in respect to spatial and temporal scales, resilience is understood here as an integral part of sustainability thinking. Sustainable development has become a paradigm, although a troubled one, in various policy and planning discourses and models. In a report, *Revisiting Sustainable Development*, the United Nations Research Institute for Social Development (UNRISD, 2015) refers to the great policy success of sustainability in development discussions. The report states that "virtually all development actors and organizations, and the public at large, have bought into the narrative of sustainable development" (Utting, 2015, p. 1). Similarly, in the context of tourism studies the idea of sustainability is often seen as "one of the great success stories of tourism research and knowledge transfer" (Hall, 2011, p. 649), making tourism and related studies highly policy relevant issues in development discussions.

A need for sustainability has been integrated into management and governance models in various planning and development scales, emphasizing the positive role and change that tourism could make for destination communities and environments (Bramwell, 2011; Butler, 1999; Hall & Lew, 1999; Lu & Nepal, 2009). This beneficial and prospective developmental role of the industry is highlighted in many international policy documents and declarations. For decades, the World Tourism Organization (UNWTO) has emphasized the positive difference the growth of international tourism makes to global and local economies. According to UNWTO (2018) international tourist arrivals have increased from 25 million in 1950 to 1.3 billion worldwide in 2017. At the same time, international tourism receipts have grown from US$2 million in 1950 to US$1.220 billion in 2016. Based on a World Travel and Tourism Council (WTTC, 2017) estimate, the direct, indirect, and induced gross domestic product (GDP) impact of the tourism and travel sector generated over 10 percent of global GDP in 2016, and in the past few years the industry has grown faster than world trade in general.

Based on the massive scale of tourism and its growth prospects, many international development agencies state that the industry could be used in tackling global scale challenges, such as extreme poverty (see Brickley, Black, & Cottrell, 2013; Saarinen, Rogerson, & Manwa, 2013; Scheyvens, 2011). The World Bank (2012), for example, has indicated that the tourism industry is an attractive vehicle for poverty alleviation and development and recently, in the context of the United Nations Sustainable Development Goals (UN SDGs), the World Bank Group (2017) launched its list of 20 reasons why tourism works for development. These elements, positioned within a sustainable tourism framework, are: sustainable economic growth; social inclusiveness, employment and poverty reduction; resource efficiency, environmental protection and climate; cultural values, diversity, and heritage; and mutual understanding, peace, and security (see also UNWTO, 2017).

Thus, in policy discourses and research sustainable tourism has been widely positioned as a "tool for development, benefitting communities in destinations around the world" (World Bank Group, 2017, p. 5). However, local and global realities may often be perceived differently as (sustainable) tourism development "comes with its own set of risks and challenges" (World Bank, 2012, p. 7; see also Mowforth & Munt, 1998; Scheyvens, 2011). Related to this, Sinclair (1998) has noted that the positive economic aspects of tourism should be placed in an equation consisting of both the advantages and disadvantages of tourism-based development. Moreover, Utting (2015, p. 1) has stated that the core elements of sustainability may "often got lost in translation" when we are actually 'doing development' (see Hunter & Green, 1995; Saarinen, 2018). In academic research this has led to increasing, and often harsh, criticism among scholars on the applicability of sustainable development thinking to tourism (see Butler, 1999; Liu, 2003; Scheyvens, 2009; Sharpley, 2000). After all, tourism is a global scale growth industry by nature and recently Hollenhorst, Houge-MacKenzie, and Ostergren (2014, p. 306), for example, have critically noted that

> tourism hides its unsustainability behind a mask that is all the more beguiling because it appears so sustainable. We too easily imagine that tourism is the embodiment of sustainability, when in reality it may represent unrealized hopes and desires for the world we want to live in.

In this respect the growth of the industry may not necessarily lead to (sustainable) development for localities where tourism takes place (see Holden, 2008; Saarinen, 2014; Schilcher, 2007).

The kind of deep frustration that emerges from three decades of active research and discussion on sustainable tourism development and management has caused some scholars to conclude that the idea and applicability of sustainable tourism has reached a dead end. Sharpley (2009, p. xiii), for example, has suggested that it is now time to move beyond sustainability as the "academic study of sustainable tourism development has reached something of an impasse." However, moving beyond the sustainable tourism paradigm has turned out to be a challenging task (McCool & Bosak, 2016; Saarinen, 2014). First, as noted above, the idea of sustainability is widely utilized by tourism policy-makers and institutions that define the goals and governance models for tourism and development at various spatial scales ranging from local to global approaches. There is also a strong body of research and study programs that specialize in sustainable tourism, which support the key role of sustainability in tourism planning and development thinking (Saarinen, Rogerson, & Hall, 2017).

Second, the position of sustainable tourism is a paradoxical one (Hall, 2011). While the concept is fuzzy and difficult to implement in tourism planning and development practices, its role and application in tourism is now more urgent than ever before. In addition to the current massive scale of global tourism, UNWTO (2011) estimates that international tourist arrivals will increase over 3 percentage points a year between 2010 and 2030 to reach 1.8 billion arrivals by 2030. These passenger numbers are largely based on air transport, which is seen as highly detrimental to the environment and a major contributor to global warming (Gössling & Hall, 2006). Thus, there is an increasing need for development thinking that would lead to better environmental management of tourism impacts at different spatial and temporal scales. Third, if the future route towards better environmental management is not to be based on sustainable development thinking, there needs to be a viable alternative governance framework. However, the search for an alternative has turned out to be a major task. Recently, one prospective approach has focused on the idea of resilience originating from dynamic systems' thinking in the environmental sciences (Berkes & Ross, 2013; see also Holling, 1973).

In general, resilience refers to the capacity of a (socio-ecological) system, such as a local ecosystem or community, to absorb disturbance and reorganize its functionality while undergoing a change (Adger, 2000; Folke, 2006). Some discussants have pondered if resilience could represent the new sustainability in resource management (see Brill, Peck, & Kramer, 2015; Davidson, 2010). Also, in tourism research "resilience planning has emerged in recent years as an alternative to the sustainable development paradigm" (Lew, 2014, p. 14). Current thinking (discussed later: see Chapters 2 and 3) does not, however, strongly support such a step or interpretation (see also Butler, 2017; Hall, Prayag, & Amore, 2018; Lew & Cheer, 2018). This was also indicated in the United Nations report *Resilient people, resilient planet: A future worth choosing*, which placed the issue of resilience within the context of global sustainability, as a tool to help put sustainable development into practice (see United Nations, 2012).

Thus, instead of seeing resilience and sustainability as alternative approaches or a matter of a zero-sum game, we argue in this book that resilience should be understood as a fundamental part of sustainable tourism thinking and destination systems, by calling for better governance in implementation and management. This aspect of 'better' governance is the key issue in sustainable tourism development (Baggio, Scott, & Cooper, 2010; Bramwell & Lane, 2011). However, it is highly sensitive to many linked 'variables,' including the scale of analysis (see Amore & Hall, 2016; Bramwell, 2011). Contemporary tourism is obviously based on a global system, in which sustainability cannot be contained at a destination level of governance alone (see Scott, Higham, Gössling, & Peeters, 2013). In a global system, which includes origins, destinations and the routes between them as well as the overall global networks of the industry, the sustainability of tourism would require a total restructuring of the industry and transition of current modes of transportation towards carbon neutral forms of mobilities. The reality, however, is that "as one of the world's largest industries, tourism is also one of the largest emitters of carbon, primarily from air transport" (Hollenhorst et al., 2014, p. 306) as noted above (see also Becken & Hay, 2007; Scott, Hall, & Gössling, 2012; Weaver, 2011).

Obviously, this is a major challenge. While it is crucial to realize the global scale problems and impacts of tourism, this global sustainability challenge is beyond the scope of this edited volume and, indeed, this introduction. Our focus is on resilient destinations from a governance perspective, in which the resilience of tourism is contextualized as an integral part of pathway creation in the process of moving towards sustainable tourism. This approach calls for rethinking the meaning of sustainable development in tourism and how sustainability and resilience are integrated. Furthermore, the role of governance and the principal conditions of tourism governance that support transitioning towards sustainability are critical issues in this debate.

Overview of contributions to this volume

In addition to the Introduction and Conclusions, the book includes two main parts: Part II, Frameworks and conceptualizations and Part III, Applications and cases. The chapters in Part II are theoretical and conceptually driven, while those in Part III are based on empirical examples and 'real world' implications. The cases cover an array of places and circumstances that represent examples of governance responses to changes and shocks due to natural disasters, environmental change threats, and economic and rural transition stresses, especially in vulnerable tourist destinations. The individual chapters are linked through the book's focus on sustainable tourism governance and resilience thinking, with the case studies illustrating and referencing the theoretical frameworks presented in Part II. The concluding chapter (Part IV) summarizes the two main parts and highlights the key issues in respect of sustainable tourism governance and resilient destinations and the challenges and opportunities that lie ahead.

At the start of Part II, Chapter 2 by Jarkko Saarinen and Alison M. Gill contextualizes resilience thinking and destination governance within the sustainable tourism discourses. Saarinen and Gill overview the idea of sustainable development and sustainable tourism and discuss the relationship between sustainability and resilience. They acknowledge that sustainable development and sustainable tourism are highly contested ideas and extremely difficult to apply in practice, especially at a global scale. Despite these challenges, they consider the call for sustainability to be one of the most urgent issues facing the tourism industry. According to Saarinen and Gill, the destination scale provides a realistic, although limited, way to work with sustainability in tourism. They highlight the idea of resilient destinations and the need for destination governance strategies that would support transitioning towards sustainable development in tourism.

In Chapter 3, C. Michael Hall provides an overview of the different theoretical groundings of resilience and the way they have been (mis)used within the tourism literature. He draws a contrast between the ecological stance that is to be found in geographical and environmental accounts of resilience in tourism and the more static engineering approaches to be found in management and organizational studies. According to Hall, the different approaches are also regarded as having substantial implications for sustainable tourism and how destination resilience is perceived and policies are enacted. He concludes by noting the dangers associated with paradigm change regarding destination management and the extent to which the notion of resilience may be used as an opportunity for the enactment of neoliberal regimes that, ironically, may only further contribute to the vulnerability of destinations to global change.

In Chapter 4, Dianne Dredge discusses the challenging interplay between governance, tourism, and resilience. In this complex context she seeks to engage in a more critical, theoretically curious, and interdisciplinary discussion of the terms "governance" and "resilience" in the tourism context. Dredge contextualizes her discussion in twentieth-century scientific thought, late modern capitalism and the Anthropocene. Based on these historically contingent societal contexts her aim is to challenge our assumptions and excavate meanings underpinning commonly used terms such as sustainability, tourism, and governance. By doing this, she aims to discuss critically the embedded ways of thinking about these concepts.

In Chapter 5, Patrick Brouder and Jarkko Saarinen focus on co-evolution and resilient regions in the sustainable tourism development process. They contextualize the discussion in the emergence of an "evolutionary turn" within economic geography over the last two decades, which has resulted in a major step forward in tourism research and regional development studies. According to Brouder and Saarinen, this has very recently created academically prolific connections to regional and community resilience thinking with fruitful implications for tourism and tourism destination governance. For them, these connections may actually enable a deeper understanding of the relationship between the tourism economy and overall community economic development of places beyond 'destinations' alone. In this respect, Evolutionary Economic Geography (EEG) potentially provides a new path forward to an understanding of the long-term sustainable development of destinations. Brouder and Saarinen believe that the important advantage of an evolutionary approach is that it takes tourism out of a tourism-centric context and into a regional-centric context, which is vital for understanding the resilience and sustainability of places used in tourism production and consumption.

In Chapter 6, Kevin Hannam seeks to develop understandings, based on the mobilities paradigm, of the complexity of contemporary connections and disconnections as people, things, and ideas move around the world. He argues that the mobilities turn in social science brings issues of movement from the margins to the center of social theory. By doing so, he recognizes that different mobilities inform and are informed by tourism and that these are highly politicized, especially in relation to resilience and sustainable tourism governance. Hannam reflects on recent work that has been developed in terms of the mobilities paradigm with respect to climate change, transport, and sustainable cities. He further examines these issues with regard to sustainable tourism governance and resilient destinations using the example of the United Arab Emirates (UAE) and concludes with reflections on future research directions in terms of policy debates concerning sustainable tourism mobilities and resilience.

At the start of Part III, Johanna Nalau, Api Movono, and Susanne Becken (Chapter 7) focus on vulnerability and the adaptive capacity of tourism from an indigenous Pacific Islands perspective. They look at some of the emerging alternative approaches in knowledge management, tourism governance, and policy that are based on indigenous systems, and see these as an attempt to increase the resilience of the tourism sector and the socio-ecological environment it depends on. They introduce some of the key drivers of change, which are an important aspect of understanding transitioning towards sustainability of the tourism sector, in the context of Fiji. They do this by investigating two central concepts of resilience theory – vulnerability and adaptive capacity – from an indigenous Pacific Islands perspective. For Nalau, Movono, and Becken, these two conceptual models integrate indigenous governance and knowledge structures and values for a more resilient and inclusive tourism governance.

In Chapter 8, Sanjay K. Nepal and Bishnu Devkota discuss post-disaster recovery in a tourism and heritage conservation context. They examine the effects of the 2015 Nepal earthquake on Kathmandu Valley's tourism hubs, especially in and around three historic palace courtyards, which are listed as UNESCO World Heritage Sites (WHS). Based on in-depth interviews with local inhabitants, they suggest that despite the damage and destruction of Kathmandu Valley's WHS, local communities remained hopeful about heritage renewal, and proactively engaged in securing and safeguarding the damaged monuments. According to Nepal and Devkota, local inhabitants were cognizant of the strong linkages between heritage conservation, tourism, and livelihood. They conclude that the actions and responses of local communities in the immediate aftermath of the earthquake indicate a positive outlook for heritage reconstruction and tourism revival.

In Chapter 9, Tina Haisch examines resilience and collective agency in a tourism destination development in the Swiss Alps. This chapter contributes to the discussion on governance for resilience in tourism destinations by focusing on human agency, which is often a neglected perspective in sustainable tourism discussions. For Haisch, the issue of human agency is key for change and regional development in the longer-term perspective. She uses an illustrative case study from a Swiss mountain tourism community, which has been undergoing major restructuring processes in recent decades. Her analysis shows that a shared perception of threats and crises, and shared agreements on informal values (growth-oriented or sustainable) and formal institutions, enable transparent communication and leads to participation that augments the possibility of collective agency towards adaptation and resilience.

In Chapter 10, Sarah Wongkee and Alison M. Gill examine the contested spaces of retailing in a destination context. They utilize a destination retail resilience framework as a heuristic device to examine retail resilience in a case study of Whistler, British Columbia, Canada. Based on a multi-method approach that employs an online survey, key informant interviews, and a review of community documents, their findings focus on issues of vulnerability, exposure, and sensitivity to stressors. According to Wongkee and Gill, the perceived threat to small independent retailers of competition from increasing numbers of corporate retail operations and the impact of this on power relationships and quality of the resort environment experience are seen as a major stressor. They further note that labor availability, retail mix, and lack of retail space are also seen as threats to resilience.

In Chapter 11, Jasper Heslinga, Peter Groote, and Frank Vanclay focus on the synergetic interactions between tourism development and landscape protection. They aim to understand changes in public thinking about the interactions between tourism development and landscape in the island of Terschelling, which is part of the UNESCO World Heritage listed Wadden Sea region in the Netherlands. Their results, based on a historical content analysis of newspaper articles and key informant interviews, reveal fluctuations over time in terms of the extent to which public opinion was oriented towards nature protection, socio-economic development, or to the synergies between them. To improve future policy relating to socio-ecological systems (SES), Heslinga, Groote, and Vanclay recommend that policy-makers seek a greater understanding of the influence of the current institutional context on policy decisions. They further suggest that an understanding of the institutional context can be helpful in finding strategies to build the socio-ecological resilience of a region.

In Chapter 12, Sayaka Sakuma discusses rural revitalization and resilience in the context of ecotourism development and governance in Okinawa, Japan. She examines the transition of Japan's tourism policy from the development of mass resort tourism to one that is based on sustainable tourism in the form of ecotourism. Drawing upon empirical research in Okinawa prefecture, her case study demonstrates how the local community responded to external policy changes and adopted a resilience-based approach to revitalize the local economy through ecotourism. Sakuma also discusses national interests in shaping regions through tourism development as well as the geographical and temporal context that enabled ecotourism to emerge as a tool for sustainable development.

Finally, in the concluding chapter (Part IV, Chapter 13), Alison M. Gill and Jarkko Saarinen synthesize and reflect on the contributions with respect to the future of tourism governance and policy and the challenges and opportunities that may lie ahead. They highlight the key issues raised by the contributors, with an emphasis on the synergistic relationships between sustainability thinking and resilience. They further stress the idea of resilient destinations and governance strategies that can lead the transition of destinations towards sustainability.

References

Adger, W.N. (2000). Social and ecological resilience: Are they related? *Progress in Human Geography, 24*, 347–364.

Amore, A., & Hall, C.M. (2016). From governance to meta-governance in tourism? Re-incorporating politics, interests and values in the analysis of tourism governance. *Tourism Recreation Research, 41*(2), 109–122.

Baggio, R., Scott, N., & Cooper, C. (2010). Improving tourism destination governance: A complexity science approach. *Tourism Review, 65*(4), 51–60.

Becken, S., & Hay, J.E. (2007). *Tourism and climate change: Risks and opportunities.* Clevedon, UK: Channel View Publications.

Berkes, F., & Ross, H. (2013). Community resilience: Toward an integrated approach. *Society and Natural Resources, 26*, 5–20.

Bramwell, B. (2011). Governance, the state and sustainable tourism: A political economy approach. *Journal of Sustainable Tourism, 19*(4–5), 459–477.

Bramwell, B., & Lane, B. (2011). Critical research on the governance of tourism and sustainability. *Journal of Sustainable Tourism, 19*(4–5), 411–421.

Brickley, K., Black, R., & Cottrell, S. (Eds.). (2013). *Sustainable tourism and millennium development goals.* Burlington, VT: Jones & Bartlett Learning.

Brill, H., Peck, C., & Kramer, M. (2015). *The resilient investor: A plan for your life, not just your money.* Oakland, CA: Berrett-Koehler.

Butler, R.W. (1999). Sustainable tourism: A state-of-the-art review. *Tourism Geographies, 1*, 7–25.

Butler, R.W. (2017). *Tourism and resilience.* Wallingford, UK: CABI.

Cheer, J., & Lew, A.A. (2017). *Tourism, resilience, and sustainability: Adapting to social, political and economic change.* London: Routledge.

Davidson, D.J. (2010). The applicability of the concept of resilience to social systems: Some sources of optimism and nagging doubts. *Society and Natural Resources, 23*, 1135–1149.

Folke, C. (2006). Resilience: The emergence of a perspective for social-ecological systems analyses. *Global Environmental Change, 16*, 253–267.

Gössling, S., & Hall, C.M. (Eds.). (2006). *Tourism and global environmental change: Ecological, social, economic and political interrelationships.* London: Routledge.

Hall, C.M. (2011). Policy learning and policy failure in sustainable tourism governance: From first- and second-order to third-order change? *Journal of Sustainable Tourism, 19*(4–5), 649–671.

Hall, C.M., & Lew, A.A. (Eds.). (1999). *Sustainable tourism: A geographical perspective.* New York: Longman.

Hall, C.M., Prayag, G., & Amore, A. (2018). *Tourism and resilience. Individual, organizational and destination perspectives.* Bristol: Channel View Publications.

Holden, A. (2008). *Environment and tourism.* London: Routledge.

Hollenhorst, S.J., Houge-MacKenzie, S., & Ostergren, D.M. (2014). The trouble with tourism. *Tourism Recreation Research, 39*(3), 305–319.

Holling, C.S. (1973). Resilience and stability of ecological systems. *Annual Review of Ecology and Systematics, 4*, 1–23.

Hunter, C., & Green, H. (1995). *Tourism and the environment: A sustainable relationship?* London: Routledge.

Lew, A.A. (2014). Scale, change and resilience in community tourism planning. *Tourism Geographies, 16*(1), 14–22.

Lew, A.A., & Cheer, J. (2018). *Tourism resilience and adaptation to environmental change: Definitions and frameworks*. London: Routledge.

Liu, Z. (2003). Sustainable tourism development: A critique. *Journal of Sustainable Tourism, 11*(6), 459–475.

Lu, J.Y., & Nepal, S.K. (2009). Sustainable tourism research: An analysis of papers published in the *Journal of Sustainable Tourism*. *Journal of Sustainable Tourism, 17*(1), 5–16.

McCool, S., & Bosak, K. (2016). *Reframing sustainable tourism*. Berlin: Springer.

Mowforth, M., & Munt, I. (1998). *Tourism and sustainability: A new tourism in the third world*. London: Routledge.

Saarinen, J. (2014). Critical sustainability: Setting the limits to growth and responsibility in tourism. *Sustainability, 6*, 1–17.

Saarinen, J. (2018). Beyond growth thinking: The need to revisit sustainable development in tourism. *Tourism Geographies, 20*(2), 337–340.

Saarinen, J., Rogerson, C., & Hall, C.M. (2017). Geographies of tourism development and planning. *Tourism Geographies, 19*(3), 307–317.

Saarinen, J., Rogerson, C.M., & Manwa, H. (Eds.). (2013). *Tourism and millennium development goals: Tourism, local communities and development*. London: Routledge.

Scheyvens, R. (2009). Pro-poor tourism: Is there value beyond the rhetoric? *Tourism Recreation Research, 34*(2), 191–196.

Scheyvens, R. (2011). *Tourism and poverty*. London: Routledge.

Schilcher, D. (2007). Growth versus equity: The continuum of pro-poor tourism and neoliberal governance. *Current Issues in Tourism, 10*(2–3), 166–193.

Scott, A., Higham, J., Gössling, S., & Peeters, P. (Eds.). (2013). *Understanding and governing sustainable tourism mobility: Psychological and behavioural approaches*. London: Routledge.

Scott, D., Hall, C.M., & Gössling, S. (2012). *Tourism and climate change: Impacts, adaptation & mitigation*. London: Routledge.

Sharpley, R. (2000). Tourism and sustainable development: Exploring the theoretical divide. *Journal of Sustainable Tourism, 8*(1), 1–19.

Sharpley, R. (2009). *Tourism development and the environment: Beyond sustainability?* London: Earthscan.

Sinclair, T. (1998). Tourism and economic development: A survey. *Journal of Development Studies, 34*(5) 1–51.

United Nations (2012). *Resilient people, resilient planet: A future worth choosing*. Report of the United Nations Secretary-General's High-level Panel on Global Sustainability. New York: United Nations.

United Nations Research Institute for Social Development (UNRISD) (2015). *Revisiting sustainable development*. Geneva: UNRISD.

Utting, P. (2015). Foreword. In P. Utting (Ed.), *Revisiting sustainable development* (pp. 1–15). Geneva: UNRISD.

Weaver, D. (2011). Can sustainable tourism survive climate change? *Journal of Sustainable Tourism, 19*, 5–15.

World Bank (2012). *Transformation through tourism: Development dynamics past, present and future* (draft). Washington, DC: World Bank.

World Bank Group (2017). *Tourism for development: 20 reasons sustainable tourism counts for development*. Washington, DC: World Bank.

World Tourism Organization (UNWTO) (2011). *Tourism towards 2030*. UNWTO: Madrid.

World Tourism Organization (UNWTO) (2017). *Tourism and the Sustainable Development Goals – Journey to 2030, highlights*. UNWTO: Madrid.

World Tourism Organization (UNWTO) (2018). *Tourism highlights – 2018 edition*. UNWTO: Madrid.

World Travel and Tourism Council (WTTC) (2017). *Global benchmarking report*. London: WTTC.

Part II

Frameworks and conceptualizations

2 Tourism, resilience, and governance strategies in the transition towards sustainability

Jarkko Saarinen and Alison M. Gill

Introduction

During the 1990s the issue of sustainability became a policy discourse, which started to direct the economic, social, and political structures and processes that constitute the contemporary operative contexts of the tourism industry (Bramwell & Lane 1993; Mowforth & Munt, 2003; Sharpley, 2000). The need for sustainable development in tourism was based on several interrelated processes (see Saarinen, 2014), but since the 1960s and 1970s the key drivers have been the growing impacts of global tourism and, in general, intensified calls for environmental protection and environmentally sound forms of production and consumption. As a result, sustainability thinking is currently firmly embedded in tourism planning, development, and governance approaches at different scales. At the same time, however, the connections and misconnections between tourism as a growth industry and sustainable development are critically debated and challenged. One of the challenging ideas has been a resilience approach in tourism destination planning and governance.

This chapter overviews and conceptualizes the key terms and ideas relating to sustainable tourism generally and, more specifically, the role of resilience thinking in sustainability planning and governance. The intention is to provide background and context for the chapters that follow in this edited volume. To provide a historical perspective, the evolution and institutionalization of sustainable development and sustainable tourism thinking and their relationships are first discussed. The idea of resilience and its relation to sustainability and sustainable tourism governance are subsequently overviewed and debated, including the acknowledgment of Anthropocentric influences.

Institutionalization of sustainable development: a short history

The conceptualization of sustainable development is a relatively recent process, but its societal background has a long history (Enders & Remig, 2015a). According to Crober (2015) and many other scholars, the basic principles of sustainability thinking have their origins in the eighteenth-century idea of 'sustained

yield' in forestry, and especially in the nineteenth-century conservation movement (see Enders & Remig, 2015b; Hall, 1998). In addition, in 1910 Gifford
Pinchot, the first Chief of the United States Forest Service, introduced 'wise use'
thinking in natural resource management which is often seen as a historical ante-
cedent of sustainable development thinking (see Butler, 1998). However, it is
difficult to evaluate in detail what role these historical processes played in the
actual institutionalization of sustainable development ideology. In addition, the
wise use tradition, for example, also has major contradictions with the sustainability approach in natural resource management as it is designed to serve extractive industries and their needs and profitability (see McCarthy & Hague, 2004;
White, 1996).

In a strict sense, sustainable development and the sustainable use of resources
involve the idea of limits to growth (see Enders & Remig, 2015b). At the global
scale, this refers to the fact that the Earth's resources are not infinite, and obviously the same applies to all geographical scales, including destinations. Thus, it
is not surprising that the term was first used in this 'sustain' or 'maintain' sense
by the Club of Rome in 1972 (Crober, 2015). In their publication titled *The
limits to growth*, the authors stated: "We are searching for a model output that
represents a world system that is: 1. sustainable without sudden and uncontrolled
collapse; and 2. capable of satisfying the basic material requirements of all of its
people" (Meadows, Meadows, Randers, & Behrens 1972, p. 152). The term was
also explicitly used in relation to the World Conservation Strategy in 1980
although, as the strategy indicates, the focus was on nature conservation but did
also involve wider social and economic aspects. A specific objective of the for-
mulated conservation strategy was influential in this respect. It specifically stated
that the objective was "to ensure the sustainable utilization of species and ecosystems [...], which support millions of rural communities as well as major
industries" (International Union for Conservation of Nature [IUCN] 1980, p. 7).
Thus, the connection and interdependency between ecological, social, and economic environments were clearly acknowledged.

Later, the IUCN and the United Nations Environment Programme (UNEP)
were active in helping to establish a World Commission on Environment and
Development (WCED) in 1982. The following year, the WCED created a commission chaired by Gro Harlem Bruntdland, which produced the highly influential report *Our common future* in 1987. That report crafted and enshrined the
idea of sustainable development into the policy and academic uses we now
know: "Sustainable development is development that meets the needs of the
present generations without compromising the ability of future generations to
meet their own needs" (World Commission on Environment and Development
[WCED], 1987, p. 43). Obviously, as the background of sustainable development and its institutionalization process is a political and an ideological one with
a clear anthropocentric 'human needs' perspective to development, such a definition involved many compromises (see Enders & Remig, 2015b). In general, it
is agreed that sustainable development is a process, a pathway to sustainability,
which is understood as a desired state of a socio-ecological system. In order to

realize that state, three core principles are necessary – namely, holism, inter-generational equity, and intragenerational equity – which are derived from the basic definition of sustainable development as referring to the needs of the present generations without compromising the ability of future generations in a system's (Planet Earth) context. In addition, there are well-known basic elements or pillars of ecological, social, and economic sustainability. In principle, they are regarded as equal in the development process. In practice, however, the economic pillar is often considered taller that the rest (United Nations, 2012, p. 4). This imbalance between ecological, social, and economic elements is frequently evident in the development of sustainable tourism and its relations to development.

Sustainable tourism

There are many definitions, principles, and criteria for sustainable tourism (see Butler, 1991, 1999; Holden, 2008). Probably the most commonly used definitions originate from various documents produced by international policy-making institutions, such as the World Tourism Organization (UNWTO). Indeed, during the past two decades the organization has committed itself to promoting sustainability in tourism development. According to a statement on the organization's website, "The World Tourism Organization (UNWTO) is the United Nations agency responsible for the promotion of responsible, sustainable and universally accessible tourism" (World Tourism Organization [UNWTO], 2018). It's original conceptual definition of sustainable tourism followed the lines of the Brundtland Commission's definition of sustainable development (see WCED, 1987) by stating that sustainable tourism is tourism development that aims to meet "the needs of present tourists and host regions while protecting and enhancing opportunities for the future" (World Tourism Organization, 1993, p. 7). Later the UNTWO, together with the UNEP, expanded the definition to include the roles and needs of the industry. According to the revised and now widely used definition, sustainable tourism is "tourism that takes full account of its current and future economic, social and environmental impacts, addressing the needs of visitors, the industry, the environment and host communities" (United Nations Environment Programme [UNEP], 2005, p. 12; see also UNWTO, 2017).

In academic tourism research, the idea of sustainability and debate over appropriate scale, scope, and application varies (Butler, 1999; Saarinen, 2006). Initially, sustainability was perceived as a realistic and suitable target for small-scale tourism operations (see Clarke, 1997), while conventional mass scale tourism was perceived negatively as something that, if it aimed to achieve sustainability in the future, needed a full transformation towards smaller scale operations. However, sustainability is now linked to all kinds of tourism activities and environments in research and policy-making (see Clarke, 1997), and the role of the industry has become more central, reflecting market driven approaches in development thinking. Swarbrooke (1999, p. 13), for example, has defined sustainable tourism as "tourism which is economically viable but does not destroy the resources on which the future of tourism will depend, notably the physical environment and the social fabric of the host community." Such definitions emphasize the needs of the industry and sustainable use of the resources it requires (Hardy, Beeton, & Pearson, 2002), which essentially, if critically interpreted, refers to an aim to sustain the industry and its rights to use local resources (Butler, 1999; Saarinen, 2014). In tourism literature this perspective, which broadly reflects wise-use thinking in natural resource use and management, is termed as a tourism-centric approach in sustainable tourism planning and development (see Burns, 1999). This has led some scholars to use the term 'sustainable development in tourism' (Butler, 1999), which terminologically is seen as respecting the ethical aspects and elements of the ideology of sustainable development (see also Lew, Ng, Ni, & Wu, 2016).

Thus, instead of having one agreed definition and understanding of sustainable tourism there are several definitions and different co-existing approaches with respect to how the limits to growth are or could be defined and set in tourism development. As shown in Table 2.1, these different approaches can, broadly speaking, be named as resource-based, industry-based, and community-based limits to growth (Saarinen, 2006). These terms follow the basic (ecological, economic, and social) elements of sustainable development with links to the conservation movement, wise-use discourses, and participatory planning models. The resource-based limits for tourism highlight the role and importance of ecological aspects of environment, while the industry-based limits emphasize the needs of tourism. The community-based limits are defined by participatory approaches and collaborative governance approaches with local stakeholders (see also Holden, 2008).

Due to their different backgrounds, these partly competing perspectives for setting the limits to growth in tourism reflect different kinds of sustainability thinking. As indicated, the industry-based approach reflects wise-use thinking by highlighting, in general, the role and needs of the businesses and markets, and the reduction of institutional regulations in natural (and cultural) resource use

Table 2.1 Perspectives for setting the limits to growth in tourism development

Background	Resource-based	Industry-based	Community-based
Orientation	Environment (physical)	Industry	Community
Origin/manifestation	Carrying capacity model	Wise use, Product cycle	Participatory planning
Limits to growth	Objective/ measurable	Relative	Constructed/ negotiated
Resource and system view	Static	Dynamic	Dynamic/static
Time scale	Long	Short	Short–medium
Governance	Institutions	Market-oriented	Collaboration

Source: Based on Saarinen (2014).

and management (see McCarthy, 2002). It highlights a governance model with a reduced role for governmental institutions in planning and decision-making (see Jessop, 2004; Rhodes, 1996). The focus of sustainable tourism research has gradually moved in this direction and towards market-oriented management, corporate social responsibility, and marketing dimensions (see Clarke, 1997; Coles, Fenclova, & Dinan, 2013; Middleton & Hawkins, 1998), which represent the hegemonic ways of current sustainability thinking in tourism (Burns, 1999; Saarinen, 2014; Scheyvens, 2011). Resource-based limits to growth rely on a contrary approach to sustainability based on stronger and external regulations that aim to safeguard the integrity of ecosystems. In this respect, Butler (1998) has specifically identified the idea of a carrying capacity approach as an integral part of the history of sustainability thinking. However, he goes even further by emphasizing that the operationalization of carrying capacity is still a fundamental step if sustainability is to be achieved in tourism in future (see Butler, 1996).

Obviously, the relation between resource-based and industry-based sustainability is problematic both in theory and practice (Saarinen, 2006), and efforts to overcome this opposition between protection and use values in destination governance have been made by utilizing participatory planning thinking, which refers to community-based limits to growth in tourism (see Murphy, 1988; Timothy & White 1999). A community approach creates a broader stakeholder context and collective action for sustainable tourism planning and development in which the limits to growth are based on negotiations and participation. It utilizes collaborative governance thinking, and places host communities and other local stakeholders and the need to empower them in a central position in the sustainable tourism development process (see Scheyvens, 1999, 2002). Although local participation involves many challenges for destination governance (see Hall, 2008; Tosun, 1999, 2000) it aims to guide tourism development in a direction that contributes to local wellbeing in socially sustainable ways. In this respect, the roles of community resilience and resilience planning have been recently highlighted in tourism literature (see Hall, Prayag, & Amore, 2018; Lew, 2014; Lew & Cheer, 2018; Strickland-Munro, Allison, & Moore, 2010).

Resilience: adapting and responding to change

The idea of resilience "is one of the major conceptual tools [...] to deal with change" (Berkes & Ross, 2013, p. 6). Originally, the concept focused on the stability of ecological systems and how systems reacted to change, disturbance, stress, and other random events. In his seminal work, Holling (1973, p. 17) conceptualized resilience as "the ability of these [natural] systems to absorb changes of state variable, driving variable, and parameters, and still persist." Soon resilience thinking began to influence research beyond ecological systems, including resource ecology; ecosystems management and adaptive management studies; and community-based natural resource management discussions (see Davidson, 2010; Davoudi, 2012; Folke, 2006; Magis, 2010). Nowadays, the concept is widely used outside the realm of ecology and ecosystem analyses, including the use of terms such as community resilience and tourism resilience (see Calgaro, Lloyd, & Dominey-Howes, 2014; Strickland-Munro et al., 2010).

There are various definitions of resilience with different characteristics and focus areas for research and management applications. Folke (2006) has categorized the scale of resilience concepts from narrowly focused to broader interpretations of the idea (see also Chapter 3). For Folke, *engineering resilience* represents the narrow interpretation, emphasizing the efficiency of a system to return to a steady state (equilibrium) that was assumed to exist before a disturbance or other change took place. Second, *ecological/ecosystem resilience* or *social resilience* represents a broader, dynamic resilience thinking, focusing on the persistence and robustness of a system to relate to change. It acknowledges that there can be multiple equilibria. Thus, in adapting to change, different ecological or social equilibrium are used for different circumstances (Lew, 2014). The third and broadest approach is *socio-ecological resilience*, which is also adopted in most tourism focused papers (see Lew et al., 2016). It is based on the integration of ecological and social processes, adaptive capacity, and transformability via learning and innovation. Thus, the notions of stability and a firm distinction between natural and human environments are overruled by a system's need to develop through continuous adaptation in transforming a multi-scalar social, ecological, and economic environment. Consequently, increasing attention is being paid to transitional aspects of establishing sustainable pathways and the manner in which they can be more resilient (e.g., Christopherson, Michie, & Tyler, 2010; Simmie & Martin, 2010). Niches (Kemp, Loorbach, & Rotmans, 2007) or 'protective spaces' (Smith & Raven, 2012) are seen as important attributes in the resilience of new ideas along these paths.

With respect to current socio-ecological resilience thinking and related sub-conceptualizations, the following are the most common aspects of resilience: change is seen as a constant state in socio-ecological systems; resilience indicates the capacity of a system to absorb disturbance and sustain itself; this takes place by adapting to and/or transforming with change (see Berkes & Ross, 2013; Davidson, 2010; Folke, 2006). With reference to these principles, Davoudi (2012) has developed the concept of evolutionary resilience and applied it to a planning context. This evolutionary idea fruitfully connects resilience thinking to regional development discourses (see Chapter 5). As Simmie and Martin (2010, p. 27) state, "the notion of 'resilience' [...] seems to be highly relevant to understanding the process and patterns of uneven regional development." For them resilience cannot be based on a "single unique state or path of an economy but several possible states or paths" in a regional development (Simmie & Martin, 2010, p. 30). Furthermore, they emphasize that from an evolutionary perspective, the important element of resilience in a regional development or a resilient region context is the adaptive capacity of a system. As an idea, the adaptive capacity is called 'adaptive' because it recognizes that the conditions of regional development (or sustainable development) are in a constant state of change (Adger, 2000; Berkes, Colding, & Folke, 2003). This perspective aligns well with the emerging area of transition management towards sustainability (see Markard, Raven, & Truffer, 2012).

In general, adaption to change can be organized as either passive or active adaptive management (Adger, 2006), depending on how learning, knowledge creation, and innovation take place (Tervo-Kankare, Kajan, & Saarinen, 2018). Passive adaptive management is reactive to change. It involves learning based on experienced situations and only if it improves decision outcomes for development. In contrast, active adaptive management involves proactive learning and decisions and actions where improving knowledge and learning are valued (Walters, 1986). Thus, active adaptation and adaptive management is driven more by a search for knowledge and information before decisions and actions, while in passive adaptive management learning is based more on experienced situations and outcomes of a changing environment. The key issue is the governance of that change, which stresses the importance of understanding the current context of changing environments in tourism and sustainable development (see Robinson & Carson, 2016). Indeed, in his review of the emergence of socioecological systems analyses, Folke (2006) connects the need for resilience thinking with the challenge of global change. For him, and many others, an increasing anthropogenic influence and presence in natural systems has progressed to a state in which humans are now one of the great forces of/in nature shaping "ecosystem dynamics from local environments to the biosphere as a whole" (Folke, 2006, p. 253; see also, Morton, 2012; Robbins & Moore, 2013). In current discussions, this increasing and visible domination by humans is seen as representing the Anthropocene.

The Anthropocene: the challenge for resilience

The Anthropocene is perceived as the new geological epoch in which human activity has become the dominant force and influence on climate and the environment (Latour, 2015; Rockström & Klum, 2012). In particular, the issue of global climate change has been linked, for example, to the socio-ecological resilience of communities, regional economies, and tourism (see Espiner & Becken, 2014; Gössling & Hall, 2006; Hall et al., 2018; Lew & Cheer, 2018). The term "Anthropocene" was popularized in the early 2000s by the Nobel Laureate Paul Crutzen (see Crutzen, 2002; Crutzen & Stoermer, 2000) and since that time the concept has come into common use (Brondizio et al., 2016). It is used as an indication of global change and environmental crisis and the Earth's limits to growth (Rockström et al., 2009). Moore (2015, p. 32) observes that, "[as] a result of population growth and resource use, humans are now a geological force in and of themselves, driving planetary change at an unprecedented rate." This view echoes the Club of Rome's limits to growth discussions and early conceptualization of sustainable development.

The Anthropocene operates at all scales and connects the global to the local and vice versa. As a process and discourse (see Castree, 2014, 2015, 2017), the Anthropocene is characterized by powerful global imaginaries of threats and disasters operating in a global–local nexus, which are estimated to have very serious consequences not only for the natural environment but also for human civilization and even the future existence of humans (Crutzen, 2002). As such the idea of the Anthropocene is also critically interpreted, especially in the social sciences and humanities (see Lorimer, 2012; Robbins & Moore, 2013; Veland & Lynch, 2016), as a doomsday prediction, strongly dominated by natural science arguments and logics. This universal natural science perspective influences and guides the ways in which the Anthropocene is understood and instrumentalized, potentially drawing our attention away from the resilience notion by emphasizing that there is a strong integration between ecological and social systems, and that these systems are also much dependent on local contextual socio-economic, cultural, and political factors.

As a discourse the Anthropocene influences many policy discussions and related practices in tourism destination systems and regions (Saarinen, 2018a). Although tourism is identified as a key component in addressing social equity and sustainable production and consumption mores and conservation (UNWTO, 2017), it also serves growth and the interest of capitalism, as noted by Dredge (see Chapter 4). Indeed, growth and changing modes of tourism production, for example, are increasingly seen as major contributors to and consequences of the Anthropocene (Hall & Saarinen, 2010), as a constantly growing and spreading tourism industry has become "a geophysical force censoriously interrelated with the capacity of the Earth to sustain the human species" (Gren & Huijbens, 2014, p. 6). By acknowledging social science perspectives on the Anthropocene, we also challenge the duality between humans and nature (Castree, 2012; Lorimer, 2012) and connect with the socio-ecological integration in resilience thinking, which provides fruitful ground for thinking about resilience in tourism and how resilient tourism relates to sustainability and sustainable tourism (see Strickland-Munro et al., 2010).

Resilient tourism and sustainability

Tourism is a dynamic and constantly changing phenomenon, which is also highly influenced by changes in its operational environments at different scales. Thus, it is not surprising that the idea of resilience has recently attracted tourism scholars. Although there has been discussion on whether resilience represents the new sustainability, it would be unmerited to claim that currently dominant views in tourism studies are based on such a standpoint. However, the concepts of resilience and sustainable development in tourism are widely perceived as highly linked and complementary (see Butler, 2017; Lew, 2014). If one wants to find conflicting views, however, those are probably related to the ways the concepts are seen to be linked (see Espiner, Orchiston, & Higham, 2017; Tobin, 1999) and what roles sustainability and resilience might play in destination development and governance. For example, McCool (2015) states that it is the role of sustainable tourism to support resilience. In contrast, Espiner et al. (2017) argue that the relationship between the concepts is actually the opposite: for them resilience is an integral part of sustainability in tourism. On the one hand, they see resilience as "necessary but not sufficient for sustainability"; on the other hand, they state that, "without resilience, sustainability cannot be realized" (Espiner et al., 2017, p. 6).

Indeed, the concepts of sustainability and resilience are highly interwoven (see Holladay & Powell, 2013) and there are many similarities between the concepts, which are well outlined in the recent literature (e.g. Lew et al., 2016). However, there are also major differences between the two. First, unlike resilience the aim of sustainable development is highly ideological and normative in nature. Sustainable development or sustainable tourism is not about adapting to and transforming environments alone or persisting with change. It does or can involve adaptation, but the very idea of sustainable development is to change the world and the course of (unsustainable) development. Therefore, some scholars see resilience as linked to adaptation, and sustainability to mitigation (see Adger, 2000; Lew et al., 2016). Second, high or good resilience in tourism or any other field does not automatically lead to sustainability. A system can be highly resilient but that situation can be based on a negative lock-in in tourism and regional development that could, for example, work against sustainability and the well-being of vulnerable communities (Simmie & Martin, 2010, p. 32). Similarly, successful adaption mechanisms that create customer comfort in tourism products, for example, can turn out to be problematic from the perspective of sustainability management (see Espiner et al., 2017; Hambira, Saarinen, Atlhopheng, & Manwa, 2013). Obviously, this relation between resilience and sustainability is essentially a question of time-scale: eventually a high path-dependency with a strong capacity to persist with change turns out to be non-resilient if a lock-in is unsustainable in the long run. Thus, there may be a scalar difference between sustainability and resilience. By definition, sustainable development is based on a very long-term commitment and evaluation of operations and impacts in a holistic and inter-generational context, while resilience analysis often operates in more local and shorter time-scales (see Lew, 2014).

In tourism, resilience thinking and research has generally evolved in two directions. First, there has been a great deal of interest in natural disasters and climate change related impacts on tourism and the vulnerability of the industry and/or tourism dependent communities (Biggs, Hall, & Stoeckl, 2012; Calgaro, Dominey-Howes, & Lloyd, 2014; Hall, Malinen, Vosslamber, & Wordsworth, 2016; Slocum & Kline, 2014; Tyrrell & Johnston, 2008). The idea of the Anthropocene has provided a framework for analyzing the resilience of tourism and tourism dependent communities in respect of change. Although the Anthropocene represents a gradual change, the research has been influenced by shocks, hazards, and extreme weather events mainly linked to global climate change processes (see Becken, 2013; Hall et al., 2018). Second, there has been a strong economic emphasis in tourism resilience with discussions focusing on livelihood diversification and economic restructuring, especially in rural and former industrial areas. In tourism studies this resilience to a slow change (Lew, 2014) has its origins in Butler's (1980) tourism area cycle of evolution (TALC) model (see

Cochrane, 2010; Hamzah & Hampton, 2013). More recently, however, economic approaches have referred to local and regional development literature and the idea of regional resilience (see Bristow, 2010; Christopherson et al., 2010) with a specific focus on evolutionary economic thinking (Davoudi, 2012; Martin & Sunley, 2014; Simmie & Martin, 2010). Thus, evolutionary thinking forms a common ground or meeting place for TALC and regional resilience studies. This approach is discussed in more detail by Brouder and Saarinen in Chapter 5.

In a regional development context, however, an evolutionary approach analyzes "the uneven distribution of economic activity in space" by focusing "on the historical processes that produce these patterns" (Boschma & Frenken, 2006, p. 286; see Martin, Sunley, Gardiner, & Tyler, 2016). By emphasizing equity and uneven distribution of benefits and costs, the evolutionary approach resonates well with the ideology of sustainable development (see Gill & Williams, 2014; Ruiz-Ballesteros, 2011). Although mainly an economic approach, evolutionary economic geography does not however exclude the other social and ecological elements of sustainable development. From this perspective, resilient tourism refers to a tourism system at a destination scale that has adaptive capacity and resources to absorb change and disturbance and sustain itself by transforming via learning and innovation (see also Tyrrell & Johnston, 2008). By understanding resilience as a tool for sustainable development, there is a need to have a destination governance structure that supports and guides the adaptive capacity and management of resiliency towards the desired common objective, that is, sustainability in tourism.

Sustainability and destination governance

As Folke (2006, p. 260) highlights, it is fundamentally important to govern and manage "a transition towards more sustainable development paths." Indeed, for him this need for better governance is a key solution to "one of the greatest challenges facing humanity" – that is, sustainability. A call for better governance is also highly evident and increasingly argued in recent sustainable tourism literature (see Espiner et al., 2017; Hall, 2008, 2011; Holden, 2008; also Dredge, Chapter 4). As noted by Bramwell (2011, p. 461) "destinations wanting to promote sustainable tourism are more likely to be successful when there is effective governance." This better governance also links with resilience thinking: as Baggio, Scott and Cooper (2010, p. 52) note, "the governance system may be considered as the tool by which the destination adapts to change." Thus, there is no doubt about the need for better destination governance given the current state of affairs characterized by increasing globalization, insecurity, and global climate change.

But what does 'better governance' mean in the context of sustainable tourism? There is a relatively simple answer with highly complex implications for destination planning and development: better destination governance strengthens resilience and adaptive capacity and leads tourism development towards sustainability by utilizing the industry as a tool for sustainable development. The challenge is the implementation. In this respect, Bramwell (2011) and Hall (2011) have identified two major broad-based and interrelated difficulties: multi-scalarism and coordination. The governance of sustainable tourism involves cross-sectoral relations and diverse policies at various levels of planning and management (Mowforth & Munt, 2003). Sustainability governance of tourism needs "to be integrated with wider economic, social and environmental policy considerations within an overall sustainable development framework" (Bramwell, 2011, p. 461). These policies often directly focus on non-tourism related issues which creates further challenges of interpretation when trying to apply them to tourism. Indeed, with respect to the coordination challenge, the multi-scalar nature of tourism related policies creates a highly complex and confusing arena of institutional arrangements for collaboration and well-coordinated actions. The tourism sector itself is also a fragmented industry, and the policy arena for sustainable tourism development involves a highly diverse set of stakeholders ranging from public to private sector and from hosts to guests in tourism and beyond (Beaumont & Dredge, 2010; Gill & Williams, 2011). Different stakeholders may have very different interests, priorities, and values related to tourism and its role in (sustainable) development. In addition, involved stakeholders have different capacities to influence and guide the development process and the impact of tourism. Thus, while governance and its coordination process involves stakeholders, resources, and knowledge it also includes power issues (Tribe, 2008). All these, especially the power issues and related potentially uneven exchange between the industry and local communities, have been noted as highly challenging matters for the sustainability of tourism (see Bramwell & Lane, 2011; Mowforth & Munt, 2003; Scheyvens, 2011).

The idea of governance itself also presents a complicated framework. There are several good definitions, reviews, and categorizations of the governance concept and its core dimensions (see Hall, 2011; O'Flynn & Wanna, 2008; Rhodes, 1996; Ruhanen, Scott, Ritchie, & Tkaczynski, 2010). Ruhanen et al. (2010), for example, analyzed 53 published governance studies in political science and management literature. Based on this, they identified 40 different dimensions of governance, which clearly highlights the complexity of the idea and research area. Among this diverse set of dimensions, the most frequently mentioned were accountability, transparency, involvement, structure, effectiveness, power, efficiency, and decentralization. All these and many other dimensions from the long list have been applied to destination governance discussion in tourism studies (see Beaumont & Dredge, 2010; Gill & Williams, 2011; Hall, 2011; Presenza, Del Chiappa, & Sheehan, 2013).

In the sustainable tourism literature, governance refers to supporting and guiding the process of collaboration and collective action towards sustainability in a multi-scalar policy environment. This calls for collective action between various stakeholders (Bramwell & Lane, 2011; Gill & Williams, 2011). The emphasis on cooperation in decision-making and development has created a relatively new collaborative governance approach (see Ansell & Gash, 2008; O'Flynn & Wanna, 2008). It is a consensus-oriented decision-making process that also incorporates links to community resilience, adaptation, and knowledge sharing (see Magis, 2010). Additional key elements in governance, especially in the context of sustainable development, are control and regulations. As defined by Rhodes (1996) in his highly cited review article, "The new governance: Governing without government," governance is positioned as a condition of ordered rule by which society is governed. In the context of tourism planning and development the key questions is: Who exercises power and controls the system, and thus, who sets the rules of the game in tourism destination development?

There are two general perspectives in organizing governance and, thus, in locating power: a political science and a corporate management approach (see Ruhanen et al., 2010). In political science, Rhodes (1997, p. 15) has defined governance as, "the self-organizing inter-organizational networks characterized by interdependence, resource exchange, rules of the game and autonomy of the state." From that perspective governance is an ideological approach that focuses on how to organize public–private sector relations in societies with the final responsibility being with institutions. In contrast to this, corporate governance deals with the issues and systems by which private sector companies and actors are managed and controlled (Ruhanen et al., 2010). Although there have been attempts to focus on the political dimensions (see Bramwell 2011; Hall 2011), a typical approach to tourism destination governance and management has been based on the corporate dimension, which utilizes current neoliberal economic thinking. There, the role of the markets in organizing better governance is usually highlighted (see Jessop, 2004; Saarinen, 2014).

For Peck and Tickell (2002) the central role of the market as a guiding frame is processed through 'roll back' and/or 'roll out' neoliberalism. The former refers to a withdrawal of government involvement, while the latter is evident in various intervention policies that enable the private sector and, thus, corporate governance to penetrate areas which were previously the domain of the public sector. In this respect, there is, for example, increasing discussion on neoliberal nature conservation, in which the tourism industry often plays a major role (see Büscher, 2013). In tourism, neoliberal governance increasingly emphasizes the role of markets – that is, a regime of accumulation with the focus on production and consumption – rather that the state or other public institutions in guiding and controlling the development discourses and practices of tourism. However, in the context of sustainable development the need for more politically driven approaches in setting the rules of destination governance would be needed. Under the current neoliberal market economy this kind of hierarchal command (Jessop, 2004), or top-down thinking, is not highly fashionable or politically acceptable in the context of resource-based sustainability. Still, hierarchical command may be urgently needed when the markets fail to support sustainable development by creating negative externalities in their operations and economic growth. This seems to be the case with respect to tourism and carbon emissions, for example, where there have been calls for government and inter-governmental regulations in respet of climate change (see Scott, Hall, & Gössling, 2012).

Concluding remarks

Tourism is generally "viewed as a renewable resource that, if cared for properly, can be utilized indefinitely" (Hollenhorst, Houge-MacKenzie, & Ostergren, 2014, p. 306). This 'proper caring' refers to the need to set the limits to growth in tourism by creating structures and collaborative processes and practices that could lead the industry towards a sustainable development path within an overall sustainability framework (Bramwell, 2011, p. 461). Critically, from the perspectives of sustainability and political governance thinking, this path can only be based on structures, regulations, collective focus and actions, and integrated policy-making that govern the industry and its impacts in the context of inter-generational and intra-generational equity. The nature of these structures and related institutional arrangements can be demonstrated by utilizing regulation theory, which involves a regime of accumulation and a mode of regulation (Cornelissen, 2005). The former refers to the organization of 'supply and demand' while the latter is focused on the structures that aim to sustain the processes of production and consumption (Mosedale, 2014). Obviously, in order to have sustainable tourism there needs to be a viable business ground that emphasizes a functioning regime of accumulation. In a sustainability context, however, the mode of regulation and related practices, norms, rules, and institutions need to include a long-term and holistic perspective involving the ideals and principles of sustainable development. Thus, these modes of sustainability regulation aim to balance the regime of accumulation with the ecological, socio-cultural, and economic environments and the overall resilience of a socio-ecological system.

Sustainable tourism governance involves the markets but also certain institutional structures that go beyond individual tourist operators, destination management organizations, or customers and their relations (Saarinen, 2018b). This call for supporting institutional arrangements and multi-scalar collective efforts are also emphasized in current resilience thinking (Biggs et al., 2012; Davidson, 2010; Espiner & Becken, 2014; Espiner et al., 2017). Indeed, as highlighted by Calgaro, Lloyd, and Dominey-Howes (2014), there is a wide spectrum of factors influencing destination vulnerability and, thus, the resilience of a destination system. These factors involve both internal and external issues, thus demonstrating the complexity and multi-scalar nature of destination governance and a collective approach. Various high-level development policy contexts, characterized by the involvement of a plethora of United Nations related institutions and acronyms, for example, manifest the collective governing aspect of sustainable tourism and resilience at the international level. A recent example is the connection between the tourism industry and the United Nations Sustainable Development Goals (SDGs) of the 2030 Agenda for Sustainable Development (see Hughes & Scheyvens, 2016). These kinds of connections underline the importance and assumed capacity of tourism, as one of the world's largest industries, to make a difference for global development and sustainability. However, the Agenda also indicates the need to rethink the current economic growth ideology in respect of social wellbeing and environmental needs in development. In this respect, the UNWTO (2017, p. 4) emphasizes that in order to make a positive contribution to the SDGs "a well-designed and managed tourism sector" is needed. This edited collection aims to contribute to these aims by thinking of tourism development, resilience, and destination governance in a sustainable development context.

References

Adger, W.N. (2000). Social and ecological resilience: Are they related? *Progress in Human Geography, 24*, 347–364.

Adger, W.N. (2006). Vulnerability. *Global Environmental Change, 16*(3), 268–281.

Ansell, C., & Gash, A. (2008). Collaborative governance in theory and practice. *Journal of Public Administration Research and Theory, 18*(4), 543–571.

Baggio, R., Scott, N., & Cooper, C. (2010). Improving tourism destination governance: A complexity science approach. *Tourism Review, 65*(4), 51–60.

Beaumont, N., & Dredge, D. (2010). Local tourism governance: A comparison of three network approaches. *Journal of Sustainable Tourism, 18*(1), 7–28.

Becken, S. (2013). Developing a framework for assessing resilience of tourism sub-systems to climatic factors. *Annals of Tourism Research, 43*, 506–528.

Berkes, F., Colding, J., & Folke, C. (Eds.). (2003). *Navigating socio-ecological systems: Building resilience for complexity and change*. Cambridge, UK: Cambridge University Press.

Berkes, F., & Ross, H. (2013). Community resilience: Toward an integrated approach. *Society and Natural Resources, 26*, 5–20.

Biggs, D., Hall, C.M., & Stoeckl, N. (2012). The resilience of formal and informal tourism enterprises to disasters: Reef tourism in Phuket, Thailand. *Journal of Sustainable Tourism, 20*(5), 645–665.

Boschma, R., & Frenken, K. (2006). Why is economic geography not an evolutionary science? *Journal of Economic Geography, 6*, 273–302.

Bramwell, B. (2011). Governance, the state and sustainable tourism: A political economy approach. *Journal of Sustainable Tourism, 19*(4–5), 459–477.

Bramwell, B., & Lane, B. (1993). Sustainable tourism: An evolving global approach. *Journal of Sustainable Tourism, 1*(1), 1–5.

Bramwell, B., & Lane, B. (2011). Critical research on the governance of tourism and sustainability. *Journal of Sustainable Tourism, 19*(4–5), 411–421.

Brill, H., Peck, C., & Kramer, M. (2015). *The resilient investor: A plan for your life, not just your money*. Oakland, CA: Berrett-Koehler.

Bristow, G. (2010). Resilient regions: re-'place'ing regional competitiveness. *Cambridge Journal of Regions, Economy and Society, 3*(1), 153–167.

Brondizio, E. O'Brien, K., Bai, X., Biermann, F. Steffen, W., Berkhout, F., … Chen, C-T.A. (2016). Re-conceptualizing the Anthropocene: A call for collaboration. *Global Environmental Change, 39*, 318–327.

Büscher, B. (2013). *Transforming the frontier: Peace parks and the politics of neoliberal conservation in southern Africa*. Durham, NC and London: Duke University Press.

Burns, P. (1999). Paradoxes in planning: Tourism elitism or brutalism? *Annals of Tourism Research, 26*, 329–348.

Butler, R.W. (1980). The concept of a tourist area life cycle of evolution: Implications for management of resources. *The Canadian Geographer, 24*(1), 5–12.

Butler, R.W. (1991). Tourism, environment, and sustainable development. *Environmental Conservation, 18*(3), 201–209.

Butler, R.W. (1996). The concept of carrying capacity for tourism destinations: Dead or merely buried? *Progress in Tourism and Hospitality Research, 2*(3–4), 283–293.

Butler, R. (1998). Sustainable tourism: Looking backwards in order to progress? In C.M. Hall & A.A. Lew (Eds.), *Sustainable tourism: A geographical perspective* (pp. 25–34). New York: Longman.

Butler, R.W. (1999). Sustainable tourism: A state-of-the-art review. *Tourism Geographies, 1*, 7–25.

Butler, R.W. (2017). *Tourism and resilience.* Wallingford, UK: CABI.

Calgaro, E., Dominey-Howes, D., & Lloyd, K. (2014). Application of the Destination Sustainability Framework to explore the drivers of vulnerability and resilience in Thailand following the 2004 Indian Ocean tsunami. *Journal of Sustainable Tourism, 22*(3), 361–383.

Calgaro, E., Lloyd, K., & Dominey-Howes, D. (2014). From vulnerability to transformation: A framework for assessing the vulnerability and resilience of tourism destinations. *Journal of Sustainable Tourism, 22*(3), 341–360.

Castree, N. (2012). *Making sense of nature.* London: Routledge.

Castree, N. (2014). The Anthropocene and geography I: The back story. *Geography Compass, 8*(7), 436–449.

Castree, N. (2015). Geography and global change science: Relationships necessary, absent, and possible. *Geographical Research, 53*(1), 1–15.

Castree, N. (2017). Unfree radicals: Geoscientists, the Anthropocene, and left politics. *Antipode, 49*(1), 52–74.

Christopherson, S., Michie, J., & Tyler, P. (2010). Regional resilience: Theoretical and empirical perspectives. *Cambridge Journal of Regions, Economy and Society, 3*(1), 3–10.

Clarke, J. (1997). A framework of approaches to sustainable tourism. *Journal of Sustainable Tourism, 5*, 224–233.

Cochrane, J. (2010). The sphere of tourism resilience. *Tourism Recreation Research, 35*(2), 173–185.

Coles, T., Fenclova, E., & Dinan, C. (2013). Tourism and corporate social responsibility: A critical review and research agenda. *Tourism Management Perspectives, 6*, 122–141.

Cornelissen, S. (2005). *The global tourism system: Governance, development and the lessons from South Africa.* Aldershot, UK: Ashgate.

Crober, U. (2015). The discovery of sustainability: A genealogy of a term. In J.C. Enders & M. Remig (Eds.), *Theories of sustainable development* (pp. 6–15). London: Routledge.

Crutzen, P.J. (2002). Geology of mankind. *Nature, 415*, 23.

Crutzen, P.J., & Stoermer, E.F. (2000). The Anthropocene. *Global Change Newsletter, 41*, 17–18.

Davidson, D.J. (2010). The applicability of the concept of resilience to social systems: Some sources of optimism and nagging doubts. *Society and Natural Resources, 23*, 1135–1149.

Davoudi, S. (2012). Resilience: A bridging concept or a dead end? *Planning Theory & Practice, 13*(2), 299–307.

Enders, J.C., & Remig, M. (2015a). Theories of sustainable development: An introduction. In J.C. Enders & M. Remig (Eds.), *Theories of sustainable development* (pp. 1–5). London: Routledge.

Enders, J.C., & Remig, M. (Eds.) (2015b). *Theories of sustainable development*. London: Routledge.

Espiner, S., & Becken, S. (2014). Tourist town on the edge: Conceptualizing vulnerability and resilience in a protected area tourism. *Journal of Sustainable Tourism, 22*(4), 646–665.

Espiner, S., Orchiston, C., & Higham, J. (2017). Resilience and sustainability: A complementary relationship? Towards a practical conceptual model for the sustainability–resilience nexus in tourism. *Journal of Sustainable Tourism, 25*(10), 1385–1400.

Folke, C. (2006). Resilience: The emergence of a perspective for social-ecological systems analyses. *Global Environmental Change, 16*, 253–267.

Gill, A.M., & Williams, P.W. (2011). Rethinking resort growth: Understanding evolving governance strategies in Whistler, British Columbia. *Journal of Sustainable Tourism, 19*(4–5), 629–648.

Gill, A.M., & Williams, P.W. (2014). Mindful deviation in creating a governance path towards sustainability in resort destinations. *Tourism Geographies, 16*(4), 546–562.

Gren, M., & Huijbens, E. (2014). Tourism and the Anthropocene. *Scandinavian Journal of Hospitality and Tourism, 14*(1), 6–22.

Gössling, S., & Hall, C.M. (Eds.). (2006). *Tourism and global environmental change: Ecological, social, economic and political interrelationships*. London: Routledge.

Hall, C.M. (1998). Historical antecedents of sustainable development and ecotourism: new labels on old bottles? In C.M. Hall & A.A. Lew (Eds.), *Sustainable tourism: A geographical perspective* (pp. 13–24). New York, NY: Longman.

Hall, C.M. (2008). *Tourism planning*. Harlow, UK: Prentice-Hall.

Hall, C.M. (2011). Policy learning and policy failure in sustainable tourism governance: From first- and second-order to third-order change? *Journal of Sustainable Tourism, 19*(4–5), 649–671.

Hall, C.M., Malinen, S., Vosslamber, R., & Wordsworth, R. (2016). *Business and post-disaster management: Business, organisational and consumer resilience and the Christchurch earthquakes*. London: Routledge.

Hall, C.M., Prayag, G., & Amore, A. (2018). *Tourism and resilience. Individual, organizational and destination perspectives*. Bristol: Channel View Publications.

Hall, C.M., & Saarinen, J. (2010). Geotourism and climate change: Paradoxes and promises of geotourism in polar regions. *Téoros, 29*(2), 77–86.

Hambira, W., Saarinen, J., Atlhopheng, J., & Manwa, H. (2013). Climate change adaptation practices in nature-based tourism in Maun in the Okavango Delta area, Botswana: How prepared are the tourism businesses? *Tourism Review International, 17*(2), 19–29.

Hamzah, A., & Hampton, M. (2013). Resilience and non-linear change in island tourism. *Tourism Geographies, 15*(1), 43–67.

Hardy, A., Beeton, R., & Pearson, L. (2002). Sustainable tourism: An overview of the concept and its position in relation to conceptualisations of tourism. *Journal of Sustainable Tourism, 10*, 475–496.

Holden, A. (2008). *Environment and tourism* (2nd edn.). London: Routledge.

Holladay, P.J., & Powell, R.B. (2013). Resident perceptions of socio-ecological resilience and the sustainability of community-based tourism development in the Commonwealth of Dominica. *Journal of Sustainable Tourism, 21*(8), 1188–1211.

Hollenhorst, S.J., Houge-MacKenzie, S., & Ostergren, D.M. (2014). The trouble with tourism. *Tourism Recreation Research, 39*(3), 305–319.

Holling, C.S. (1973). Resilience and stability of ecological systems. *Annual Review of Ecology and Systematics, 4*, 1–23.

Hughes, E., & Scheyvens, R. (2016). Corporate social responsibility in tourism post-2015: A development first approach. *Tourism Geographies, 18*(5), 469–482.

International Union for Conservation of Nature (IUCN). (1980). *World conservation strategy*. Morges, Switzerland: IUCN.

Jessop, B. (2004). Hollowing out the "nation-state" and multilevel governance. In P. Kenneth (Ed.), *A handbook of comparative social policy* (pp. 11–25). Cheltenham, UK: Edward Elgar.

Kemp, R., Loorbach, D., & Rotmans, J. (2007). Transition management as a model for managing processes of co-evolution towards sustainable development. *International Journal of Sustainable Development and World Ecology, 14*, 1–15.

Latour, B. (2015). Telling friends from foes in the time of the Anthropocene. In C. Hamilton, F. Gemenne, & C. Bonneuil (Eds.), *The Anthropocene and the global environmental crisis: Rethinking modernity in a new epoch* (pp. 145–155). Abingdon, UK: Routledge.

Lew, A.A. (2014). Scale, change and resilience in community tourism planning. *Tourism Geographies, 16*(1), 14–22.

Lew, A.A., & Cheer, J. (2018). *Tourism resilience and adaptation to environmental change: Definitions and frameworks*. Routledge: London.

Lew, A.A., Ng, P.T., Ni, C., & Wu, T. (2016). Community sustainability and resilience: Similarities, differences and indicators. *Tourism Geographies, 18*(1), 18—27.

Lorimer, J. (2012). Multinatural geographies for the Anthropocene. *Progress in Human Geography, 36*, 593–612.

McCarthy, J. (2002). First World political ecology: Lessons from the Wise Use movement. *Environment and Planning A, 34*, 1281–1302.

McCarthy, J., & Hague, E. (2004). Race, nation, and nature: The cultural politics of "Celtic" identification in the American West. *Annals of the Association of American Geographers, 94*(2), 387–408.

McCool, S. (2015). Sustainable tourism: Guiding fiction, social trap or path to resilience? In T.V. Singh (Ed.), *Challenges in tourism research* (pp. 224–234). Bristol: Channel View Publications.

Magis, K. (2010). Community resilience: An indicator of social sustainability. *Society and Natural Resources, 23*, 401–416.

Markard, J., Raven, R., & Truffer, B. (2012). Sustainability transitions: An emerging field of research and its prospects. *Research Policy, 41*, 955–967.

Martin, R., & Sunley, P. (2014). On the notion of regional economic resilience: Conceptualization and explanation. *Journal of Economic Geography, 15*(1), 1–42.

Martin, R., Sunley, P., Gardiner, B., & Tyler, P. (2016). How regions react to recessions: Resilience and the role of economic structure. *Regional Studies, 50*(4), 561–585.

Meadows, D., Meadows, D., Randers, J., & Behrens, W. (1972). *The limits to growth: A report for the Club of Rome's project on predicament of mankind*. London: Earth Island.

Middleton, V., & Hawkins, R. (1998). *Sustainable tourism: A marketing perspective*. London: Routledge.

Moore, A. (2015). Tourism in the Anthropocene Park? New analytic possibilities. *International Journal of Tourism Anthropology, 4*(2), 186–200.

Morton, T. (2012). From modernity to the Anthropocene: Ecology and art in the age of asymmetry. *International Social Science Journal, 63*(207–208), 39–51.

Mosedale, J. (2014). Political economy of tourism: Regulation theory, institutions, and governance networks. In A.A., Lew, C.M. Hall, & A.M. Williams (Eds.), *The Wiley Blackwell companion to tourism* (pp. 55–65). Chichester, UK: John Wiley.

Mowforth, M., & Munt, I. (2003). *Tourism and sustainability: A new tourism in the Third World*. London: Routledge.

Murphy, P. (1988). Community driven tourism planning. *Tourism Management, 9*(2), 96–104.

O'Flynn, J., & Wanna, J. (Eds.). (2008). *Collaborative governance: A new era of public policy in Australia?* Canberra: ANU E-Press.

Peck, J., & Tickell, A. (2002). Neoliberalising space. *Antipode, 34*, 208–216.

Presenza, A., Del Chiappa, G., & Sheehan, L. (2013). Residents' engagement and local tourism governance in maturing beach destinations. Evidence from an Italian case study. *Journal of Destination Marketing & Management, 2*, 22–30.

Rhodes, R.A.W. (1996). The new governance: Governing without government. *Political Studies, 44*, 652–667.

Rhodes, R.A.W. (1997). *Understanding governance: Policy, networks, governance, reflexivity and accountability*. Buckingham, UK: Open University Press.

Robbins, P., & Moore, S.A. (2013). Ecological anxiety disorder: Diagnosing the politics of the Anthropocene. *Cultural Geographies, 20*(1), 3–19.

Robinson, G.M., & Carson, D.A. (2016). Resilient communities: Transitions, pathways and resourcefulness. *The Geographical Journal, 182*(2), 114–122.

Rockström, J., & Klum, M. (2012). *The human quest – Prospering within planetary boundaries*. Stockholm: Bokförlaget Langenskiöld.

Rockström, J., Steffen, W., Noone, K., Persson, Å., Stuart Chapin III, F., Lambin, E.F., … & Foley, J.A. (2009). A safe operating space for humanity. *Nature, 461*, 472–475.

Ruhanen, L., Scott, N., Ritchie, B., & Tkaczynski, A. (2010). Governance: A review and synthesis of the literature. *Tourism Review, 65*, 4–16.

Ruiz-Ballesteros, E. (2011). Socio-ecological resilience and community-based tourism: An approach from Agua Blanca, Ecuador. *Tourism Management, 32*, 655–666.

Saarinen, J. (2006). Traditions of sustainability in tourism studies. *Annals of Tourism Research, 33*(4), 1121–1140.

Saarinen, J. (2014). Critical sustainability: Setting the limits to growth and responsibility in tourism. *Sustainability, 6*, 1–17.

Saarinen, J. (2018a). What are wilderness areas for? Tourism and political ecologies of wilderness uses and management in the Anthropocene. *Journal of Sustainable Tourism*. Advance online publication. doi: org/10.1080/09669582.2018.1456543

Saarinen, J. (2018b). Beyond growth thinking: The need to revisit sustainable development in tourism. *Tourism Geographies, 20*(2), 337–340.

Scheyvens, R. (1999). Ecotourism and the empowerment of local communities. *Tourism Management, 20*, 245–249.

Scheyvens, R. (2002). *Tourism for development: Empowering communities*. Harlow, UK: Prentice Hall.

Scheyvens, R. (2011). *Tourism and poverty*. London: Routledge.

Scott, D., Hall, C.M., & Gössling, S. (2012). *Tourism and climate change: Impacts, adaptation and mitigation*. London: Routledge.

Sharpley, R. (2000). Tourism and sustainable development: Exploring the theoretical divide. *Journal of Sustainable Tourism, 8*(1), 1–19.

Simmie, J., & Martin, R. (2010). The economic resilience of regions: Towards an evolutionary approach. *Cambridge Journal of Regions, Economy and Society, 3*(1), 27–43.

Slocum, S., & Kline, C. (2014). Regional resilience: Opportunities, challenges and policy messages from Western North Carolina. *Anatolia, 25*(3), 403–416.

Smith, A., & Raven, R. (2012). What is protective space? Reconsidering niches in transitions to sustainability. *Research Policy, 41*, 1025–1036.

Smith, A., & Stirling, A. (2010). The politics of social-ecological resilience and sociotechnical transitions. *Ecology and Society, 15*(1), 1–13 [online]. Retrieved from www.ecologyandsociety.org/vol15/iss1/art11/.

Strickland-Munro, J., Allison, H., & Moore, S. (2010). Using resilience concepts to investigate the impacts of protected area tourism on communities. *Annals of Tourism Research, 37*(2), 499–519.

Swarbrooke, J. (1999). *Sustainable tourism management*. Wallingford, UK: CAB International.

Tervo-Kankare, K., Kajan, E., & Saarinen, J. (2018). Costs and benefits of environmental change: Tourism industry's responses in Arctic Finland. *Tourism Geographies, 20*(2), 202–223.

Timothy, D., & White, K. (1999). Community-based ecotourism development on the periphery of Belize. *Current Issues in Tourism, 2*, 226–242.

Tobin, G.A. (1999). Sustainability and community resilience: The holy grail of hazards planning? *Environmental Hazards, 1*, 13–25.

Tosun, C. (1999). Towards a typology of community participation in the tourism development process. *Anatolia, 10*(2), 113–134.

Tosun, C. (2000). Limits to community participation in the tourism development process in developing countries. *Tourism Management, 21*, 613–633.

Tribe, J. (2008). Tourism: A critical business. *Journal of Travel Research, 46*, 245–255.

Tyrrell, T.J., & Johnston, R.J. (2008). Tourism sustainability, resiliency and dynamics: Towards a more comprehensive perspective. *Tourism and Hospitality Research, 8*(1), 14–24.

United Nations. (2012). *Resilient people, resilient planet: A future worth choosing*. Report of the United Nations Secretary-General's High-level Panel on Global Sustainability. New York: United Nations.

United Nations Environment Programme (UNEP). (2005). *Making tourism more sustainable – A guide for policy makers*. Paris: UNEP.

UNWTO (World Tourism Organization). (2017). *Tourism and the sustainable development goals – Journey to 2030, highlights*. Madrid: UNWTO.

Veland, S., & Lynch, A.H. (2016). Scaling the Anthropocene: How the stories we tell matter. *Geoforum, 72*, 1–5.

Walters, C.J. (1986). *Adaptive management of renewable resources*. New York: McGraw-Hill.

White, R. (1996). Are you an environmentalist or do you work for a living? In W. Cronon (Ed.), *Uncommon ground: Rethinking human place in nature* (pp. 171–185). New York: W.W. Norton & Company.

World Commission on Environment and Development (WCED). (1987). *Our common future*. Oxford: Oxford University Press.

World Tourism Organization (1993). *Sustainable tourism development: Guide for local planners*. Madrid: Word Tourism Organization.

World Tourism Organization (UNWTO). (2018). Who we are. Retrieved from www2.unwto.org/content/who-we-are-0.

3 Resilience theory and tourism

C. Michael Hall

Introduction

Resilience has become a new buzzword in the lexicon of tourism studies. Whereas at one time seemingly everything had to be sustainable, now everything has to be resilient as well! Undoubtedly, the notion of resilience shares a number of significant characteristics with the concept of sustainability. First, there are overlaps between the concepts with respect to the management and maintenance of ecological and social systems. However, while related they are different. Sustainability and resilience are not identical concepts and cannot be substituted for each other (Hall, Prayag, & Amore, 2018). Xu, Marinova, and Guo (2015), for example, argue that the main difference is that resilience thinking does not emphasize the long-term time dimension and equity, whereas intergenerational equity is the core concept of sustainability. Nevertheless, strong definitions of sustainable development that emphasize that stocks of natural capital need to be maintained at or above existing threshold levels require sufficiently resilient socio-ecosystems in order to endure external perturbations and pressures (Ruiz-Ballesteros, 2011). Second, both resilience and sustainability are a 'boundary object' (Brand & Jax, 2007) or 'bridging concept' (Beichler, Hasibovic, Davidse, & Deppisch, 2014), which allows different disciplinary perspectives and knowledge domains of stakeholders, including business and public policy, to interface with each other and find common ground.

Bridging concepts can be extremely useful in providing a conceptual umbrella under which different stakeholder viewpoints can be brought together. The blurring of boundaries between different approaches to conceptual definition can clearly be useful in policy development terms as well as in developing disciplinary, public policy, and stakeholder debates (Strunz, 2012). Vale (2014), for example, argues that "the biggest upside to resilience, however, is the opportunity to turn its flexibility to full advantage by taking seriously the actual interconnections among various domains that have embraced the same terminology" (Vale, 2014, p. 198). Similarly, in the field of urban resilience, Meerow and Newell (2016), suggest that the concept of resilience has helped bring together the different agendas surrounding climate change adaptation and disaster risk reduction, as well as security and sustainability concerns.

Yet while bridging concepts can help find common ground they can also create significant conceptual confusion as a result of their flexibility – a point raised by Elmqvist, Barnett and Wilkinson (2014) and Meerow and Newell (2016), the latter noting the way that resilience sometime became interchangeable with "like-minded terms such as sustainability, vulnerability, and adaptation" (Meerow & Newell, 2016, p. 2). As a result, the notion of resilience has been criticized as being laden with so much ambiguity that it has been labelled as an 'empty signifier' (Weichselgartner & Kelman, 2015) and potentially a difficult concept to operationalize in disaster risk management policy-making (Matyas & Pelling, 2014). Arguably, such issues are also beginning to plague the growing use of the resilience concept in tourism studies in which there are substantial inconsistencies in the way the term is used, not only with respect to understandings of the concepts of perturbation and change, but also of the 'state' to which a system returns post-disturbance, the composition of the tourism system, and scale.

Conceptualizing resilience

The etymological origins of the concept of resilience date to the late sixteenth and early seventeenth centuries and stem from the Latin term *resilio*, which literally means 'to spring back' (Klein, Nicholls, & Thomalla, 2003). In the academic literature the notion of resilience has been in use since before the 1960s. It was a term that originally was mainly used in engineering and material science fields with its migration to ecology and environmental studies not really occurring in a substantial form until the 1980s and until post-2000 for the social sciences, with the greatest overall growth in use occurring in the medical literature (Hall, 2018). The wide range of disciplines that utilize the concept of resilience and the range of definitions that exist reflect its polysemic nature (Sharifi & Yamagata, 2016). The implications of this situation are well described by Cutter, Burton, and Emrich (2010, p. 1):

> Lingering concerns from the research community focus on disagreements as to the definition of resilience, whether resilience is an outcome or a process, what type of resilience is being addressed (economic systems, infrastructure systems, ecological systems, or community systems), and which policy realm (counterterrorism; climate change; emergency management; long-term disaster recovery; environmental restoration) it should target.

Yet despite the meaning of the term often being ambiguous in an academic context, and there being many different definitions and interpretations (Meerow, Newell, & Stults, 2016), there has been phenomenal growth in its use in the research literature (Hall, 2018). Such a situation also occurs in tourism studies with Hall (2018) noting that two-thirds of all uses of 'resilience' in tourism occurred since 2005 even though the first use was in the 1970s. Many of the early writings on resilience in tourism used the term in an economic context

(Holder, 1980; O'Hare & Barrett, 1994; Rensel, 1993). Much of this early work focussed on the contribution of tourism to the wider economy as a way of diversifying and strengthening it in the face of external shock, e.g., Holder (1980) in the Caribbean, or the capacity of tourism itself to survive and even grow in the face of perturbations, e.g., O'Hare and Barrett (1994) on Sri Lanka.

The first paper to draw on the ecological dimensions of resilience in a tourism context was by Lovejoy (1994), who discussed the role and value of biodiversity as an asset for the tourism industry, although the first to utilize specific ecological conceptions of resilience was by Tyler and Dangerfield (1999) in relation to ecotourism. However, as Hall (2018) notes, Tyler and Dangerfield's paper also contributed early on to the considerable and ongoing confusion that exists in tourism studies with regard to the relationships between resilience and sustainable development (Hall et al., 2018; Lew, Ng, Ni, & Wu, 2016). The resilience literature in tourism has also been dominated by the use of the term in relation to the economic dimensions of tourism, with Hall (2018) reporting that about half of the research he evaluated in his bibliometric analysis fell into this category. The next most researched theme was work on resilient communities within a policy and planning context. According to Hall (2018) approximately one-third of the journal articles published in relation to tourism and resilience related to conservation themes and, perhaps as a refection of their susceptibility to climate change, coastal regions and islands accounted for almost one-quarter of papers (e.g., Biggs, Hicks, Cinner, & Hall, 2015; Hall, 2012). Despite the broad significance of the theme, issues of crisis, disaster, and security in tourism are not strongly linked to the resilience literature, although issues of vulnerability are important (Hall, 2010). Nevertheless, this lack of linkage is surprising given the overarching theme of capacity to respond to change and perturbations in the resilience literature (Hall et al., 2018).

With respect to the scale of analysis, the majority of research in tourism is at community or regional level, although Hall et al. (2018, p. 56) do suggest that: "Given its centrality as a framing concept in tourism studies, there is also surprisingly limited overt research on destinations." Similarly, there is also only limited research on significant elements of the tourism system such as organizations (e.g., Orchiston & Higham, 2016; Prayag & Orchiston, 2016), supply chains, or direct research on individuals, whether as tourists, community members, or entrepreneurs (e.g., Biggs, Hall, & Stoeckl, 2012). Although not necessarily completely tourism specific, useful destination level studies of resilience in relation to disasters include Gotham (2007) on New Orleans, Gotham and Greenberg's (2014) comparative study of New Orleans and New York, and Hall, Malinen, Vosslamber, and Wordsworth's (2016) edited work on post-disaster management following the Christchurch earthquakes.

Tourism's use of resilience as a research framework is further complicated by the lack of consistency in use of the term or in seeking to explain how it is being used in particular studies or publications. According to Hall et al. (2018, pp. 56, 59), in the main, notions of resilience are not made clear, with often no attempt to delineate between the different approaches towards resilience and, in many cases, no definition at all. Resilience is extremely important so it seems, but not so important for many authors that it should be clearly conceptualised.

They then go on to suggest that in the tourism literature the concept of resilience appears to be becoming a positive normative concept, but without an appreciation of its application beyond metaphorical description. Tourism studies is not alone in its methodological and conceptual confusion regarding resilience, and reflects concerns in the wider social sciences. Pendall, Foster, and Cowell (2010), for example, observe the 'fuzziness' of the idea of resilience in social science and urge caution with respect to the simplistic transfer of the idea into public policy and social science research (Hall, 2016).

In social policy, for example, resilience is usually framed with respect to 'positive thinking' and 'successful' adaptation to adversity or risk (Jenson & Fraser, 2015a), and resilience is regarded as,

> the outcome of an interactive process involving risk, protection, and promotion. Thus, adaptation, which is expressed through individual behavior, is interpreted as an interactive product involving the presence or absence of specific risk; level of exposure to risk; and the strength of the specific risk, protective, and promotive factors present in a child's life.
>
> (Jenson & Fraser, 2015b, p. 15)

Hayward (2013, p. 37), however, argues that

> the idea of resilience as a personal quality must be treated with caution:

> Given that human resilience is best understood as the interrelationships among the individuals and their community, environment, and social institutions, it has been disturbing to witness the plethora of consultancies that have sprung up in the wake of our local disaster to offer courses in personal resilience, aimed at helping employees to adapt to the "new normal" of life lived in ongoing aftershocks. The implicit subtext of many of these self-help resilience courses appears to be to restore individuals to their roles as willing workers to aid an economic recovery as quickly as possible.

The resilience of tourism organizations, and particularly smaller businesses, is an under-explored topic, and has usually been studied with respect to tourism businesses' response to disaster. Biggs et al. (2015) define resilience as a business's ability to maintain and adapt in the face of disturbance while maintaining its identity. At the organizational level resilience is usually associated with survival in the face of severe shocks (Shaw & Maythorne, 2013), although it is also sometimes used more positively to describe businesses and organizations that embrace change (Sheffi, 2015) or recover quickly after an adverse event

(Herbane, 2010). Nilakant et al. (2016) therefore argue that organizational resilience should be regarded as a continuum, ranging from 'bouncing back' (surviving a crisis) to 'bouncing forward' (thriving after a crisis). Following Cutter et al. (2008) they suggest that organizational resilience should be viewed as consisting of: (a) inherent resilience that enables positive function in the absence of any adverse events and reduces the probability of failure; and (b) adaptive resilience, which refers to flexibility in response during adverse events and enables a quick recovery. Such perspectives have also been influential at the community level. For example, Sharifi and Yamagata (2016) suggest that community resilience in response to disaster is usually understood in the context of four abilities: the ability to prepare and plan for, absorb, recover from, and successfully adapt to adverse events.

Nevertheless, one of the most significant ways to frame understandings of resilience across different disciplines, as well as in tourism, is in terms of the differences between engineering resilience and ecological resilience (Holling, 1996, 2001). Engineering resilience, which is an approach that dominates engineering, economics, and much of business studies, is a measure of the speed at which a system can return to its previous equilibrium or reference state and is also referred to as 'elasticity.' Ecological resilience refers to a return to the reference dynamics after a temporary disturbance but does not assume equilibrium. In fact, from an ecological resilience perspective bouncing back to a previous equilibrium may be impossible in complex systems because they can shift between multiple stable states. According to Holling (1973, p. 17):

> resilience determines the persistence of relationships within a system and is a measure of the ability of these systems to absorb changes of state variables, driving variables, and parameters, and still persist. In this definition resilience is the property of the system and persistence or probability of extinction is the result.

The various key elements of engineering and ecological resilience are outlined in Table 3.1. As Holling (2010, p. 54) observed, "The two contrasting aspects of

Table 3.1 Engineering and ecological resilience

Engineering resilience	Ecological resilience
Static/constant	Dynamic/change
Complicated systems	Complex systems
Equilibrium	Domain of attraction (regimes)
Predictable	Unpredictable
Numerical values of state variables	Relationships between structure and function
Rate of recovery after perturbation (elasticity)	Ability to absorb the effects of disturbance
Maximising system performance	Preserving desirable system function
Optimal control	Monitoring and predicting

Sources: Based on Grimm and Calabrese (2011); Song et al. (2015); Hall et al. (2018).

stability – essentially one that focuses on maintaining efficiency of function (engineering resilience) and one that focuses on maintaining existence of function (ecological resilience) – are so fundamental that they can become alternative paradigms." Yet despite the fundamental differences between the two approaches and their implications for how resilience is conceptualized and understood, the majority of studies of tourism and resilience have not clearly defined how their research relates to the different framings of resilience and the important assumptions made with respect to the nature of the system, equilibrium, and change (Hall, 2016, 2018).

Hall (2016, p. 279) argues that,

> In ecology, resilience is neither a positive nor a negative: while longer-term survival may be appreciated by an individual of a species (if they are cognizant enough to appreciate such things), it may make no difference to the survival of a species or to ecosystem stability.

However, if human agency is included in formulating notions of resilience and their application and value, especially when the focus shifts from the resilience of a system to the resilience or survival of a firm, organization, or individual, then this suggests a shift towards a more deterministic understanding of change in which communities, organizations, and individuals supposedly possess the attributes with which to adapt to external change (Hall, 2016; Hall et al., 2018). The expansion of resilience concepts to include human elements and encompass a much wider social-ecological systems perspective therefore "represents a shift not only in focus and from single and multiple and interdisciplinary analysis, it also integrates a new set of ideas around adaptation and adaptive capacity, learning and innovation" (Brown, 2016, p. 79). Such a perspective of resilience "acknowledges that people themselves are able to shape the trajectory of change … and play a central role in the degree and type of impact caused by the change" (Maguire & Cartwright, 2008, p. 5).

Destinations and resilience

From a socio-ecological resilience perspective, resilience practice is very much concerned with the thresholds at which one regime shifts to another. In such a shift the system behaves in a different way and has a different identity (Walker & Salt, 2012). Such shifts are often difficult to identify until after they have occurred because the variables in the system do not demonstrate a simple linear response (as may be suggested from an engineering resilience perspective). Grimm and Calabrese (2011, p. 10) note that from such an approach

> management should not be concerned about equilibria and some kind of "balance of nature," but should instead focus on the key mechanisms that allow a system to persist, and on the fact that these mechanisms have only a certain capacity, which can be reduced by environmental change and human impact.

Critical to these are the notions of the adaptive cycle and panarchy.

The adaptive cycle model is a way of describing the progression of a socio-ecological system over time and its associated resilience in terms of its various stages of function and organization. The four stages of the cycle are rapid growth, conservation, release, and reorganization, followed again by rapid growth (Holling, 2001). Adaptive cycles tend to apply to smaller spatial units, rather than to entire ecosystems (Grimm & Calabrese, 2011), but this is also a function of the temporal unit used to measure change and potentially the nature of the disturbance (Hall et al., 2018). However, as well as the significance of the adaptive cycles within scales it is also important to recognize that processes and structures are linked – "what happens at one scale can influence or even drive what's happening at other scales" (Walker & Salt, 2006, p. 90). For understandings of destination resilience this is potentially a crucial observation as it means that that the resilience of the destination system, which is the only meaningful notion of destination resilience from an ecological resilience perspective, needs to be seen within the context of what is happening at other scales and in their interaction with the destination system.

The "adaptive and evolutionary nature of adaptive cycles that are nested one within the other across space and time scales" (Holling, Gunderson, & Peterson, 2002, p. 74) is known as a panarchy. Adaptive cycles are nested in a hierarchy across time and space. Larger and slower structures tend to set the conditions in which faster ones function. However, the structures and the relationships between them are not static (Hall et al., 2018). For example, destination systems are embedded within the wider tourism system which is, in turn, subject to broader changes in the socio-economic system. Yet such cross-scale interactions do not just feed 'down' to a destination, they can also come from below – for example, from specific organizational and community systems which are, in turn, potentially influenced by individuals. In addition, Hall et al. (2018) note that as well as vertically nested relations, the tourism system is also characterized by horizontal linkages and relations to other destinations and regions, including at the organizational and individual level, and the inherent mobility of tourists and the potential mobility of organizations and capital. Furthermore, change to a system does not just come from fast external shocks, such as a disaster or crisis, but may also arise from gradual (e.g., impacts of new technological practices such as the internet) or slow cumulative change, as the result, for example, of evolutionary change or changes in socio-technical systems that give rise to habits and social and economic practices. Hall et al. (2018) suggest that the latter has been very poorly explicitly studied in the case of tourism with respect to resilience, including in regard to behavioral responses to environmental change.

Figure 3.1 provides a representation of the panarchical nature of tourism-related resilience. Even though they act differently, social and environmental systems have a symbiotic relationship and the resilience of the tourism system, as well as other socio-economic systems, such as regions, communities, and countries, cannot be resilient if the environmental system is vulnerable (Ruiz-Ballesteros, 2011). The resilience of the tourism system is a product of the

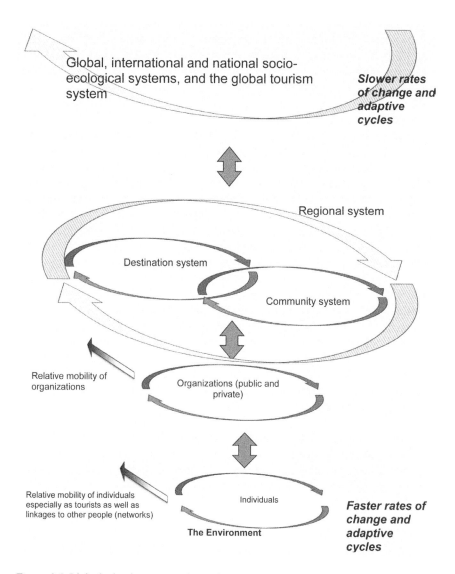

Figure 3.1 Linked adaptive systems in tourism.

Source: Author's own work.

interconnections and linkages between the different parts of the system at different scales. Smaller scale elements such as individuals and, although not included here, physical infrastructure such as rooms and their furnishings, have much higher rates of change than large scale elements, such as regions or the layout of cities (Hall, 2008). Different adaptive capacities also exist at different scales.

However, as noted above, changes at one scale do not necessarily lead to changes at another to which it is connected. From an ecological resilience perspective, the relationships between the elements of a system are not linear (Hall, 2016). Such a situation with respect to the holistic nature of systems clearly creates predictive issues with respect to destination resilience, as well as other elements of the tourism system. Nevertheless, a number of significant observations can be reported that have implications for destinations and their overall sustainability.

First, although connectedness is an important attribute of systems and the panarchical nature of the global tourism system, there is a risk that separate groups, organizations, or destinations may actually become less resilient the more they interact and engage with larger regional, national, and global systems – what can be described as vertical connectedness – as this leads to increased vulnerability to externally induced change (Adger, 2006; Bec, McLennan, & Moyle, 2016). Second, community resilience and cohesion is an important component of destination resilience. Destinations and community systems are not identical but they do substantially overlap. Such horizontal connectness (see Figure 3.1) allows the development of shared communities of interest including, most importantly, given some of the research undertaken on resilience in tourism, a shared place (Biggs et al., 2012, 2015). Third, factors such as diversity, connectivity, and heterogeneity are assumed to contribute to greater resilience (Glassop, 2007; Hall et al., 2018). Redundancy in critical functional groups, which allows for a diversity of responses to different forms of disturbance and environmental variability but maintains similar effects on system function, potentially increases resilience (Brand & Jax, 2007). However, as Hall et al. (2018, p. 155) observed,

> such ecological resilience thinking, which also applies to social, infrastructural and supply-chain resilience, does not transfer very well to dominant modes of engineering and economic thought that focus on efficiency, equilibrium and return time as being the key characteristics of resilience, and that usually seek to remove any perceived system redundancies or inefficiencies.

Indeed, a focus on "efficiency" and "return time" is also one of the hallmarks of neoliberal economic policy which usually seeks to remove any perceived system redundancies or inefficiencies, often by seeking to encourage 'market forces' (Amore & Hall, 2016, 2017; Johnson, 2011; Klein, 2007). For example, in commenting on the Christchurch earthquakes, Hayward (2013, p. 36) observes:

> the rhetoric of resilience is used to justify authorities making decisions quickly and measuring their impact on recovery by the speed with which the city returns to a "new normal" or experiences "certainty" as firm centralized decision making ... the drive for efficiency is all too frequently used to

justify expert command-and-control decision making with little or no meaningful local scrutiny or community leadership in decision making.

All too often the desire of policy-makers to be seen to be 'doing something' and responding quickly to a crisis or disaster has only served to intensify business as usual decision-making, rather than change the paradigms by which the social bases of crisis are ignored (Hall, 2011). As Vale (2014, p. 198) critically observes, "It is all too easy to talk about 'bouncing back to where we were' without asking which 'we' is counted, and without asking whether 'where we were' is a place to which a return is desirable."

Conclusions

In ecology, resilience is neither a positive nor a negative (Hall, 2016). However, the adoption of more normative socio-ecological and other approaches to resilience, such as those informed by disaster capitalism and neoliberalism (Amore & Hall, 2017; Klein, 2007), means that consideration of the role of human agency in both formulating and applying notions of resilience to communities and destinations, and the individuals and organizations within them, becomes extremely important. Tourism researchers have not given enough consideration to these issues, including the significance of defining the tourism system itself. For example, following the 2004 Boxing Day tsunami which hit coastal Sri Lanka, the residents of poor fishing villages were relocated inland, and hotel and resort developments were constructed on land they had previously occupied (Vale, 2014). Hall et al. (2018) suggest that if the 'tourism system' was defined only in narrow terms, this would be regarded as a positive development for the hospitality sector and the tourism system of Sri Lanka overall. However, if the destination system was defined in broader terms to include the communities affected by tourism development, then the loss of livelihood as a result of relocation would be regarded as a negative for the system. Or, at the very least, issues of trade-off could be considered much more explicitly and transparently (Hall et al., 2018). Nevertheless, while the Sri Lankan case provides a particularly graphic example of system definition and response to change it should also be noted that most change is not so sudden. Students of destinations and tourism in general need to develop a far better understanding of gradual change in tourism as well as the significance of tipping points for regime shift.

Notions such as 'bounce back' and 'adaptive capacity' make the implicit assumption that there is a return to a 'new' normal (Pizzo, 2015). Yet the notion of what is normal and what is change is highly contextualized and a product of perspective and the time and spatial scale that is being used. For example, much tourism is built on the unsafe assumption that growth is normal, yet growth cannot last forever. No population, including that of tourists, can increase indefinitely (Hall, 2015). Change, the movement from one state to another, is actually the norm.

But what is important, from a human and ethical perspective, is what sort of change and what sort of state we want to move to and how we are going to get there. It is perhaps this normative issue that lies at the heart of much discussion about resilience, as it does about sustainability.

(Hall et al., 2018, p. 158)

Finally, much more attention needs to be given to analysis of the vulnerability of a destination system before a crisis occurs. A resilient system is not invulnerable to change and perturbation but it retains the capacity to manage the impacts and adapt to circumstances. Resilience means that the connection between the elements in a system is maintained in the face of vulnerability. Not all tourism organizations or individuals are necessary for system maintenance. It is our normative judgements that determine just exactly what, who, where, when, and why such elements are valued and maintained.

References

Adger, W.N. (2006). Vulnerability. *Global Environmental Change, 16*(3), 268–281.

Amore, A., & Hall, C.M. (2016). From governance to meta-governance in tourism?: Re-incorporating politics, interests and values in the analysis of tourism governance. *Tourism Recreation Research, 41*(2), 109–122.

Amore, A., & Hall, C.M. (2017). National and urban public policy agenda in tourism. Towards the emergence of a hyperneoliberal script? *International Journal of Tourism Policy, 7*(1), 4–22.

Bec, A., McLennan, C.L., & Moyle, B.D. (2016). Community resilience to long-term tourism decline and rejuvenation: A literature review and conceptual model. *Current Issues in Tourism, 19*(5), 431–457.

Beichler, S., Hasibovic, S., Davidse, B.J., & Deppisch, S. (2014). The role played by social-ecological resilience as a method of integration in interdisciplinary research. *Ecology and Society, 19*(3), 1–8.

Biggs, D., Hall, C.M., & Stoeckl, N. (2012). The resilience of formal and informal tourism enterprises to disasters: Reef tourism in Phuket, Thailand. *Journal of Sustainable Tourism, 20*(5), 645–665.

Biggs, D., Hicks, C.C., Cinner, J.E., & Hall, C.M. (2015). Marine tourism in the face of global change: The resilience of enterprises to crises in Thailand and Australia. *Ocean & Coastal Management, 105*, 65–74.

Brand, F.S., & Jax, K. (2007). Focusing the meaning(s) of resilience: Resilience as a descriptive concept and a boundary object. *Ecology and Society, 12*(1), 1–23.

Brown, K. (2016). *Resilience, development and global change.* Abingdon, UK: Routledge.

Cutter, S.L., Barnes, L., Berry, M., Burton, C., Evans, E., Tate, E., & Webb, J. (2008). A place-based model for understanding community resilience to natural disasters. *Global Environmental Change, 18*(4), 598–606.

Cutter, S.L., Burton, C., & Emrich, C. (2010). Disaster resilience indicators for benchmarking baseline conditions. *Journal of Homeland Security and Emergency Management, 7*(1), 1–22.

Daily, G., & Matson, P. (2008). Ecosystem services: From theory to implementation. *Proceedings of the National Academy of Sciences, 105*, 9455–9456.

Elmqvist, T., Barnett, G., & Wilkinson, C. (2014). Exploring urban sustainability and resilience. In L.J. Pearson, P.W. Newman, & P. Roberts (Eds.), *Resilient sustainable cities: A future* (pp. 19–28). New York: Routledge.

Glassop, L. (2007). The three Rs of resilience: Redundancy, requisite variety and resources. In R. Kay & K.A. Richardson (Eds.), *Building and sustaining resilience in complex organizations. Pre-proceedings of the 1st International workshop on complexity and organizational resilience* (pp. 19–34). Marblehead, MA: ISCE Publishing.

Gotham, K.F. (2007). (Re)branding the Big Easy: Tourism rebuilding in post-Katrina New Orleans. *Urban Affairs Review*, *42*(6), 823–850.

Gotham, K.F., & Greenberg, M. (2014). *Crisis cities: Disaster and redevelopment in New York and New Orleans*. New York: Oxford University Press.

Grimm, V., & Calabrese, J.M. (2011). What is resilience? A short introduction. In G. Deffuant & N. Gilbert (Eds.), *Viability and resilience of complex systems: Concepts, methods and case studies from ecology and society* (pp. 3–13). Heidelberg: Springer.

Hall, C.M. (2008). *Tourism planning*. Harlow, UK: Pearson.

Hall, C.M. (2010). Crisis events in tourism: Subjects of crisis in tourism. *Current Issues in Tourism*, *13*(5), 401–417.

Hall, C.M. (2011). Policy learning and policy failure in sustainable tourism governance: From first and second to third order change? *Journal of Sustainable Tourism*, *19*(4–5), 649–671.

Hall, C.M. (2012). Island, islandness, vulnerability and resilience. *Tourism Recreation Research*, *37*(2), 177–181.

Hall, C.M. (2015). Economic greenwash: On the absurdity of tourism and green growth. In V. Reddy & K. Wilkes (Eds.), *Tourism in the green economy* (pp. 339–358). London: Earthscan.

Hall, C.M. (2016). Putting ecological thinking back into disaster ecology and responses to natural disasters. In C.M. Hall, S. Malinen, R. Vosslamber, & R. Wordsworth (Eds.), *Business and post-disaster management: Business, organisational and consumer resilience and the Christchurch earthquakes* (pp. 269–292). Abingdon, UK: Routledge.

Hall, C.M. (2018). Resilience in tourism: Development, theory and application. In J.M. Cheer & A. Lew (Eds.), *Tourism, resilience and sustainability: Adapting to social, political and economic change* (pp. 18–33). Abingdon, UK: Routledge.

Hall, C.M., Malinen, S., Vosslamber, R., & Wordsworth, R. (Eds.). (2016). *Business and post-disaster management: Business, organisational and consumer resilience and the Christchurch earthquakes*. Abingdon, UK: Routledge.

Hall, C.M., Prayag, G., & Amore, A. (2018). *Tourism and resilience: Individual, organisational and destination perspectives*. Bristol: Channel View Publications.

Hayward, B. (2013). Rethinking resilience: Reflections on the earthquakes in Christchurch, New Zealand, 2010 and 2011. *Ecology and Society*, *18*(4), 34–42.

Herbane, B. (2010). The evolution of business continuity management: A historical review of practices and drivers. *Business History*, *52*(6), 978–1002.

Holder, J.S. (1980). Buying time with tourism in the Caribbean. *International Journal of Tourism Management*, *1*(2), 76–83.

Holling, C.S. (1973). Resilience and stability of ecological systems. *Annual Review of Ecology and Systematics*, *4*(1), 1–23.

Holling, C.S. (1996). Engineering resilience versus ecological resilience. In P. Schulze (Ed.), *Engineering within ecological constraints* (pp. 31–44). Washington, DC: National Academies Press.

Holling, C.S. (2001). Understanding the complexity of economic, ecological, and social systems. *Ecosystems, 4*(5), 390–405.

Holling, C.S. (2010). Engineering resilience versus ecological resilience. In L.H. Gunderson, C.R. Allen, & C.S. Holling (Eds.), *Foundations of ecological resilience* (pp. 51–66). Washington, DC: Island Press.

Holling, C.S., Gunderson, L.H., & Peterson, G.D. (2002). Sustainability and panarchies. In L.H. Gundersson & C.S. Holling (Eds.), *Panarchy: Understanding transformations in human and natural systems* (pp. 63–102). Washington, DC: Island Press.

Jenson, J.M., & Fraser, M.W. (Eds.). (2015a). *Social policy for children and families: A risk and resilience perspective* (3rd ed.). Thousand Oaks, CA: Sage.

Jenson, J.M., & Fraser, M.W. (2015b). A risk and resilience framework for child, youth, and family policy. In J.M. Jenson and M.W. Fraser (Eds.), *Social policy for children and families: A risk and resilience perspective* (3rd ed.) (pp. 5–24). Thousand Oaks, CA: Sage.

Johnson, C. (2011). *The neoliberal deluge: Hurricane Katrina, late capitalism, and the remaking of New Orleans*. Minneapolis, MN: University of Minnesota Press.

Klein, N. (2007). *The shock doctrine: The rise of disaster capitalism*. New York: Metropolitan Books.

Klein, N., Nicholls, R.J., & Thomalla, F. (2003). Resilience to natural hazards: How useful is this concept? *Environmental Hazards, 5*(1), 35–45.

Lew, A.A., Ng, P.T., Ni, C.C., & Wu, T.C. (2016). Community sustainability and resilience: Similarities, differences and indicators. *Tourism Geographies, 18*(1), 18–27.

Lovejoy, T.E. (1994). The quantification of biodiversity. *Philosophical Transactions of the Royal Society of London. Series B: Biological Science, 345*(1311), 81–87.

Maguire, B., & Cartwright, S. (2008). *Assessing a community's capacity to manage change: A resilience approach to social assessment*. Canberra: Bureau of Rural Sciences.

Matyas, D., & Pelling, M. (2014). Positioning resilience for 2015: The role of resistance, incremental adjustment and transformation in disaster risk management policy. *Disasters, 39*(Suppl. 1), S1–S18.

Meerow, S., & Newell, J.P. (2016). Urban resilience for whom, what, when, where, and why? *Urban Geography, 147*, 38–49.

Meerow, S., Newell, J.P., & Stults, M. (2016). Defining urban resilience: A review. *Landscape and Urban Planning, 147*, 38–49.

Nilakant, V., Walker, B., Kuntz, J., de Vries, H., Malinen, S., Näswall, K., & van Heugten, K. (2016). Dynamics of organisational response to a disaster: A study of organisations impacted by earthquakes. In C.M. Hall, S. Malinen, R. Vosslamber, & R. Wordsworth (Eds.), *Business and post-disaster management: Business, organisational and consumer resilience and the Christchurch Earthquakes* (pp. 35–47). Abingdon, UK: Routledge.

O'Hare, G., & Barrett, H. (1994). Effects of market fluctuations on the Sri Lankan tourist industry: Resilience and change, 1981–1991. *Tijdschrift voor Economische en Sociale Geografie, 85*(1), 39–52.

Orchiston, C., & Higham, J.E.S. (2016). Knowledge management and tourism recovery (de)marketing: The Christchurch earthquakes 2010–2011. *Current Issues in Tourism, 19*(1), 64–84.

Pendall, R., Foster, K., & Cowell, M. (2010). Resilience and regions: Building understanding of the metaphor. *Cambridge Journal of Regions, Economy and Society, 3*, 71–84.

Pizzo, B. (2015). Problematizing resilience: Implications for planning theory and practice. *Cities*, *43*, 133–140.

Prayag, G., & Orchiston, C. (2016). Earthquake impacts, mitigation, and organisational resilience of business sectors in Canterbury. In C.M. Hall, S. Malinen, R. Vosslamber, & R. Wordsworth (Eds.), *Business and post-disaster management: Business, organisational and consumer resilience and the Christchurch earthquakes* (pp. 97–120). Abingdon, UK: Routledge.

Rensel, J. (1993). The Fiji connection: Migrant involvement in the economy of Rotuma. *Pacific Viewpoint*, *34*(2), 215–240.

Ruiz-Ballesteros, E. (2011). Social-ecological resilience and community-based tourism: An approach from Agua Blanca, Ecuador. *Tourism Management*, *32*(3), 655–666.

Sharifi, A., & Yamagata, Y. (2016). On the suitability of assessment tools for guiding communities towards disaster resilience. *International Journal of Disaster Risk Reduction*, *18*, 115–124.

Shaw, K., & Maythorne, L. (2013). Managing for local resilience: Towards a strategic approach. *Public Policy and Administration*, *28*(1), 43–65.

Sheffi, Y. (2015). *The power of resilience: How the best companies manage the unexpected*. Boston, MA: MIT Press.

Song, H.-S., Renslow, R.S., Fredrickson, J.K., & Lindemann, S.R. (2015). Integrating ecological and engineering concepts of resilience in microbial communities. *Frontiers in Microbiology*, *6*, 1298.

Strunz, S. (2012). Is conceptual vagueness an asset? Arguments from philosophy of science applied to the concept of resilience. *Ecological Economics*, *76*, 112–118.

Tyler, D., & Dangerfield, J.M. (1999). Ecosystem tourism: A resource-based philosophy for ecotourism. *Journal of Sustainable Tourism*, *7*(2), 146–158.

Vale, L. (2014). The politics of resilient cities: Whose resilience and whose city? *Building Research & Information*, *42*(2), 37–41.

Walker, B., & Salt, D. (2006). *Resilience thinking: Sustaining ecosystems and people in a changing world*. Washington, DC: Island Press.

Walker, B., & Salt, D. (2012). *Resilience practice: Building capacity to absorb disturbance and maintain function*. Washington, DC: Island Press.

Weichselgartner, J., & Kelman, I. (2015). Geographies of resilience: Challenges and opportunities of a descriptive concept. *Progress in Human Geography*, *39*(3), 249–267.

Xu, L., Marinova, D., & Guo, X. (2015). Resilience thinking: A renewed system approach for sustainability science. *Sustainability Science*, *10*, 123–138.

4 Governance, tourism, and resilience

A long way to go?

Dianne Dredge

Introduction

Welcome to tourism under late modern capitalism in the Anthropocene. The starting point for this chapter is that there are deeply ambiguous tensions between tourism under the extractive practices of late modern capitalism and the sustainability challenge represented by the Anthropocene. This chapter aims to engage in a more complex, critical, theoretically curious, and interdisciplinary discussion about tourism, governance, and resilience than characterizes the extant literature. It seeks to challenge readers' assumptions and excavate meanings underpinning commonly used terms such as sustainability, tourism, resilience, and governance with the intent of provoking deeper thinking, and challenging embedded ways of thinking about these key concepts.

I start by drawing attention to a prevailing tension between tourism and sustainability. On the one hand, tourism under late modern capitalism has enjoyed a long boom; it has doubled down on profit and growth, and showed incredible resilience after the 2008 financial crisis. Advocates continue to argue that tourism contributes to sustainability by valuing the natural and cultural resources on which it relies. On the other hand, tourism is deeply implicated in a range of environmental and ecological changes that affect the Anthropocene including CO_2 emissions, climate change, ecological diversity, and marine pollution (Gössling, Scott, & Hall, 2013; Higham & Miller, 2018; Hollenhorst, Houge-Mackenzie, & Ostergren, 2015). The consensus among scientists is that how we address the challenges captured by the Anthropocene, an epoch in the Earth's evolution marked by significant and sustained anthropogenic impacts on its geology and ecosystems, will determine human survival (Rockström et al., 2009). In this context then, questions about governance strategies for tourism fall within this larger challenge, and cannot be addressed in isolation.

The governance of tourism is concerned with how tourism is steered; who steers, and to what ends does this steering take place. Incorporating sustainability issues into tourism governance strategies has, however, proven to be difficult, with the challenge often being seen as too grand and too complex due to the binary divide between growth and sustainability, or too long-term for the short-term nature of destination politics (Dredge, 2016a; Dredge & Jamal, 2013). To fill this gap, emerging discourses about socio-ecological resilience argue that by decoding the sustainability challenge into smaller parts, social-economic-ecological systems can adapt, rebalance, and cope with change more effectively (Davoudi et al., 2012; Folke, Carpenter, Elmqvist, Gunderson, & Walker, 2002). *Can resilience be decoded into a framework that might assist tourism destinations to adapt and transform on their way to becoming more sustainable?* This is the question addressed in this chapter.

Approach

The departure point for this chapter is to take a complex systems perspective that recognizes that tourism governance takes place in much broader and more complex settings than is often acknowledged. Tourism governance research is often focused on episodes of governance or destination contexts and, for the sake of expediency, word limits, journal scope, and other reasons, researchers often reduce and simplify complexity and de-emphasize factors not immediately evident or relevant to their research (Dredge, 2016a). There is also a tendency for early movers to jump on a term borrowed from other fields, to colonize it, and to argue for its utility, significance, and contribution. Scholarly publishing practices and incentives only exacerbate this approach. Later waves of research usually offer more balanced and critical perspectives and evaluations. This chapter, and Saarinen and Gill's ambition in this volume more generally, is positioned as a contribution within these secondary waves of critical and creative thinking.

To address the above aim, this chapter engages in a more complex, critical, theoretically curious, and interdisciplinary discussion about tourism, governance, and resilience by interrogating two alternative contexts within which the governance of tourism can be positioned. The first of these explores the governance of tourism in the context of the Anthropocene, and the second explores the governance of tourism under late modern capitalism. These two contexts render alternative ways of understanding the challenge of sustainability and governance, and thus provide different departure points for understanding and giving meaning to resilience. Furthermore, while the departure point of this book is resilient destinations, this chapter adopts a non-scalar perspective on destinations. That is, destinations are not seen as compartmentalized, nested territorial concepts but rather sets of interconnected, networked, socio-economic practices simultaneously occurring on multiple scales. They do not exist at a predetermined spatial scale, although governance and policy practices work to constitute destinations (Lagendijk, 2009). The destination management organization (DMO) only prevails because of emphasis given to its socio-economic practices; however, destinations are rarely fixed by these organizational boundaries. By conceptualizing destinations as fluidly constituted through governance practices, we can open up to destination regions being manifested at different scales, overlapping, intersecting, and dynamic. This conceptualization of destinations has important implications for how governance strategies for tourism are framed.

Drawing upon this fluid conceptualization of destinations, the intention of this chapter is not to unfold a single linear narrative about the strengths, weaknesses, and contributions of resilience thinking to the governance of spatially defined tourism destinations. Rather, the chapter seeks to demonstrate that alternative paths exist in how we might conceptualize and understand how resilience thinking might inform the governance strategies of tourism in the transition towards sustainability. Through this approach, and by painting two different scenarios of tourism governance influenced by two different interpretations of the tourism world, the chapter starts to demonstrate how ontology shapes governance. In order to provide structure for the chapter, three key questions are posed to excavate, first, the governance of tourism in the Anthropocene and, second, under late modern capitalism:

- What is the system within which the governance of tourism takes place?
- To what ends is the governance of tourism?
- What/who is present/absent in the governance of tourism?

Following on from a discussion of these three questions in each of the two tourism worlds, the chapter will then address the key question raised earlier: Can resilience be decoded into a framework that assists tourism destinations to adapt and transform on their way to becoming more sustainable?

To illustrate and ground abstract discussion, I draw from previous work in the collaborative economy (Dredge & Gyimóthy, 2017). The intention of using tourism and the collaborative economy is not to present a case study, but rather to provide a complex rendering of the inter-scalar and multi-actor complexity of the wicked problem space that contemporary tourism governance operates within, and how, as discussed above, destinations are fluid constructions. This approach has been adopted as a reflexive response to observation that, all too often, the focus of those responsible for setting up, implementing, and overseeing the governance of tourism is solution-focused, jumping quickly to resolve issues and take action. Not enough time is spent on understanding and tracing the problems, the choices available, or the complexity of the issues (Bason, 2010). Stretching the boundaries of issue identification by conceptualizing the challenge of governance and resilience differently can foster new ways of understanding the challenge and new solutions can emerge. That is, by immersing oneself in the problem identification stage for longer, drawing from alternative ways of thinking about the tourism governance challenge, we might start to identify, unpack, and uncover alternative approaches beyond path dependent ways of thinking, that are fit for complex purposes.

Tourism governance in the Anthropocene

What is the system within which the governance of tourism takes place in the Anthropocene?

While the governance of wicked problems such as tourism calls for a complex systems perspective, there are different ways of conceptualizing that system. It is this ontology, or how we see the world, that shapes the governance strategies that emerge. In rendering a picture of governance in the Anthropocene, I call upon what Abram (1996) refers to as a more-than-human world, the departure point of which is to de-center and draw into question the prevailing human-centered values that underpin the way we understand and frame the challenge of tourism governance and sustainability.

The scientific community supports this call for a philosophical shift in the way we see, understand, and respond to the human-centered imperative of sustainability with scientists coining the term "Anthropocene" (Waters et al., 2016) and the concept of planetary boundaries (Rockström et al., 2009). Put simply, the Anthropocene refers to the current period in the Earth's evolution where the scale of human-induced environmental impact is so great that a transition into a new (and, quite possibly, catastrophic) geological period has been identified (Foster, 2017; Waters et al., 2016). The significance of the Anthropocene is that it brings into sharper focus the entanglements between humans and nature, highlighting that the survival of people and planet is a complex challenge that cannot be addressed by placing human interests at the center.

The conceptual appeal of the Anthropocene as a heuristic construct is that it enables an understanding of the problem as a blending of the needs of the ecological system with socio-economic interests. This socio-ecological system provides the departure point for resilience thinking (Walker & Cooper, 2011). However, there are important critiques emerging about the Anthropocene that go to the heart of how we conceptualize, interpret, and operationalize socio-ecological systems, and that make governance at the scale of the Anthropocene problematic (Biermann et al., 2016; Olsson, Jerneck, Thoren, Persson, & O'Byrne, 2015). First, while an ecological system can be operationalized and analyzed by tracing the functional relationships between elements (e.g., water, fauna, flora, soil, atmosphere, etc.), social systems are more difficult to conceptualize due to their open, discontinuous, and multi-scalar properties. As a consequence, social scientists argue that ecological and social domains cannot be reduced to a common conceptual, theoretical, or analytical framework (Olsson et al., 2015).

Using the example of a forest, Nightingale (cited in West et al., 2015) illustrates the challenge:

> Imagine a forest: the forest consists of relations between all sorts of organisms, the structure of the forest is affected by the harvesting activities of people as well as by various other creatures, the biophysical processes of vegetation growth are affected by atmospheric chemistry, which in turn is shaped by human activities across the globe, the content of the soil reflects the chemicals used by surrounding agricultural areas, and perhaps the forest only exists because it sits on land designated as a "conservation area." What in the forest is "social" and what is "natural?"

Thinking about the role and effects of tourism within the forest landscape only further complicates the challenge. Governance actions are required to manage the natural–social forest at global to micro scales, and across different aspects of both natural resource management regimes and socio-economic regimes. Our divided governance systems reinforce the difficulty of conceptualizing an integrated socio-ecological system, because we have not yet managed to satisfactorily figure out how to think outside the categories of human and nature.

Some researchers have argued that conceptualizing hybrid non-human actors gives these landscapes a presence that can be made explicit and potentially incorporated in governance. For example, the Plastic Gyre – multiple patches of debris comprising mostly plastic pollution and chemical sludge that stretches over the Pacific Ocean – illustrates how complex socio-ecological landscapes or, in this case, marine-scapes, become elevated or explicated in governance systems (Eriksen et al., 2013). The Pacific Gyre has been produced as a result of complex social and ecological processes. Plastics are cheap to produce and have become a ubiquitous part of consumerism; ecological processes in the world's oceans are complex and have received less attention than the terrestrial environment; and environmental governance of the world's oceans have suffered from an 'out-of-sight, out-of-mind' approach for much of the twentieth century. Accordingly, treating the causes and consequences of the Gyre is bigger than any actor or organization, and the floating mass of debris has become a hybrid socio-ecological marine-scape with its own trajectory capable of causing considerable damage to both human and ecological systems. The difficulty here is how we conceptualize what to do about it, and the global to micro scales at which governance action needs to take place.

While the Gyre is often framed as an environmental catastrophe, capitalism, a ubiquitous driver of social, economic, ecological, and political change across the globe, has been largely ignored but is deeply bound up with the production of this hybrid marine-scape (McKinnon & Driscoll Derickson, 2012). This difficulty of understanding, balancing, blending, and developing actions within this hybrid socio-ecological system is always underpinned by values, priorities, and end goals that are generated at different levels and in different actor groups, illustrating that careful integration at local, regional, and global levels is needed.

To what ends is the governance of tourism in the Anthropocene?

Sustainable development is almost universally understood to be the goal of tourism governance for the management of socio-ecological systems. However, sustainable development has been criticized as being too human-centered. To understand why this critique has emerged it is important to contextualize the concept of sustainable development within its twentieth century rational scientific roots. In environmental studies, ecosystems and their capacity to maintain a steady-state have been much discussed (Holling, 1973). Ideally, a steady-state is one in which a system's inputs and outputs are sufficiently balanced so that the system continues to function without any reduction in its capacity to maintain itself. It is this steady-state rationale that lies at the origin of sustainability thinking. Applied in complex, open socio-ecological systems however, the notion of a steady-state is highly problematic. Not only can ecological processes be disrupted as a result of external factors outside what may be anticipated (suggesting that the traditional systems approach is limited by the boundedness of human cognition), but the dominance of political, cultural, economic, and behavioral influences means that a human-centered approach to sustainable goals and practices prevails (Caldwell, 2013). This has led some to declare "the end of sustainability" (Benson & Craig, 2014). Others have declared that, while the term might be 'past its use-by date,' we will just have to live with the consequences and adapt to the disruptive consequences of the current trajectory (Foster, 2017).

Looking for a way to overcome the criticisms associated with sustainability, and based on the observation that ecosystems can adapt over time, ecologists were among the first to observe how complex systems absorb shocks, adapt to disruption, and build resilience (Adger, 2000; Bergen, Bolton, & Fridley, 2001; Holling, 1973). The implication from this thinking was that understanding more about how natural systems adapt and build resilience might provide a window to understanding how we might progressively adapt towards the shifting goals of sustainability. As a result, resilience thinking has received considerable attention as a more action-oriented, adaptive, and achievable response to the longer-term goals of sustainability. In resilience thinking, the emphasis is on decoding the sustainability challenge into smaller adaptive actions that allow socio-ecological systems to rebalance and cope with change (Davoudi et al., 2012; Folke et al., 2002).

What/who is present/absent in the governance of tourism in the Anthropocene?

At the core of the tourism governance challenge in the Anthropocene there is a paradox. On one hand, the growth of tourism has unleashed a range of well-documented ecological, social, and cultural impacts that have triggered concerns about ecological sustainability, wellbeing, and quality of life (Higham & Miller, 2018). On the other hand, tourism has also been positioned as part of the sustainability solution with advocates adopting an ecosystem services approach, arguing that tourism adds value to the social, cultural, and environmental resources on which it is based (Rode, Wittmer, Emerton & Schröter-Schlaack, 2016). These divergent arguments about the value of tourism have often been positioned as binary opposites with researchers claiming that we need to place more attention on governance and the steering of tourism so that we can achieve win–win outcomes for both sustainability and tourism. However, both sustainability and tourism growth are human-centered constructs. Both serve the interests of capitalism, economic growth, and social priorities, where one set of interests advocate for no/low growth tourism and the other for higher growth. In this traditional approach to tourism governance, the interests of the non-human world, its ecological processes, and nature, are absent.

If we are to adopt a more holistic approach to tourism governance under the Anthropocene (notwithstanding the challenges discussed above), it requires that we acknowledge the boundedness of our human-centered approach, and extend our thinking beyond what we currently know, to incorporate broader non-human interests. I argued above for a more-than-human approach to governance, which would incorporate the rights of nature to be represented in governance processes. Ecuador was the first country to enshrine the rights of nature within its constitution in 2008 (Youatt, 2017). New Zealand has also given legal personhood to the Te Urewera forest, the Whanganui River, and Mount Taranaki and a number of other countries are also responding to the global rights for nature movement. In this approach, the human element of the socio-ecological system is trying to listen better to the non-human components (Dryzek, 2016).

Youatt (2017) unpacks a range of vexed issues and contradictions in the rights for nature movement, which are outside the scope of this chapter to consider in detail. In relation to governance, however, he rightly points out that by giving legal rights and a political voice to nature, this movement brings nature into the human world. Moreover, by personifying nature, this implies a capacity to voice concerns and act, and thus the question of who/what qualifies to give voice and act as the collective person emerges (Dryzek, 2016). In both Ecuador and New Zealand, indigenous voices are positioned as being the guardians of nature and, while there are still questions about representation, in principle this has opened up the opportunity for indigenous knowledge and cultural values of nature to be represented and for nature to be incorporated into governance without being reduced to an economic construct.

In summarizing the line of argument in the earlier section, the approach was to draw attention to the ontological shift captured in a rendering of the more-than-human world and, if we accept this, the need to step up to a more complex sustainability challenge. Not only is a philosophical–ethical repositioning in the way we see and understand the world required, but we also need governance systems that can reconcile ecological and human values. This demands that we address the historical divide between humans and nature that has, historically, led us to privilege human values over nature in governance. The implications for governance are powerful. In a more-than-human world, governance strategies for tourism would incorporate and treat equally the imperative of sustaining healthy ecological systems alongside human considerations. The dominance of the destination as a spatially defined and territorially nested unit of governance would need to be backgrounded in favor of more complex global to local governance practices that mainstream ecological considerations alongside socio-economic interests (e.g., Dryzek, 2016). The focus on industry interests would need to be balanced against a range of environmental governance activities at different scales and in different policy sectors. This would require vastly different governance infrastructures and a political commitment that would be difficult to garner under late modern capitalism, and it also brings into question whether the current DMO configurations are fit-for-purpose under the Anthropocene.

Tourism under late modern capitalism

What is the system within which the governance of tourism takes place under late modern capitalism?

The Anthropocene, discussed above, identifies the industrial revolution as the turning point when humans began to change nature. However, Moore (2017) argues that the history of capitalism reveals that nature started to be reshaped when colonialism became a global force in the late sixteenth century, and that the term Anthropocene does not adequately take into account the various periods of capitalism and the way these have affected human–nature relationships. For the purposes of this chapter, we focus on late modern capitalism, the term used to describe the current iteration of capitalism under late modernity (see Harvey, 2010; Piketty, 2014). Late modern capitalism is the period that began in the 1980s, starting around the same time as Reaganism and Thatcherism, and we focus on this period because it represents a period of sustained tourism growth under accelerated neoliberalism. Under late modern capitalism, ideologically-driven neoliberal governments began to focus more heavily on capital accumulation, and there has been a reassignment in the value of nature as being of service to capitalism. Cheap nature became a world-praxis (Moore, 2017), which refers to a period wherein the previous respect for, and dependency upon, natural systems has been backgrounded in pursuit of wealth. Nature has become a resource to dominate and exploit, a resource to power economic growth, a 'tap' and a 'sink' to serve capitalism (Sandler, 2009).

In tourism, mass industrialization has flourished under late modern capitalism (World Tourism Organization [UNWTO], 2018). Natural resources and cultural heritage are low-cost resources for exploitation, and governments have become complicit in privatizing and facilitating the appropriation of nature by rolling back established environmental protections. At the same time, there is a trend towards the cheapening of labor by reassigning the value of different types of work; a war is being waged on welfare recipients, and there is a peeling back of long-established social obligations in health, education, and social services (Moore, 2017). Politicians and policymakers wax lyrical about the benefits of trickle-down economics, and yet it has been increasingly argued that there is little or no evidence that the increased profits generated by corporate interests are reinvested in the commons or in nature (Grossberg, 2010; Harvey, 2010; Stiglitz, 2002). Removing labor protections and employer obligations, and providing tax relief for the corporate sector, are also in the crosshairs of government action, all in the pursuit of creating fiscal environments conducive to private sector innovation, growth, investment, and profit. Under these conditions, wages in many countries have stagnated, and there is increased underemployment and casualization of labor. In tourism, this is evident in low wage growth, limited career progression, and increasing casualization. So, along with cheap nature, cheap labor has also facilitated tourism growth (Baum, 2012). The effects of accelerated capitalism have led to what some call the Capitalocene, a term that

Moore (2017) suggests more aptly describes the deepening rift between humans and nature that sits at odds with the Anthropocene. The recent rise of platform capitalism in the tourism collaborative economy provides an insightful example of these processes.

A detour into the tourism collaborative economy

The rise of the collaborative economy has occurred at a time when many destinations are feeling the impacts of decades of pro-growth tourism strategies. Late modern capitalism has fueled the cheapening of nature which has significantly benefited the tourism sector. For example, growth in low cost airline passenger capacity has been stimulated by government policies that have reduced both investment and environmental barriers so that the full environmental cost of travel is not factored into the market. City branding and promotion efforts, as well as the staging of events as economic development tools, have contributed to the intensification of mass tourism activity, where accessing new markets and inventing new products are directed towards the interests of capitalism (Dredge & Gyimóthy, 2017). The digital or platform collaborative economy burst into this space, promising that sharing was less resource consumptive, more authentic, and sustainable (Botsman & Rogers, 2011).

Looked at another way, the rise of the collaborative economy is a new form of capitalism empowered by information and communications technology (ICT) that enables easy entry for micro-entrepreneurs, as well as immediate and seamless financial transactions, and allows the global companies that own such platforms to access and profit from assets they do not own (Slee, 2016). So, instead of destinations having to attract investment in hotel room stock, which requires navigating financial and land use planning systems (which takes time), collaborative economy accommodation has been a tool to grow tourism at the fringes of planning and regulation. Historically, these planning and regulation systems were designed through democratic processes to protect public interests, including nature. However, the rise of the collaborative economy illustrates the drive and resilience of capitalism to innovate its way through obstacles such as local regulations.

As a consequence of the rapid uptake of collaborative economy accommodation, housing shortages and affordability issues have emerged (Dredge, 2016a). The causes of these housing issues are complex and historically embedded in, for example, the evolution of national and regional housing policies and infrastructure and investment policies, which have shaped the supply and demand for housing; they have shaped the behaviors of markets and capital investment and, in turn, contributed to current housing shortages and affordability issues. The collaborative economy accommodation sector has grown, in part, due to the natural tendency of capital to maximize its return on investment. One impact of this is that short-term tourism rental is more profitable than renting to local residents. As a result, investors seeking to maximize their returns have been drawn to the collaborative economy accommodation sector where small investors with as little as one apartment to rent can access the global marketplace. This illustrates the power of capitalism to individualize the market place, making it increasingly difficult to regulate (Dredge & Jenkins, 2012).

A 'perfect storm' is the expression used to describe the confluence of issues where dynamics of a wicked policy problem produce synergies – a composite problem – that are significantly more complex and difficult to deal with than if individual issues were addressed separately. The metaphor is particularly apt to describe what is going on in destinations where a number of policy and regulatory issues coalesce, where there are diverse stakeholder interests at play, and the complexity of taking action involves weighing up a range of interconnected actions, interventions, and policy options and evaluating their unknown/known consequences. In this messy space, destination management organizations (DMOs) have provided the traditional governance structure for tourism; however, it is increasingly questioned and, if it is to survive, metamorphosis is required (Dredge, 2016b; Munar, 2016).

What this brief detour has illustrated is that the governance of the collaborative economy as it affects tourism is one aspect of the wider tourism domain. It is messy, it overlaps with a range of other policy sectors and, despite the fact that destinations provide the institutional basis of tourism governance, the tourism collaborative economy cannot be territorially defined. So, instead of viewing destinations as bounded objects, they are better described as an assemblage of open, discontinuous spaces where different aspects of tourism are treated within networks of interest operating across different scales. There are no clear responsibilities; the system is in a constant state of flux. Nature and labor are cheapened in the tourism collaborative economy, having been removed from sight in platform capitalism's use of hosts' assets and subsuming the cost of labor into the product price (Slee, 2016). The liquid mobile business logics of this form of global capitalism ignore local regulatory environments, and the sovereignty of destinations to manage what is happening in tourism at a local level is compromised (Dredge & Jamal, 2013).

To what ends is the governance of tourism under late modern capitalism?

This question has been partially addressed in the above discussion, where it has been argued that the capitalist system that underpins mass tourism also defines the ends of tourism governance. There is no separation between the system and its ends. Global tourism businesses have benefited through tourism policies that have directed public resources towards the opening up of, and increased access to, cheap nature and cheap labor. Direct tourism policies have, for example, sought to reduce government regulation on transport and travel, privatize public assets such as national parks and cultural attractions for tourism use, and stimulate markets through place branding. Indirectly, a range of broader social, economic development, and environmental policy developments, has facilitated travel and mobility. ICT developments have increased awareness of new tourism opportunities, opened up new markets and business logics, and allowed entry into the marketplace of new and hybrid actors (e.g., prosumers). Examples include new digital markets and technological innovations, new modes of exchange such as the digital collaborative economy epitomized by global corporations such as Airbnb and Uber, and distributed production systems that make it easier for consumers to customize their travel and tourism experiences (Dredge & Gyimóthy, 2017). These innovations combined with an increasingly liberalized economic environment and employment conditions have stimulated massive and sustained disruption to traditional tourism systems, often with big winners and losers (Dredge & Gyimóthy, 2017). Some destinations have recorded a massive uplift in visitation leading to exaggerated tourism demand – but overtourism illustrates that these destinations are not necessarily 'winners.' Community resistance and conflict have emerged in a wide range of urban and rural areas, as well as in the peripheral areas, where limits of acceptable change have been reached or exceeded. These outcomes illustrate that despite the claims by international organizations with responsibility for tourism, the ends of the tourism governance system are not focused on nature, community, and labor.

What/who is present/absent in the governance of tourism under late modern capitalism?

Under late modern capitalism, then, the system in which tourism governance takes place is not only dominated by human interests, but capitalism has reasserted itself, reworking and degrading both nature and labor in the process. The economic crisis of 2008 that ricocheted around the world had a patchy but little overall effect on tourism growth, illustrating the ability of capitalism to reshape and re-engineer itself (see Harvey, 2010). Indeed, what is interesting about the post-2008 epoch is not simply the speed of recuperation and the resilience shown by capitalism, but

> the dramatic changes in ways of thought and understanding, of institutions and dominant ideologies, of political allegiances and processes, or political subjectivities, of technologies and organisational forms, or social relations, of the cultural customs and tastes that inform daily life.
>
> (Harvey, 2015, p. x)

In Harvey's view, the institutional environment has adapted to become increasingly focused on growth, profit, and capital accumulation to the exclusion of other non-aligned interests.

To illustrate this, Dredge (2017) explains the changing governance landscape that is unfolding as a result of the increasing power of Airbnb, the emergence of new actors and pressure groups, and the political pressure placed on governments. Since 2008 relations between governments, corporate interests, and lobby groups have strengthened even further and policy has become increasingly closed to outside interests in an effort to consolidate and reinforce the power of capitalism. In this context, science generated from established research institutions about the impact of capitalism on nature can be discarded and alternative, politically motivated evidence is easily generated (Frankfurt, 2005). Following Harvey (2015) as cited above, the system in which governance takes place is then vested in (re)constructing its own interests, and the ideologies, allegiances, and power dynamics at play tend towards dominating and exploiting nature rather than integrating its interests in governance. Not only, as discussed above, is the human–nature binary reinforced, but public and private interests have coalesced under neoliberal ideologies and trickle-down economics. Under these ideologies, the state progresses private interests claiming that a robust private sector is in the public good, and the public good becomes synonymous with the narrow interests of capitalism. The governance system in this context is liquid, defined in relational–functional terms in its pursuit of the self-interest of capitalism (Bauman, 2010).

Discussion

What is the use of resilience?

Returning to the overarching intention of this chapter, to investigate whether resilience thinking has a useful role to play in tourism governance, we can now turn to explore resilience in the context of destinations. Discussions of resilience have tended to adopt a fixed territorial notion of the destination region, with two broad interpretations emerging. First, a common-sense understanding of resilience is a single step 'bounce-back' version where the region returns to its previous state. Second, complex-systems thinking has contributed the idea of a multi-equilibrium model where the system adapts to a new steady-state (Pendall, Foster, & Cowell, 2010). In this variation, the region has the ability to bounce-back and transform, changing its economic structure, labor, and/or institutional systems in an adaptive manner (Simmie & Martin, 2010). Resilience then, is the capacity of a region to be moved off its equilibrium path (i.e., sensitivity to shock) and its adaptive response (i.e., recovery back to equilibrium) (Simmie & Martin, 2010). Applied to tourism, resilience is the capacity of the tourism system not only to respond to shocks, but also the capacity of that system to rebalance and adapt and, in the process, build in long-term measures to guard against future shocks. This conceptualization fits comfortably with a tourist destination defined as a territorial region, but if the earlier challenge of governance in the Anthropocene is taken up, then resilience takes on a new global to local complexity.

How regions build resilience has been a subject of much interest, especially in evolutionary economics and institutional geography (Pendall et al., 2010; Simmie & Martin, 2010), as well as in tourism (Brouder, 2014). The influence of path dependency has been explored, where resilience is thought to be affected by a region's dependency, or lock-in, to a particular development trajectory. In tourism, the nature of its assets and resources, the structure of labor supply, institutional systems, and infrastructure may contribute to lock-in. Depending upon the extent of this lock-in to a particular economic path, a region may find it difficult to recover and adapt. In complex systems, the challenge of adapting and recalibrating is even greater because various interdependent components of the system work in complex feedback loops and self-reinforcing ways. The concept of the self-organizing system, where micro-scale interactions occur interdependently and contribute to the co-evolutionary behavior of the macro-system, has been used to describe how large complex systems adapt and maintain themselves. In tourism, evolutionary economics has been used to describe and explain complex destination systems, and how they adapt and transform after disruption, and concepts such as equilibria, thresholds, and feedback mechanisms provide the analytical tools.

Two alternative renderings of the world in which tourism governance takes place have been presented in this chapter: tourism governance in the Anthropocene, and tourism governance under late modern capitalism. These two threads above have drawn attention, first, to the fact that planetary survival depends on recalibrating the way we conceptualize and understand the challenge of sustainability in a more-than-human world. Second, under late modern capitalism (the Capitalocene, according to Moore, 2017), governance systems have adapted to become less open to incorporating non-aligned interests, and the cheapening of both nature and labor has driven a chasm between them and their participation in governance systems. The above discussions raise a series of theoretical questions and practical challenges in considering whether resilience might be a useful concept in governance strategies for tourism.

Is resilience good, bad, or neutral?

Resilience thinking has become a popular theme of research and discussion because it captures the importance of being able to cope with and recover after some disturbance or shock to a system (Olsson et al., 2015). However, is resilience good, bad, or neutral? Our two scenarios reveal important ambiguities and challenges. Under the Anthropocene, ecological resilience is positioned as good and desirable, yet under late modern capitalism we reveal its resilience as being detrimental to both nature and labor due to their cheapening and revaluing as a service to growth, profit, and capital accumulation. Most of the literature on tourism and resilience takes a normative starting point that resilience is good and something to strive towards. But is it? The pertinent questions are: What kind of resilience, and what/who benefits?

What kind of resilience and for what/whom?

In any attempt to answer whether resilience is good, bad, or neutral, we need to ask what kind of resilience are we talking about, and who/what is the subject of resilience. Researchers in tourism have, so far, applied the concept of resilience to regions and their communities, to industry, and to ecological systems. Yet discussions of the ontological foundations on which these case studies have been built tend to lack detail, or lip service is given to socio-ecological resilience without full disclosure of the analytical lens and how humans and nature are reconciled in the one approach. Moreover, the literature has revealed two broad types of resilience: bounce-back resilience and adaptive resilience wherein the system adapts to a new steady-state. Is bouncing back to the same state, or movement to a new state, desirable? In what direction is this adaptation taking place? These are political questions, the answers to which depend on context, but the political response might also be quite different at different levels, in different networks, and among different actors. For example, what might be considered a resilient state at a national level may not be considered resilient at a local level. In terms of how resilience might inform governance strategies for tourism, then, clarity is required about what kind of resilience is being targeted, and who/what is the target of resilience.

What kind of a system are we conceptualizing?

Resilience thinking is based on a complex systems approach, and the rendering of two different kinds of systems in this chapter illustrates that resilience can be conceptualized in terms of a human system or a more-than-human world. The rendering of the two different approaches to the system remind us that the complexity of tourism governance is bounded by our own cognition of the world, the sociocultural knowledge worlds we inhabit, and the analytical lenses and tools we employ to assist in building our understandings. To date, the emphasis has been on governance, resilience, and tourism within an economic system under late modern capitalism, focusing on recuperating visitor numbers or industry recovery (Lew, 2014). Governance strategies usually respond, for example, to how the tourism industry can be more resilient to external shocks and disruptive events (e.g., Biggs, Hall, & Stoeckl, 2012), and how communities can adapt to change (e.g., Bec, McLennan, & Moyle, 2016). Resilience concepts have also been used to explore the management of natural resources under pressure from tourism, climate change, and natural disasters (e.g., Becken, 2013; Becken & Hay, 2012; Strickland-Munro, Allison, & Moore, 2010). The default position is the engineering approach to resilience, which remains human-centered and scientific in its knowledge inputs (Cheer & Lew, 2018; Lew, 2014). While these discussions have often claimed to adopt human–environment systems approaches, details about how social and ecological knowledge, priorities, and processes are reconciled in a single approach are less than clear. That said, resilience shows potential to be a boundary object through which understanding can be shared across different knowledge worlds.

Can resilience be a boundary object that facilitates socio-ecological approaches to governance?

Star and Griesemer (1989) propose the notion of boundary objects as translation devices that are flexible enough to be translated into different socio-technical worlds to produce hybrid understandings. Boundary objects are weakly structured when commonly used, but can be strongly structured in individual cases. Star (2010) has gone on to observe that systems of boundary objects can grow into boundary infrastructures, providing fertile ground for understanding interdisciplinary complexity. Davoudi et al. (2012), for example, have translated resilience from ecology to the social world and then to planning, illustrating its bridging potential. This is an approach also supported in principle by Baggio, Brown, and Hellebrandt (2015, p. 2):

> The broad interpretation of resilience as an ensemble of ideas and theories on how to understand and analyze dynamics of complex systems in different fields may lead us to assume that resilience is a boundary object and therefore able to foster interdisciplinary collaboration. Resilience is thus proposed as a boundary object and a bridging concept, actually fostering communication and collaboration across fields, in other words, fostering interdisciplinarity.

In their analysis of citation networks, however, these authors found that despite the above optimism, resilience was weakly used as a bridge across fields in research practice. There was limited standardization of key concepts, and there has been limited evolution from a vague concept to a more tailored concept that can be used to bridge science and policy realms (Baggio et al., 2015). Herein lies the challenge ahead for tourism and governance research.

Conclusions

In conclusion, we return to the key question raised at the beginning of this chapter: *Can resilience be decoded into a framework that might assist tourism destinations to adapt and transform on their way to becoming more sustainable?* In addressing this question, the chapter has rendered two different approaches to understanding how resilience might be framed. In the process, I have built a complex systems perspective placing tourism and the challenge of resilience and sustainability within a complex, more-than-human world. This approach has moved discussions of tourism governance beyond a relatively tame, human-centered approach to industry resilience, and placed it within the more complex and less certain Anthropocene.

Duit et al. (2010) observe that a first wave of resilience thinking occurred when ecologists picked up the notion and applied it to environmental systems to understand concepts such as equilibrium and adaptation. The second wave of discussion focused on theorizations of resilience within socio-ecological systems, taking as a starting point that any attempt to define, implement, and manage resilience was socially constructed. The third wave, which we now contribute to, carries a more sensitive appreciation of the intertwined influence of ecological, social, political, and institutional realms, and seeks to move beyond normative claims that resilience is good, towards more complex perspectives and understandings (Sawyer, 2005). In this vein, the ambition of this chapter has been to engage in a more complex, critical, theoretically curious, and interdisciplinary discussion about tourism, governance, and resilience from which some final contributions of the chapter can be drawn.

First, this chapter has demonstrated that different applications of resilience thinking open up alternative ways of understanding how resilience can be framed, interpreted, and valued. Governance strategies that pursue resilience under late modern capitalism value very different outcomes to resilience under the Anthropocene. Accordingly, there is a need for governance strategies that engage in purposive and reflexive discussion about what is resilience, equilibrium, adaptation, and other resilience concepts, and to be conscious of assumptions generated from within the socio-technical knowledge world of tourism which predominantly focus on human/industry values. *Second*, the rendering of resilience under late modern capitalism and the Anthropocene opens up the opportunity to compare and contrast the way resilience can be operationalized according to different values. These different approaches demonstrate that resilience can be a boundary object possessing some interpretive flexibility across disciplines. That said, however, resilience terminology and concepts need refinement before interdisciplinary understandings can evolve. *Third*, any development of resilience within governance strategies needs to be clear about what kind of resilience and to what ends. In other words, who/what are the winners in framing resilience in a particular way, and at what cost to other human and non-human interests? Put simply, perhaps, will resilience strategies targeting industry adaptation be at a cost to nature? What will the value to industry be of framing resilience under the Anthropocene? *Fourth*, and finally, resilience thinking has a long way to go before it consolidates its promise of being a socio-ecological approach to progress sustainability. Not only does it require reflexive understanding of the way the system and the ends of resilience are framed, but also the capacity to absorb and/or adapt.

References

Abram, D. (1996). *The spell of the sensuous: Perception and language in a more-than-human world*. New York: Pantheon Books.

Adger, W.N. (2000). Social and ecological resilience: Are they related? *Progress in Human Geography*, *24*(3), 347–364.

Baggio, J.A., Brown, K., & Hellebrandt, D. (2015). Boundary object or bridging concept? A citation network analysis of resilience. *Ecology and Society*, *20*(2), 2.

Bason, C. (2010). *Leading public sector innovation: Co-creating for a better society*. Bristol: Policy Press.

Baum, T. (2012). *Migrant workers in the international hotel industry* (International Migration Paper No. 112). Geneva: International Labour Organization.

Bauman, Z. (2010). *Liquid modernity*. Cambridge, UK: Policy Press.

Bec, A., McLennan, C., & Moyle, B. (2016). Community resilience to long-term tourism decline and rejuvenation: A literature review and conceptual model. *Current Issues in Tourism*, *19*(5), 431–457.

Becken, S. (2013). Developing a framework for assessing resilience of tourism sub-systems to climatic factors. *Annals of Tourism Research*, *43*(4), 506–528.

Becken, S., & Hay, J. (2012). *Climate change and tourism: From policy to practice.* London: Routledge.

Benson, M., & Craig, R. (2014). The end of sustainability. *Society and Natural Resources*, *27*, 777–782.

Bergen, S.D., Bolton, S.M., & Fridley, J. (2001). Design principles for ecological engineering. *Ecological Engineering*, *18*(2), 201–210.

Biermann, F., Bai, X., Bondre, N., Broadgate, W., Chen, C.-T.A., Dube, O.P., … Seton, K.C. (2016). Down to earth: Contextualising the Anthropocene. *Global Environmental Change*, *39*, 341–350.

Biggs, D., Hall, C.M., & Stoeckl, N. (2012). Understanding resilience of formal and informal enterprises to disasters: Reef tourism in Phuket, Thailand. *Journal of Sustainable Tourism*, *20*(5), 645–665.

Botsman, R., & Rogers, R. (2011). *What's mine is yours: How collaborative consumption is changing the way we live.* New York: Collins.

Brouder, P. (2014). Evolutionary economic geography: A new path for tourism studies? *Tourism Geographies: An International Journal of Tourism Space, Place and Environment*, *16*(1), 2–7.

Caldwell, L. (2013). The concept of sustainability: A critical approach. In J. Lemons, L. Welstra, & R. Goodland (Eds.), *Ecological sustainability and integrity: Concepts and approaches* (pp. 1–15). Dordrecht: Springer.

Cheer, J., & Lew, A. (2018). *Tourism, resilience and sustainability: Adapting to social, political and economic change.* Abingdon, UK: Routledge.

Davoudi, S., Shaw, K., Haider, L., Quinlan, A., Peterson, G., Wilkinson, C., … Porter, L. (2012). Resilience: A bridging concept or a dead end? *Planning Theory & Practice*, *13*(2), 299–333.

Dredge, D. (2016a). Tourism and governance. In G. Moscardo & P. Benckendorff (Eds.), *Education for sustainability in tourism: A handbook of processes, resources and strategies* (pp. 75–90). Berlin: Springer.

Dredge, D. (2016b). Are DMOs on a path to redundancy? *Tourism Recreation Research*, *41*(3), 235–253.

Dredge, D. (2017). Policy and regulatory perspectives in the collaborative economy. In D. Dredge & S. Gyimóthy (Eds.), *Collaborative economy and tourism: Perspectives, politics, policies and prospects* (pp. 75–91). Berlin: Springer.

Dredge, D., & Gyimóthy, S. (Eds.). (2017). *Collaborative economy and tourism: Perspectives, politics, policies and prospects.* Berlin: Springer.

Dredge, D., & Jamal, T. (2013). Mobilities on the Gold Coast, Australia: Implications for destination governance and sustainable tourism. *Journal of Sustainable Tourism*, *21*(4), 557–559.

Dredge, D., & Jenkins, J. (2012). Australian national tourism policy: Influences of reflexive and political modernisation. *Tourism Planning and Development*, *9*(3), 231–251.

Dryzek, J. (2016). Institutions for the Anthropocene: Governance in a changing earth system. *British Journal of Political Science*, *46*(4), 937–956.

Duit, A., Galaz, V., Eckerberg, K., & Ebbesson, J. (2010). Governance, complexity, and resilience. *Global Environmental Change*, *20*, 363–368.

Eriksen, M., Maximenko, N., Thiel, M., Cummins, A., Lattin, G., Wilson, S., … Rifman, S. (2013). Plastic pollution in the South Pacific subtropical gyre. *Marine Pollution Bulletin*, *68*, 71–76.

Folke, C., Carpenter, S., Elmqvist, T., Gunderson, L., & Walker, B. (2002). Resilience and sustainable development: Building adaptive capacity in a world of transformations. *Ambio, 31*(5), 437–440.

Foster, J. (2017). Hope after sustainability – Tragedy and transformation. *Global Discourse, 7*(1), 1–9.

Frankfurt, H. (2005). *On bullshit*. Princeton, NJ: Princeton University Press.

Garmestani, A.S., & Benson, M.H. (2013). A framework for resilience-based governance of social–ecological systems. *Ecology and Society, 18*(1), 9.

Gössling, S., Scott, D., & Hall, C.M. (2013). Challenges of tourism in a low-carbon economy. *Wiley Interdisciplinary Reviews: Climate Change, 4*(6), 525–538.

Grossberg, L. (2010). Standing on a bridge: Rescuing economies from economists. *Journal of Communication Inquiry, 34*(4), 316–336.

Harvey, D. (2010). *The enigma of capital and the crisis of capitalism*. London: Profile Books.

Harvey, D. (2015). *Seventeen contradictions and the end of capitalism*. London: Profile Books.

Higham, J., & Miller, G. (2018). Transforming societies and transforming tourism: Sustainable tourism in times of change. *Journal of Sustainable Tourism, 26*(1), 1–8.

Hollenhorst, S.J., Houge-Mackenzie, S., & Ostergren, D.M. (2015). The trouble with tourism. *Tourism Recreation Research, 39*, 305–319.

Holling, C.S. (1973). Resilience and stability of ecological systems. *Annual Review of Ecology and Systematics, 4*, 1–23.

Lagendijk, A. (2009). The accident of the region: A strategic perspective on the construction of a region's significance. In A. Pike (Ed.), *Wither regional studies?* (pp. 49–63). Abingdon, UK: Routledge.

Lew, A. (2014). Scale, change and resilience in community tourism planning. *Tourism Geographies, 16*(1), 14–22.

McKinnon, D., & Driscoll Derickson, K. (2012). From resilience to resourcefulness: A critique of resilience policy and activism. *Progress in Human Geography, 37*(2), 253–270.

Moore, J.W. (2017). The Capitalocene, part I: On the nature and origins of our ecological crisis. *Journal of Peasant Studies, 44*, 594–630.

Munar, A.-M. (2016). Surviving metamorphosis. *Tourism Recreation Research, 41*(3), 358–361.

Olsson, L., Jerneck, A., Thoren, H., Persson, J., & O'Byrne, D. (2015). Why resilience is unappealing to social science: Theoretical and empirical investigations of the scientific use of resilience [online]. *Science Advances, 1*(4), e1400217. Retrieved from http://advances.sciencemag.org/content/1/4/e1400217.full.

Pendall, R., Foster, K., & Cowell, M. (2010). Resilience and regions: Building understanding of the metaphor. *Cambridge Journal of Regions, Economy and Society, 3*, 71–84.

Pike, A., Dawley, S., & Tomaney, J. (2010). Resilience, adaptation and adaptability. *Cambridge Journal of Regions, Economy and Society, 3*, 1–12.

Piketty, T. (2014). *Capital in the twenty-first century*. Cambridge, MA: Belknap Press/ Harvard University Press.

Rockström, J., Steffen, W., Noone, K., Persson, A., Chapin III, F.S., Lambin, E., … Foley, J. (2009). Planetary boundaries: Exploring the safe operating space for humanity. *Ecology and Society, 14*(2), 472–475.

Rode, J., Wittmer, H., Emerton, L., & Schröter-Schlaack, C. (2016). "Ecosystem service opportunities": A practice-oriented framework for identifying economic instruments to enhance biodiversity and human livelihoods. *Journal for Nature Conservation*, *33*, 35–47.

Sandler, B. (2009). Grow or die: Marxist theories of capitalism and the environment. *Rethinking Marxism: A Journal of Economics, Culture and Society*, *7*(2), 38–57.

Sawyer, R.K. (2005). *Social emergence. Societies as complex systems*. New York: Cambridge University Press.

Simmie, J., & Martin, R. (2010). The economic resilience of regions: Towards an evolutionary approach. *Cambridge Journal of Regions, Economy and Society*, *3*, 27–43.

Slee, T. (2016). *What's yours is mine: Against the sharing economy*. New York: OR Books.

Star, L. (2010). This is not a boundary object: Reflections on the origins of a concept. *Science, Technology and Human Values*, *35*(5), 601–617.

Star, S.L., & Griesemer, J. (1989). Institutional ecology, "translations", and boundary objects: Amateurs and professionals on Berkeley's museum of vertebrate zoology. *Social Studies of Science*, *19*, 387–420.

Stiglitz, J. (2002, December 20). There is no invisible hand. *Guardian*. Retrieved from www.theguardian.com.

Strickland-Munro, J.K., Allison, H.E., & Moore, S.A. (2010). Using resilience concepts to investigate the impacts of protected area tourism on communities. *Annals of Tourism Research*, *31*(2), 499–519.

Walker, J., & Cooper, M. (2011). Genealogies of resilience: From systems ecology to the political economy of crisis adaptation. *Security Dialogue*, *43*, 143–160.

Waters, C.N., Zalasiewicz, J., Summerhayes, C., Barnosky, A.D., Clément Poirier, C., Gałuszka, A., ... Wolfe, A.P. (2016). The Anthropocene is functionally and stratigraphically distinct from the Holocene [online]. *Science*, *351*(6269). doi: 10.1126/science.aad2622.

West, S., Galafassi, D., Haider, J., Marin, A., Merrie, A., Ospina-Medina, D., & Schill, C. (2015). *Critically reflecting on social–ecological systems research*. Retrieved from http://rs.resalliance.org/2015/02/11/critically-reflecting-on-social-ecological-systems-research/.

World Tourism Organization (UNWTO). (2018). *UNWTO world tourism barometer*. Retrieved from http://cf.cdn.unwto.org/sites/all/files/pdf/unwto_barom17_06_december_excerpt_.pdf.

Youatt, R. (2017). Personhood and the rights of nature: The new subjects of contemporary earth politics. *International Political Sociology*, *11*, 39–54.

5 Co-evolution and resilient regions

Moving towards sustainable tourism development

Patrick Brouder and Jarkko Saarinen

Introduction

The emergence of an 'evolutionary turn' within economic geography over the last two decades (Coe, 2010; Grabher, 2009; Pike, MacKinnon, & Cumbers, 2015) has recently resulted in a major step forward in tourism research and regional development studies (see Brouder, Anton Clavé, Gill, & Ioannides, 2017). As a framework, the evolutionary turn enables a deeper understanding of the relationship between the tourism economy and the overall community economic development of places (which are more than just 'destinations' and bounded territorial spaces). Evolutionary Economic Geography (EEG) is proving to be a new path towards understanding the long-term sustainable development of destinations (Brouder, 2017). An important advantage of an evolutionary approach is that it takes tourism out of a tourism-centric focus into broader regional and relational contexts, which are vital for understanding the resilience of places.

Indeed, the recent emergence of EEG thinking highlights the resilience perspective and multi-scalar approaches in regional development discussions (Martin, Sunley, Gardiner, & Tyler, 2016). In this respect, Simmie and Martin (2010, p. 27) have indicated that ideas such as resilience "seem to be highly relevant to … understanding the process and patterns of uneven regional development." Resilience itself is a much debated issue in the literature (see Davidson, 2010; Davoudi, 2012; Folke, 2006; Walker & Salt, 2006; also see Chapters 2 and 3 in this book). Its conceptual origins are based on natural sciences with a focus on ecological systems, their stability, and how systems react to disturbance, stress, and shock (Holling, 1973). Nowadays, the concept is widely used in broader socio-ecological system analyses in community, regional, and tourism development contexts, for example (see Berkes & Ross, 2016; Calgaro, Lloyd, & Dominey-Howes, 2014; Lew, 2014; Martin et al., 2016; Strickland-Munro, Allison, & Moore, 2010).

As a conceptual approach, resilience aims to deal with change (Berkes & Ross, 2013). It involves both the ability to recover from a shock but also to resist that disturbance by processing a transition from one socio-economic structure to another (Hill, Wial, & Wolman, 2008). Thus, in regional and tourism development studies the issue of resilience relates to a long-running core question: Why do some places manage to succeed and overcome difficulties while others fail (see Christopherson, Michie, & Tyler, 2010; Coe, 2010)? In this context, the term 'regional resilience' has become much used, partly due to the recent economic crisis as well as uncertainties and inequalities in global and regional development (Boschma, 2015). It has various meanings in the literature (see Bristow, 2010; Martin et al., 2016; Slocum & Kline, 2014), but in general the term refers to an ongoing process in which regions are not just coping with and accommodating shocks and other disturbances in order to recover to a stable equilibrium state (Simmie & Martin, 2010). Rather, the concept extends "to the ability of regions to reconfigure their socio-economic and institutional structures to develop new growth paths" (Boschma, 2015, p. 734). In this respect, resilience thinking involves both reactive and proactive dimensions in tourism destination development (see Chapter 2).

In this chapter we highlight the position of evolutionary studies within tourism in terms of its ability to lead to a deeper understanding of regional resilience in destinations. By drawing on the literature on institutions in tourism and the emerging concept of co-evolution from EEG, we show how destinations might better approach tourism development opportunities with a view to maximizing local benefits and reducing long-term risks. At the same time, they would remain open to the long-term changes in the place/destination which may alter the importance of tourism, in some cases even reducing tourism's share of the regional economy.

Tourism destination development in an evolutionary context

Studying how tourism evolves in a place over time has been a major subject of study for tourism geographers and other scholars for decades. From Butler's very well-known tourist area cycle of evolution (TALC) (Butler, 1980) through to Lew's recent study of fast and slow resilience in destinations (Lew, 2014) there has been great interest in understanding change. While the recent turn towards resilience within tourism has been welcome, many studies of destination resilience still fall into the trap of looking only at the tourism sector, a critique which has been levelled against the TALC and almost all tourism development models since (and before!). We argue that destination resilience can only be fully understood in the context of regional evolution and that this holds true whether the emphasis is on the economic, ecological, or sociocultural aspects of resilience (though a thorough analysis of resilience should include all three!). From a tourism evolution perspective, EEG enables a broader approach by incorporating evolution between tourism paths and between tourism and other sectors, although the emphasis within EEG in tourism has focused on the economic aspect.

The existing literature on tourism and resilience has shown a greater need to understand short-term and long-term change and how the processes which cause changes are manifested in destinations. This builds on past studies of sustainability in tourism where calls were made to move from sustainability as a desired state to understanding the processes which lead to a more sustainable development in destinations. In this chapter we build on the significant legacy of sustainable development in tourism studies (Saarinen, 2006) and resilience studies in tourism (see Butler, 2017; Cheer & Lew, 2018; Hall, Prayag, & Amore, 2018; Lew & Cheer, 2018) and try to further nuance these approaches through an evolutionary lens.

The twenty-first century has seen a rise in the so-called 'evolutionary turn' in economic geography (Grabher, 2009) and papers inspired by evolutionary theory have had a significant impact on economic geography (Coe, 2010). More than just another 'turn' the evolutionary project in geography has started to challenge other epistemological approaches to more deeply consider how change occurs over time. EEG is based on three theoretical antecedents: path dependence, complexity theory, and generalized Darwinism (Boschma & Martin, 2010). The central place of complexity theory, in particular, forms a natural epistemological bridge to resilience theory (Meekes, Parra, & de Roo, 2016). From a tourism studies perspective, complexity theory has for a long time been a subject of interest (Baggio, 2008; Milne & Ateljevic, 2001) and the recent renewal of interest in complexity has been driven by the rise of evolutionary and resilience approaches to understanding destination change. What has been lacking until now is a conceptual interrogation of the potential links between tourism resilience and tourism evolution – an area with fertile ground for conceptual development and empirical inquiry.

One area of common ground for investigation is the role of agency in destination development. Agency is central to evolutionary studies in tourism as demonstrated in the case of Whistler, a resort municipality in western Canada where sustainable development principles have guided local tourism development for decades (Gill & Williams, 2011, 2014). One potential distinction between tourism evolution and tourism resilience is the notion of new-path creation (or indeed path plasticity) in tourism which opens the potential for completely new development paths rather than attempts to maintain the status quo (a simplistic critique of resilience!). It is important to note here that EEG appears more open to considerations of non-tourism development. Larsson and Lindström (2014), for example, compared how new tourism developments co-evolved with the traditional boat-building industry in Sweden. While they showed that such co-evolution is not without its problems, the very fact that theirs was a cross-sectoral approach is something that needs to be considered more often in tourism studies since most destinations are actually regional economies with the destination being only one layer of the economy or, indeed, society. Thus, "potential exists for studies to include the multiple, co-evolving, tourism development paths within a regional economy of multiple, co-evolving, non-tourism development paths" (Brouder & Eriksson, 2013, p. 374). The extant studies on resilience in tourism have tended towards a tourism-only focus. While this makes for prudent methodological reductionism, it also tends towards a limiting epistemological reductionism – which is not fully reflective of what resilience truly means in a place-based context (as most places are made up of more than just tourism) that is also part of a wider network of places and processes in between places.

The evolutionary perspective: evolving towards resilient destinations

One constructive way forward is to explore the potential fusion of different theoretical frames. For example, Patchell and Hayter (2013) have called for closer links between environmental economic geography and EEG, which sounds very much like a clarion call for resilience researchers. Basically, there are three types of approaches in regional resilience studies (Boschma, 2015), emerging from different understandings of resilience thinking (Davoudi, 2012). The first is based on an engineering approach to resilience (see Lew, 2014), and refers to the ability of a regional economy to return to a pre-existing steady state after a disturbance/shock. This assumption of a pre-existing stable equilibrium state has turned out to be problematic, in both theory and practice, in regional development research (Simmie & Martin, 2010).

Instead of a single equilibrium state, the second approach is based on multiple equilibria (Boschma, 2015), and originates from ecological studies (Holling, 1973). As noted earlier, this approach was later extended to include both ecological and social systems (see Berkes & Folke, 1998). In principle, the (socio-)ecological approach has a long tradition in economic geography and tourism research. The TALC, for example, can be interpreted as being based on a multiple equilibria approach. In short, the model depicts the change process of a destination from the early exploration and involvement stages through the development and consolidation stages, and finally to the stagnation stage (Butler, 1980). According to the model, every destination has a carrying capacity, a limit to its growth, and eventual emergent stagnation indicates that this limit has been reached. However, although somewhat deterministic (Ma & Hassink, 2013) in its path-dependency, the model is cyclical (Baum, 1998; Butler, 2004): after stagnation the evolution cycle can start again and exhibit new growth. This 'path-creation' leading the growth of tourism over the limits of carrying capacity (based on a specific 'destination product') may be highly problematic for the sustainability of tourism development (Saarinen, 2006). This highlights the challenges between resilience and sustainability in a short-term analysis (see Martin & Sunley, 2014; Chapter 2 in this book) as a resilient destination can be locked-in to unsustainable practices and structures in a long-term perspective. Here, however, this cyclical development path does indicate that there may be multiple equilibria for destination development based on the TALC. Thus, in this situation the previous development path 'disappears' (Christopherson et al., 2010) and a resilient destination shifts its weight from one equilibrium to another. Obviously, a shock or other disturbance can lead destination development to decline after the stagnation phase. This demon-strates the idea of multiple equilibria, with negative cycles due to over-development and loss of attractiveness in tourism, for example, or due to a wider socio-economic shift since sector-specific disturbances are often echoes of developments in other sectors, as well as other processes beyond a destination-specific scale.

The third and most recent approach in research on resilient regions has been based on an evolutionary perspective. It focuses on long-term evolution (Simmie & Martin, 2010), making the relationship between resilience and sustainability less problematic for the governance of tourism destination system and development. Evolutionary resilience refers to the capacity of a destination to "sustain long-term development" and "respond positively to short-term shocks" (Boschma, 2015, p. 735). From this perspective, destination resilience is an ongoing process without thinking of recovery to steady and pre-defined equilibrium states (Simmie & Martin, 2010). Thus, EEG does not use equilibrium-based assumptions for the development of the spatial economy, focusing instead on the historically-contingent, geographically-rooted, long-term processes of economic transformation over time. Evolution is driven by continuous change from within a given region (Boschma & Martin, 2007), which is not understood as a bounded space with fixed territorial boundaries. Instead, regions and destinations are regarded as relational spaces (see Hassink, Klaerding, & Marques, 2014) and part of multi-scalar processes (see Saarinen, 2004), wherein resilience depends on the ability of destinations to cope with and work with change. This ability to maintain and create new growth relates to the adaptive capacity (adaptation and adaptability) (Adger, 2000) of destination systems (see Grabher, 1993).

In the evolutionary context of resilient regions, EEG research involves three foundations: path dependence, complexity theory and generalized Darwinism (Boschma & Martin, 2010; Coe, 2010). These conceptual foundations are the bedrock on which empirical work is built, although recently the aspect of generalized Darwinism has faced criticism (see Martin & Sunley, 2015). While methodological reductionism leads researchers to focus on one or other of these, the holistic epistemology of EEG requires that all three must be kept in mind when designing empirical work so that studies may fit into the overarching framework.

Research in EEG is concerned with economic novelty (innovation), how spatial structures emerge (as economic activity self-organizes over time), and how path dependence (and new path creation) are inherently place dependent (Martin & Sunley, 2006). The more mature field of evolutionary economics sees the 'creative destruction' of firm routines as causing change in the economy and EEG adds to this by investigating whether these processes of creative destruction are also place dependent. Rigby and Essletzbichler (2006) examined the routines and technologies of firms across US regions and found that they differ geographically, thus affecting economic performance across space. EEG is then distinct as it focuses on the regional scale; learning tends to be geographically-bounded (Boschma & Martin, 2007) and analysis spatially grounded (see Harvey, 1993) – facts which are highly intuitive to tourism scholars as the tourism sector is place-based, yet we know there is more to tourism development than simply location.

Evolutionary studies within tourism have focused on two main areas: path dependence (and new path creation) and co-evolution (mostly of tourism paths within a destination region). Studies of path dependence in tourism (see Williams & Baláž, 2000, 2002) have shown how the historical legacy in a given region can impact (both positively and negatively) the evolution of the tourism economy over time (Saarinen & Kask, 2008). More recent studies of path dependence in tourism (see Gill & Williams, 2011; Halkier & Therkelsen, 2013) have shifted the focus to the agency of tourism stakeholders in breaking away from negative development paths and creating new ones. Such studies answer the call of EEG scholars who call for studies of just how change occurs rather than post hoc analyses showing various stages of local convergence (Coe, 2010; Martin & Sunley, 2010). There is great potential in aligning such studies with the emerging literature on regional resilience in tourism as individual agency and new path creation are fundamental to long-term resilience.

There has been a relentless gap between economic geography and tourism studies (Ioannides, 2006; Ioannides & Brouder, 2017) despite the strong potential for new research paths (see Brouder et al., 2017; Ioannides & Debbage, 1998). For instance, Sanz-Ibáñez and Anton Clavé (2014) have called for relational approaches to be linked to evolutionary studies in tourism, and Meekes et al. (2016) have also argued for a complex adaptive systems approach to evolutionary studies in tourism. Tourism research is also adding to understandings of co-evolution in EEG. Papatheodorou (2004) noted how evolutionary economics could aid understanding of the inter-relations between tourism stakeholders. EEG now "has potential to develop academic understanding of small-scale tourism in regions where it is not the dominant sector, or where it is made up of multiple (perhaps even contesting) paths" (Brouder & Fullerton, 2015), with EEG approaches seeing complexity as including intra-regional and inter-sectoral co-evolution. Such an approach is fully in line with resilience thinking for sustainable tourism governance (Bramwell, 2011).

Discussion and conclusion

There is great potential in utilizing evolutionary theory in studies of destination resilience and in connecting it to sustainability governance in tourism. In this chapter we have called for a hybrid approach using EEG in tourism studies in a heuristic manner to better understand destination resilience. We are not suggesting the privileging of EEG over resilience theory per se, but rather see this as an innovative way to investigate the possibilities for conceptual hybridity as well as a means to investigate the limitations of such an approach. The simplistic critique that evolutionary theory has no telos does not hold up in studies of EEG, as Essletzbichler (2009) has argued. In fact, by embracing resilience theory EEG gains two important insights – the environmental perspective which is central to resilience theory and the need for a vision of long-term sustainability for regions. What EEG brings to the table is a strong focus on the mechanisms of change and on the agency of stakeholders as well as a broader perspective beyond tourism through the concepts of path creation and regional sectoral branching.

Tourism researchers are increasingly concerned with questions of sustainable destination governance with various models and best practices presented on how to successfully manage destinations. This chapter has provided an alternative approach to destination governance thinking. Highlighting the concept of co-evolution, a new approach is outlined for a more organic destination governance system. Co-evolution occurs in a number of ways: between distinct groups of tourism businesses (grouped by sub-region or sub-sector), between tourism development paths and other economic development paths (across the regional economy), and between tourism businesses and regional institutions (standard co-evolutionary approach) (Brouder & Fullerton, 2017). Brouder and Fullerton (2015) also used EEG to explore the under-researched rural tourism development paths within the mass tourism destination of Niagara, Canada, showing that these distinct rural and mass paths are co-evolving over time.

This type of organic destination governance system must focus on the institutional geographies of the region since successful long-term regional tourism development requires some regional institutional reconfiguration. The role of tourism researchers then is to analyze the level of institutional coherence and cohesion across the region in order to reveal the level of stasis in destination governance. Ultimately, policy should be directed towards encouraging the dynamism which is inherent to regional tourism evolution but which is often stifled by the prevailing governance framework. Such broader and more dynamic understandings of destination change, with destinations as one layer of complex, co-evolving places, will strengthen future studies of tourism resilience.

References

Adger, W.N. (2000). Social and ecological resilience: Are they related? *Progress in Human Geography, 24*, 347–364.

Baggio, R. (2008). Symptoms of complexity in a tourism system. *Tourism Analysis, 13*(1), 1–20.

Baum, T. (1998). Taking the exit route: Extending the tourism area life cycle model. *Current Issues in Tourism, 1*, 167–175.

Berkes, F., & Folke, C (Eds.). (1998). *Linking social and ecological systems*. Cambridge, UK: Cambridge University Press.

Berkes, F., & Ross, H. (2013). Community resilience: Toward an integrated approach. *Society and Natural Resources, 26*, 5–20.

Berkes, F., & Ross, H. (2016). Panarchy and community resilience: Sustainability science and policy implications. *Environmental Science and Policy, 61*, 185–193.

Bramwell, B. (2011). Governance, the state and sustainable tourism: A political economy approach. *Journal of Sustainable Tourism, 19*(4–5), 459–477.

Bristow, G. (2010). Resilient regions: Re-"place"ing regional competitiveness. *Cambridge Journal of Regions, Economy and Society, 3*(1), 153–167.

Boschma, R. (2015). Towards an evolutionary perspective on regional resilience. *Regional Studies, 49*(5), 733–751.

Boschma, R., & Martin, R. (2007). Editorial: Constructing an evolutionary economic geography. *Journal of Economic Geography, 7*(5), 537–548.

Boschma, R., & Martin, R. (2010). The aims and scope of evolutionary economic geography. In R. Boschma & R. Martin (Eds.), *The handbook of evolutionary economic geography* (pp. 3–39). Cheltenham, UK: Edward Elgar.

Brouder, P. (2017). Evolutionary economic geography: Reflections from a sustainable tourism perspective. *Tourism Geographies, 19*(3), 438–447.

Brouder, P., Anton Clavé, S., Gill, A., & Ioannides, D. (Eds.). (2017). *Tourism destination evolution*. London: Routledge.

Brouder, P., & Eriksson, R.H. (2013). Tourism evolution: On the synergies of tourism studies and evolutionary economic geography. *Annals of Tourism Research, 43*, 370–389.

Brouder, P., & Fullerton, C. (2015). Exploring heterogeneous tourism development paths: Cascade effect or co-evolution in Niagara? *Scandinavian Journal of Hospitality and Tourism, 15*(1–2), 152–166.

Brouder, P., & Fullerton, C. (2017). Co-evolution and sustainable tourism development: From old institutional inertia to new institutional imperatives in Niagara. In P. Brouder, S. Anton Clavé, A. Gill, & D. Ioannides (Eds.), *Tourism destination evolution* (pp. 149–164). London: Routledge.

Butler, R.W. (1980). The concept of a tourist area life cycle of evolution: Implications for management of resources. *The Canadian Geographer, 24*(1), 5–12.

Butler, R.W. (2004). The tourism area life cycle in the twenty-first century. In A.A. Lew, C.M. Hall, & A.M. Williams (Eds.), *A companion to tourism* (pp. 159–169). Oxford: Blackwell.

Butler, R.W. (2017). *Tourism and resilience*. Chichester, UK: CABI.

Calgaro, E., Lloyd, K., & Dominey-Howes, D. (2014). From vulnerability to transformation: A framework for assessing the vulnerability and resilience of tourism destinations. *Journal of Sustainable Tourism, 22*(3), 341–360.

Cheer, J., & Lew, A.A. (Eds.). (2018). *Tourism, resilience, and sustainability: Adapting to social, political and economic change*. London: Routledge.

Christopherson, S., Michie, J., & Tyler, P. (2010). Regional resilience: Theoretical and empirical perspectives. *Cambridge Journal of Regions, Economy and Society, 3*(1), 3–10.

Coe, N.M. (2010). Geographies of production I: An evolutionary revolution. *Progress in Human Geography, 35*(1), 81–91.

Davidson, D.J. (2010). The applicability of the concept of resilience to social systems: Some sources of optimism and nagging doubts. *Society and Natural Resources, 23*, 1135–1149.

Davoudi, S. (2012). Resilience: A bridging concept or a dead end? *Planning Theory & Practice, 13*(2), 299–307.

Essletzbichler, J. (2009). Evolutionary economic geography, institutions, and political economy. *Economic Geography, 85*(2), 159–165.

Folke, C. (2006). Resilience: The emergence of a perspective for social–ecological systems analyses. *Global Environmental Change, 16*, 253–267.

Gill, A.M., & Williams, P.W. (2011). Rethinking resort growth: Understanding evolving governance strategies in Whistler, British Columbia. *Journal of Sustainable Tourism, 19*(4–5), 629–648.

Gill, A.M., & Williams, P.W. (2014). Mindful deviation in creating a governance path towards sustainability in resort destinations. *Tourism Geographies, 16*(4), 546–562.

Grabher, G. (Ed.). (1993). *The embedded firm: On the socio-economics of industrial networks*. London: Routledge.

Grabher, G. (2009). Yet another turn? The evolutionary project in economic geography. *Economic Geography, 85*(2), 119–127.

Halkier, H., & Therkelsen, A. (2013). Exploring tourism destination path plasticity: The case of coastal tourism in North Jutland, Denmark. *Zeitschrift für Wirtschaftsgeographie, 57*(1–2), 39–51.

Hall, C.M., Prayag, G., & Amore, A. (2018). *Tourism and resilience: Individual, organizational and destination perspectives*. Bristol: Channel View Publications.

Harvey, D. (1993). From space to place and back again: Reflections on the condition of postmodernity. In J. Bird, B. Curtis, T. Putnam, G. Robertson, & L. Tickner (Eds.), *Mapping the futures: Local cultures, global change* (pp. 3–29). London: Routledge.

Hassink, R., Klaerding, C., & Marques, P. (2014). Advancing evolutionary economic geography by engaged pluralism. *Regional Studies, 48*(7), 1295–1307.

Henning, M., Stam, E., & Wenting, R. (2013). Path dependence research in regional economic development: Cacophony or knowledge accumulation? *Regional Studies, 47*(8), 1348–1362.

Hill, E., Wial, H., & Wolman, H. (2008). *Exploring economic regional resilience* (Institute of Urban and Regional Development Working Paper 2008/04). Berkeley, CA: University of California.

Holling, C.S. (1973). Resilience and stability of ecological systems. *Annual Review of Ecology and Systematics, 4*, 1–23.

Ioannides, D. (2006). The economic geography of the tourist industry: Ten tears of progress in research and an agenda for the future. *Tourism Geographies, 8*(1), 76–86.

Ioannides, D., & Brouder, P. (2017). Tourism and economic geography redux: Evolutionary economic geography's role in scholarship bridge construction. In P. Brouder, S. Anton Clavé, A. Gill, & D. Ioannides (Eds.), *Tourism destination evolution* (pp. 183–193). London: Routledge.

Ioannides, D., & Debbage, K.G. (1998). *The economic geography of the tourist Industry: A supply-side analysis*. London: Psychology Press.

Larsson, A., & Lindström, K. (2014). Bridging the knowledge-gap between the old and the new: Regional marine experience production in Orust, Västra Götaland, Sweden. *European Planning Studies, 22*(8), 1551–1568.

Lew, A.A. (2014). Scale, change and resilience in community tourism planning. *Tourism Geographies, 16*(1), 14–22.

Lew, A.A., & Cheer, J. (Eds.). (2018). *Tourism resilience and adaptation to environmental change: Definitions and frameworks*. London: Routledge.

Ma, M., & Hassink, R. (2013). An evolutionary perspective on tourism area development. *Annals of Tourism Research, 41*(1), 89–109.

Martin, R., & Sunley, P. (2006). Path dependence and regional economic evolution. *Journal of Economic Geography, 6*(4), 395–437.

Martin, R., & Sunley, P. (2010). The place of path dependence in an evolutionary perspective on the economic landscape. In R. Boschma & R. Martin (Eds.), *The handbook of evolutionary economic geography* (pp. 62–92). Cheltenham, UK: Edward Elgar.

Martin, R., & Sunley, P. (2014). On the notion of regional economic resilience: Conceptualization and explanation. *Journal of Economic Geography, 15*(1), 1–42.

Martin, R., & Sunley, P. (2015). Towards a developmental turn in evolutionary economic geography. *Regional Studies, 49*(5), 712–732.

Martin, R., Sunley, P., Gardiner, B., & Tyler, P. (2016). How regions react to recessions: Resilience and the role of economic structure. *Regional Studies, 50*(4), 561–585.

Meekes, J.F., Parra, C., & de Roo, G. (2016). Regional development and leisure in Fryslân: A complex adaptive systems perspective through evolutionary economic geography. In P. Brouder, S. Anton Clavé, A. Gill, & D. Ioannides (Eds.), *Tourism destination evolution* (pp. 165–182). London: Routledge.

Milne, S., & Ateljevic, I. (2001). Tourism, economic development and the global–local nexus: Theory embracing complexity. *Tourism Geographies, 3*(4), 369–393.

Papatheodorou, A. (2004). Exploring the evolution of tourism resorts. *Annals of Tourism Research, 31*(1), 219–237.

Patchell, J., & Hayter, R. (2013). Environmental and evolutionary economic geography: Time for EEG[2]? *Geografiska Annaler: Series B, Human Geography, 95*(2), 111–130.

Pike, A., MacKinnon, D., & Cumbers, A. (2015). Doing evolution in economic geography. *Economic Geography, 92*(2), 123–144.

Rigby, D.L., & Essletzbichler, J. (2006). Technological variety, technological change and a geography of production techniques. *Journal of Economic Geography, 6*(1), 45–70.

Saarinen, J. (2004). Destinations in change: The transformation process of tourist destinations. *Tourist Studies, 4*(2), 161–179.

Saarinen, J. (2006). Traditions of sustainability in tourism studies. *Annals of Tourism Research, 33*(4), 1121–1140.

Saarinen, J., & Kask, T. (2008). Transforming tourism spaces in changing socio-political contexts: The case of Pärnu, Estonia, as a tourist destination. *Tourism Geographies, 10*(4), 452–473.

Sanz-Ibáñez, C., & Anton Clavé, S. (2014). The evolution of destinations: Towards an evolutionary and relational economic geography approach. *Tourism Geographies, 16*(4), 563–579.

Simmie, J., & Martin, R. (2010). The economic resilience of regions: Towards an evolutionary approach. *Cambridge Journal of Regions, Economy and Society, 3*(1), 27–43.

Slocum, S., & Kline, C. (2014). Regional resilience: Opportunities, challenges and policy messages from Western North Carolina. *Anatolia, 25*(3), 403–416.

Strickland-Munro, J., Allison, H., & Moore, S. (2010). Using resilience concepts to investigate the impacts of protected area tourism on communities. *Annals of Tourism Research, 37*(2), 499–519.

Walker, B., & Salt, D. (2006). *Resilience thinking: Sustaining ecosystems and people in a changing world.* Washington, DC: Island Press.

Williams, A.M., & Baláž, V. (2000). *Tourism in transition: Economic change in central Europe.* London: I.B. Tauris.

Williams, A.M., & Baláž, V. (2002). The Czech and Slovak Republics: Conceptual issues in the economic analysis of tourism in transition. *Tourism Management, 23*(1), 37–45.

6 The mobilities paradigm, resilience, and sustainable tourism

Kevin Hannam

Introduction

Tourism is widely seen as a somewhat resilient industry – as it has continued to grow despite the many economic and political shocks it has faced (Crotti & Misrahi, 2015). But clearly such economic resilience is only one part of the picture. Resilience also refers to the ways in which, as well as the extent to which, communities may adapt or change in the face of internal or external threats or challenges. In addition to economic resilience then, and drawing upon systems thinking, we can think of cultural resilience, social resilience, ecological resilience, as well as political resilience, as being connected. In the context of connectivity, the theoretical development of the concept of mobilities has emphasized the ways in which tourism is connected to other forms of movement and the ways in which, together, these may lead to breakdowns or even innovations in transport systems. In this chapter I discuss key aspects of the mobilities paradigm and then go on to examine the concept of resilience in relation to tourism mobilities. I conclude that research into tourism mobilities helps us to better understand the complexity of resilience for future sustainable tourism.

The mobilities paradigm

The mobilities paradigm develops a more sophisticated interdisciplinary analysis of movement within societies. It also helps to develop mobile methodologies that are useful for collecting and analyzing data relating to contemporary social, cultural, and environmental aspects of mobilities, in order to capture the messiness of everyday life. In terms of policy and politics, the mobilities paradigm arguably also helps us to understand and think critically about some of the key problems that face contemporary societies through the movement of people and things.

The mobilities paradigm does not argue that mobilities are something new (although the global volume of mobilities has continually increased) but that studies of tourism are too static, focusing on particular sites when in fact tourism can often be much more fluid: tourists and tourism are on the move literally and imaginatively (Salazar, 2012). As Hannam (2009, p. 109) has argued:

[n]ot only does a mobilities perspective lead us to discard our usual notions of spatiality and scale, but it also undermines existing linear assumptions about temporality and timing, which often assume that actors are able to do only one thing at a time, and that events follow each other in a linear order.

This chapter thus reviews and develops work from what has been termed the 'new mobilities paradigm' (Adey, Bissell, Hannam, Merriman, & Sheller, 2013; Hannam, Sheller, & Urry, 2006; Sheller & Urry, 2006, 2016) and what has become known more recently as the study of tourism mobilities (Hannam, Butler, & Paris, 2014; Sheller & Urry, 2004). Tourism research has paid attention to various forms of human mobility such as migration through, for example, second homes, ancestry tourism, and Visiting Friends and Relatives (VFR). Developing this expansion of research focus, Salazar (2012, p. 576) notes however that, "as a polymorphic concept, mobility invites us to renew our theorizing, especially regarding conventional themes such as culture, identity, and transnational relationships."

A mobilities approach further develops such research through a critical approach to our understandings of the complex and dynamic integration of environmental impacts that have been the mainstay of much tourism management research (Hannam, 2018). Although tourism research has, for example, considered its relationships with transport, the mobilities paradigm allows us to develop a more critical perspective; for instance, on how discourses and practices of 'freedom' underpin the contemporary tourism experiences of transport (Freudendal-Pedersen, 2009; Hannam, 2016; Sager, 2006; Sheller & Urry, 2016).

The study of tourism has often been seen as on the periphery of the social sciences; however, the mobilities paradigm arguably allows us to place tourism at the core of social and cultural life rather than at the margins (Coles & Hall, 2006; Hannam, 2009). Tourism mobilities, then, are analyzed not as an ephemeral aspect of social life that is practiced outside normal, everyday life but seen as integral to wider processes of economic and political development processes, and even constitutive of everyday life (Coles & Hall, 2006; Edensor, 2007; Franklin, 2003; Franklin & Crang, 2001; Hannam & Knox, 2010; Hannam et al., 2014).

It is not just that tourism is a form of mobility like other forms of mobility – such as commuting or migration – but that different mobilities inform and are informed by tourism (Sheller & Urry, 2004). In any situation, mobilities involve the movement of people, the movement of a wide range of material things, and the movement of more intangible thoughts and imaginaries. Mobilities also involve the use of a range of new and old technologies. As tourists assimilate mobile technologies into their daily practices and expand these practices into digital spaces, they often replicate and reconfigure their performativities and sociabilities. Tourism can be viewed as a complex assemblage (Germann Molz & Paris, 2016) of portable technologies, infrastructure, virtual and networked spaces, and bodies that flow through various mobilities.

In short, proponents of the mobilities paradigm argue that the concept of mobilities is concerned, simultaneously as assemblages, with mapping and understanding the large-scale movement of people, objects, capital, and information across the world, as well as the more local processes of daily transportation, movement through public space, and the travel of material things within everyday life (Hannam et al., 2006). As Cresswell argues,

> When mobility is thought of as constellations of movement, representation, and practice, we can think through a more finely developed politics of mobility, one that works with mobilities and immobilities so as to deduce particular facets, such as motive force, speed, rhythm, route, experience and friction.
>
> (Cresswell 2010, p. 17, cited in Rickly, Hannam, & Mostafanezhad, 2016, pp. 1–2)

The mobilities paradigm thus presents a new configuration for applied management-orientated research, integrating the study of complex systems, notions of transition, and analyses of how mobilities inform various social practices such as tourism (Sheller & Urry, 2016).

The development of the new *Applied Mobilities* journal, which focuses on the sustainability of future mobilities, brings forth a planning and management orientation for the mobilities paradigm. In their editorial in the first issue of *Applied Mobilities*, Freudendal-Pedersen, Hannam and Kesselring (2016, p. 1) argue that:

> Mobilities have brought about positive economic and social effects, such as wealth, international cultures of collaboration and exchange. But at the same time, issues such as increasing inequalities, climate change, urban sprawl and highly mobile energy-consuming lifestyles have put questions of sustainability centre stage.

In the following sections I outline the significance of the mobilities paradigm for understanding resilience and sustainable tourism.

Resilience and tourism mobilities

Resilience in tourism research has been developed as a way of understanding how communities might adapt and ultimately sustain their livelihoods through tourism (Espiner, Orchiston, & Higham, 2017). A critical aspect of resilience is adaptation or the ability to re-organize in the face of conditions that make previous ways of working or living untenable. Much tourism literature has focused on resilience to the immediate challenges posed by the local impacts of natural disasters. For example, Biggs, Hall, and Stoeckl (2012) have explored the resilience of vulnerable tourism sectors to disasters in their research into the coral reef tourism industry in Phuket, Thailand following the 2004 tsunami and the 2008 political crisis. They demonstrate how both formal and informal tourism enterprises enjoy high lifestyle benefits from reef tourism that in turn supports local resilience.

However, a mobilities perspective takes this a stage further and incorporates more elements into the system of resilience. Hofmann (2016), for instance, argues that in the case of Laos the bombing campaign during the 1960s left behind a complex legacy of destruction, "but also stories of resilience centered on various translations and enactments of bombs (and specifically bomb-remade-spoons) considered as non-human actors." War, conflict, and mobilities are closely interrelated, because "[m]obility is at the heart of modern warfare. One could claim that movement is at the very core of any kind of group aggression – moving from one place to another is required in acts of war" (Kaplan, 2006, p. 1).

The mobilities paradigm also provides a critical perspective on the emergent tourism geographies instigated by different modes of travel. While the relations between tourism and transport have been studied previously, the mobilities paradigm recognizes the importance of transport for tourism practices and the meaning of social lives more generally. In particular, the concepts of aeromobility (Urry 2007) and automobility (Featherstone, 2004; Urry, 2004), the two dominant forms of travel today, have rapidly developed to become important topics of debate in the social sciences, theorized from a mobilities perspective.

An interesting example of aeromobilities research that considered resilience from the perspective of tourism mobilities, was the impact of the disruptions to air travel triggered by Iceland's Eyjafjallajökull eruptions in April and May 2010. In an introduction to a special issue of the journal *Mobilities*, Birtchnell and Buscher (2011) argue that this natural disaster provides insights into some of the connecting themes of mobilities and highlights the sometimes strange and surprising aspects of human strandedness in a world of mobile lives. Furthermore, Benediktsson, Lund, and Huijbens (2011) develop the complex meaning of risk for tourism mobilities in this context. They focus on the response of the Icelandic tourist authorities and demonstrate that for many tourists the eruptions added considerable depth to their travel experiences. Indeed, Iceland now has some claim to being a much more resilient tourism destination as a result of the impact of this natural event as well as the subsequent financial crisis (Johannesson & Huijbens, 2010).

Such event mobilities have also been examined as things that interrupt the normal order such that they have wider repercussions in time and space (Hannam, Mostafanezhad, & Rickly, 2016). As a number of philosophers have noted, events and the acquisition of them have become a defining feature of contemporary life, bound up with our identities (Badiou, 2013; Žižek, 2014). The number of events as well as their different scales also leads to various stresses: in transport systems, through congestion; in security, through geopolitical systems of control; as well as both individuals' and societies' abilities to cope with attending and organizing multiple events at the same time (Hannam et al., 2016). Tourism, events, and mobilities co-exist in various foldings and unfoldings through time and space which are difficult to control through contemporary scheduling. They are also subject to national and international geopolitical structures as well as the creation of atmospheres (Tzanelli, 2018). Events may also serve as contexts that provide meanings and purpose to a specific action – such as frantically leaving one's home to escape from a mudslide (Cook & Butz, 2016). Research into event mobilities, then, leads us to question the resilience of destinations at various scales.

From an applied perspective, the mobilities paradigm has been at the forefront of developing critiques of the systems of urban planning that have given rise to the dominance of automobility in western and non-western societies fueled, literally and figuratively, by a dependence on oil (Urry, 2016). Ferreira, Bertolini, and Naess (2017, p. 16) argue that:

> Contemporary transport systems lack resilience. They are prone to congestion, vulnerable to multiple threats, constitute a great financial burden, and are environmentally unsustainable. Research and policies have been developed aimed at solving these problems by means of improving transport technologies and governance; however, success has been limited.

Ferreira et al. (2017) question whether resilience can be increased by means of promoting localism, slowness, and stillness, or what they term "immotility" – the propensity not to travel. At a micro-scale we can also consider the various frictions of tourism mobilities in relation to technological resilience. For example, the frictions of campervan travel may involve various technological 'breakdowns'; here, the lack of resilience of this form of travel becomes one of its affordances and attractions (Wilson & Hannam, 2017).

Resilience also pertains to the contemporary geopolitics of human mobilities: the refugee, the migrant, the expatriate, and the tourist are all involved in practices of cultural resilience. This comes to the fore in particular instances where different categories of mobile humans 'collide' – such as on the beaches of Greece where images of refugees were juxtaposed with sunbathing tourists. In his account of the impact of the refugee crisis in Greece, Papataxiarchis (2016) describes how the complexity of the encounters between locals, volunteers, professional humanitarian workers, and refugees on the 'front-line' beaches involve symbolic hierarchies. He further notes the emergence of 'e-volunteers' who send various performative signifiers, in the form of words and photos online, leaving electronic traces as markers of their identities; in addition, there are other humanitarian 'pilgrims' and tourists in search of 'journalistic' intelligence. These encounters have had a profound impact on the resilience of tourism destinations, where refugees, locals, volunteers, and tourists become bundled together (Hannam, 2017).

In countries of the Middle East and North Africa (MENA region), cultural resilience has also been foregrounded due to the numbers of expatriates and tourists working in and visiting destinations such as Dubai. Within most Gulf countries, the number of expatriates greatly exceeds the number of local citizens, filling the demand for labor that has been driven by ambitious tourism and real estate development plans. This has resulted in heavy reliance on a foreign work-force to alleviate staff shortages and/or provide technical expertise. To counter the reliance on foreign workers and unemployment within the growing local youth populations, most Gulf Cooperation Council (GCC) governments have established labor localization policies aimed at increasing local participation in the private sector as part of wider national strategies for economic and cultural resilience and sustainability (Hannam & Paris, 2018).

According to the Abu Dhabi Tourism and Culture Authority, Emiratis account for only 1 percent of employment in the tourism and hospitality sector in the United Arab Emirates. Low participation in the hospitality sector in GCC coun-tries has been attributed to lack of capacity and necessary skills, lack of aware-ness of the range of opportunities available, the low salaries offered in comparison to public sector jobs, and a lack of prestige (Sadi & Henderson, 2005; Stephenson, Russell, & Edgar, 2010). To address these challenges, recent initiatives have sought to provide training and increase awareness about career opportunities for nationals in the tourism and hospitality industry. In the United Arab Emirates, Emiratization programs for the tourism sector have focused on education and training for youth. For example, the Dubai Department of Tourism and Commerce Marketing recently launched Dubai Tourism College as a means of recruiting and training Emirati youth for tourist-facing roles and encouraging them to become role models within the industry.

The focus on knowledge and education development in tourism and hospital-ity is seen as a way to overcome some of the challenges of cultural resilience and sustainability. Previous policies in countries such as Oman and Saudi Arabia set quotas for local employment that were not aligned with or sustainable in the context of overall growth and development plans. With this realization, policies are now focused on more gradual and organic growth in local skills, manage-ment competencies, and participation in the private sector (Hannam & Paris, 2018). Nevertheless, there is an increasing number of MENA expatriates employed in management and upper-management positions in the tourism indus-try in the region. Managers, many with more than five or ten years of experience, from Lebanon, Syria, Palestine, and Egypt, are increasingly common in inter-national hotel chains. Steiner (2007) has argued that the integration of MENA expatriates into management structures can increase companies' local embed-dedness through local knowledge and experience, thus increasing local cultural resilience. Companies with a higher degree of local embeddedness are able to moderate perceptions during crisis, a key for both resilience and destination recovery in MENA countries.

It has been further noted that more attention ought to be given to the role of cultural resilience in the making of cities in the Gulf countries (Radoine, 2013). Here, the concept of resilience, in relation to cultural heritage, refers to the capacity of cities "to recover dormant dynamic cultural resources.... It is the ability of a city to regenerate its latent cultural memory and image" (Radoine, 2013, p. 243). However, Elsheshtawy (2004, p. 193) has argued that in the case of Dubai:

The city is ... being re-created through the gaze of the tourist, the look of multi-national corporations, and the stare of real estate development companies. In such a context it becomes quite natural for developments to become isolated and fragmented islands.

The development of touristic urban mega-projects such as the Palm Islands has had little consideration for the long-term consequences on local flora and fauna in Dubai, threatening cultural and environmental resilience (Radione, 2013) as well as future sustainable tourism mobilities.

Conclusions

This chapter has sought to give some insights into the multiple mobilities relevant to the study of tourism and the way in which these might be related to the conceptualization of resilience for future sustainable mobilities. The 'new mobilities paradigm' arguably allows us to place travel and tourism at the center of social and cultural life rather than at the margins, and this chapter has discussed how this might be applied in the development of a research agenda for understanding sustainable tourism mobilities. The transition to a post-carbon future will potentially open up many new technological configurations for tourism mobilities but at present the demand for further auto- and aeromobilities is continuing to grow (Urry, 2016). Moreover, as recent discussions of human mobilities and immobilities continue to suggest, places and politics will remain paramount in our discussions of tourism mobilities (Rickly et al., 2016), particularly when we consider issues of cultural resilience.

References

Adey, P., Bissell, D., Hannam, K., Merriman, P., & Sheller, M. (Eds.). (2013). *Handbook of mobilities*. London: Routledge.

Badiou, A. (2013). *Philosophy and the event*. New York: Polity.

Benediktsson, K., Lund, K.A., & Huijbens, E. (2011). Inspired by eruptions? Eyjafjallajökull and Icelandic tourism. *Mobilities*, *6*(1), 77–84.

Biggs, D., Hall, C.M., & Stoeckl, N. (2012). The resilience of formal and informal tourism enterprises to disasters: Reef tourism in Phuket, Thailand. *Journal of Sustainable Tourism*, *20*(5), 645–665.

Birtchnell, T., & Buscher, M. (2011). Stranded: An eruption of disruption. *Mobilities*, *6*(1), 1–9.

Coles, T., & Hall, C.M. (2006). Editorial: The geography of tourism is dead. Long live geographies of tourism and mobility. *Current Issues in Tourism*, *9*(4–5), 289–292.

Cook, N., & Butz, D. (2016). Mobility justice in the context of disaster. *Mobilities*, *11*(2), 400–419.

Cresswell, T. (2010). Towards a politics of mobility. *Environment and Planning D: Society and Space*, *28*(1), 17–31.

Crotti, R., & Misrahi, T. (2015). *The Travel & Tourism Competitiveness Index 2015: T&T as a resilient contribution to national development*. Retrieved from World

Economic Forum website: www3.weforum.org/docs/TT15/WEF_TTCR_Chapter1.1_
2015.pdf.

Edensor, T. (2007). Mundane mobilities, performances and spaces of tourism. *Social &
Cultural Geography*, *8*(2), 201–215.

Elsheshtawy, Y. (2004). Redrawing boundaries: Dubai, an emerging global city. In Y.
Elsheshtawy (Ed.), *Planning Middle Eastern cities: An urban kaleidoscope in a glo-
balizing world* (pp. 169–199). London: Routledge.

Espiner, S., Orchiston, C., & Higham, J. (2017). Resilience and sustainability: A complementary relationship? Towards a practical conceptual model for the sustainability–
resilience nexus in tourism. *Journal of Sustainable Tourism*, *25*, 1385–1400.

Featherstone, M. (2004). Automobilities: An introduction. *Theory, Culture & Society*,
21(4–5), 1–24.

Ferreira, A., Bertolini, L., & Naess, P. (2017). Immotility as resilience? A key consideration for transport policy and research. *Applied Mobilities*, *2*(1), 16–31.

Franklin, A. (2003). *Tourism: An introduction*. London: Sage.

Franklin, A., & Crang, M. (2001). The trouble with tourism and travel theory? *Tourist
Studies*, *1*(1), 5–22.

Freudendal-Pedersen, M. (2009). *Mobility in daily life: Between freedom and unfreedom.*
Farnham, UK: Ashgate.

Freudendal-Pedersen, M., Hannam, K., & Kesselring, S. (2016). Applied mobilities,
transitions and opportunities. *Applied Mobilities*, *1*(1), 1–9.

Germann Molz, J., & Paris, C. (2016). The social affordances of flashpacking: Exploring
the mobility nexus of travel and communication. *Mobilities*, *10*(2), 173–192.

Hannam, K. (2009). The end of tourism? Nomadology and the mobilities paradigm. In J.
Tribe (Ed.), *Philosophical issues in tourism* (pp. 101–113). Clevedon, UK: Channel
View Publications.

Hannam, K. (2016). Gendered automobilities: Female Pakistani migrants driving in Saudi
Arabia. In J. Rickly, K. Hannam, & M. Mostafanezhad (Eds.), *Tourism and leisure
mobilities* (pp. 54–64). London: Routledge.

Hannam, K. (2017). Tourism, mobilities and the geopolitics of erasure. In D. Hall (Ed.),
Tourism and geopolitics: Issues and concepts from Central and Eastern Europe
(pp. 345–353). Wallingford, UK: CABI.

Hannam, K. (2018). The mobilities paradigm and tourism management. In C. Cooper, S.
Volo, W. Gartner, & N. Scott (Eds.), *The Sage handbook of tourism management*
(pp. 5–11). London: Sage.

Hannam, K., Butler, G., & Paris, C. (2014). Developments and key concepts in tourism
mobilities. *Annals of Tourism Research*, *44*(1), 171–185.

Hannam, K., & Knox, D. (2010). *Understanding tourism*. London: Sage.

Hannam, K., Mostafanezhad, M., & Rickly, J. (Eds.). (2016). *Event mobilities: Politics,
place and performance*. London: Routledge.

Hannam, K., & Paris, C. (2018). Migration and an expatriate workforce. In D. Timothy
(Ed.), *The Routledge handbook on tourism in the Middle East and North Africa* (forth-
coming). London: Routledge.

Hannam, K., Sheller, M., & Urry, J. (2006). Editorial: Mobilities, immobilities and moor-
ings. *Mobilities*, *1*(1), 1–22.

Hofmann, A. (2016). Material semiotics, ontological politics and im/mobilities of bomb-
spoons in Laos. *Applied Mobilities*, *1*(1), 102–118.

Johannesson, G.T., & Huijbens, E. (2010). Tourism in times of crisis: Exploring the discourse of tourism development in Iceland. *Current Issues in Tourism*, *13*(5), 419–434.

Kaplan, C. (2006). Mobility and war: The cosmic view of US "air power". *Environment and Planning A, 38*(2), 395–407.

Papataxiarchis, E. (2016). Being "there": At the front line of the "European refugee crisis'" – Part 1. *Anthropology Today, 32*(2), 3–9.

Radoine, H. (2013). Cultural resilience in contemporary urbanism: The case of Sharjah, UAE. *International Development Planning Review, 35*(3), 241–260.

Rickly, J., Hannam, K., & Mostafanezhad, M. (Eds.). (2016). *Tourism and leisure mobilities*. London: Routledge.

Sadi, M., & Henderson, J. (2005). Local versus foreign workers in the hospitality and tourism industry: A Saudi Arabian perspective. *Cornell Hotel and Restaurant Administration Quarterly, 46*(2), 247–257.

Sager, T. (2006). Freedom as mobility: Implications of the distinction between actual and potential travelling. *Mobilities, 1*(3), 465–488.

Salazar, N. (2012). Tourism imaginaries: A conceptual approach. *Annals of Tourism Research, 39*(2), 863–882.

Sheller, M., & Urry, J. (Eds.). (2004). *Tourism mobilities: Places to play, places in play*. London: Routledge.

Sheller, M., & Urry, J. (2006). The new mobilities paradigm. *Environment and Planning A, 38*(2), 207–226.

Sheller, M., & Urry, J. (2016). Mobilizing the new mobilities paradigm. *Applied Mobilities, 1*(1), 10–25.

Steiner, C. (2007). Political instability, transnational tourist companies and destination recovery in the Middle East after 9/11. *Tourism Hospitality Planning & Development, 4*(3), 167–188.

Stephenson, M., Russell, K., & Edgar, D. (2010). Islamic hospitality in the UAE: Indigenization of products and human capital. *Journal of Islamic Marketing, 1*(1), 9–24.

Tzanelli, R. (2018). *Mega-events as economies of the imagination*. London: Routledge.

Urry, J. (2004). The "system" of automobility. *Theory, Culture & Society, 21*(4–5), 25–39.

Urry, J. (2007). *Mobilities*. Cambridge, UK: Polity.

Urry, J. (2008). Climate change, travel and complex futures. *British Journal of Sociology, 59*(2), 261–279.

Urry, J. (2016). *What is the future?* Cambridge, UK: Polity.

Wilson, S., & Hannam, K. (2017). The frictions of slow tourism mobilities: Conceptualising campervan travel. *Annals of Tourism Research, 67*, 25–36.

Žižek, S. (2014). *Event: Philosophy in transit*. Harmondsworth, UK: Penguin.

Part III
Applications and cases

7 Conceptualizing vulnerability and adaptive capacity of tourism from an indigenous Pacific Islands perspective

Johanna Nalau, Api Movono, and Susanne Becken

Introduction

Climate is one of the most decisive attraction and risk factors for the tourism industry as a whole (Scott & Lemieux, 2010) and weather is often the driving factor in tourism decision-making. Climate change will have significant impacts on destination choice as parameters change, for example, with respect to visitor comfort in terms of increased heat stress due to rises in temperature (Matzarakis, 2006), and changing seasonality with impacts on the potential range of available leisure activities (Yu, Schwartz, & Walsh, 2009). Furthermore, increases in the number of extreme weather events have the potential to alter tourists' perceptions of 'safe' destinations, leading to a decrease in tourism arrivals for some areas (Jeuring & Becken, 2013), while extreme events can damage ecosystems that tourism depends on such as coral reefs (Nalau, Schliephack, & Becken 2017a; World Meteorological Organization, United Nations Environmental Programme, & World Tourism Organization, 2008). Changes in weather and climatic conditions such as longer warm seasons can, however, also open up new areas and opportunities for tourism (Johnston, Johnston, Stewart, Dawson, & Lemelin, 2012; Uyarra et al., 2005). With such changes, the tourism industry at large is facing a somewhat uncertain operational environment. This means that the sector overall needs to plan and take into account changing environmental conditions, and increase its resilience by investing in strategies that can enable it to continue to flourish, including actions around climate change adaptation.

Tourism businesses, especially those in tropical island destinations, are highly dependent on weather and climate. In the Pacific Small Island Developing States (PSIDS), tourism is the only economic sector to grow relatively consistently in recent years. In 2012, the sector peaked at 1.77 million international arrivals; after a setback in 2013 due to severe tropical cyclones, it rebounded in 2014 to 1.69 million arrivals (South Pacific Tourism Organisation n.d.). Sustainable tourism can be defined as "achieving quality growth in a manner that does not deplete the natural and built environments and preserves the culture, history and heritage of the local community" (Edgell, Allen, Smith, & Swanson, 2008, p. 183).

Yet, Small Island Developing States (SIDS) are simultaneously highly vulnerable to climate change impacts, including increases in extreme events, sea level rises, salt water intrusion, increases in temperature, and subsequent land loss and inhabitability of islands (Nurse et al., 2014). The unique characteristics of SIDS further increases their vulnerability as they often include a large number of remote low-lying islands, rural–urban migration, high population growth rates, and high dependency on external economic inputs including remittances, international trade, and development aid (Hay, Forbes, & Mimura, 2013; Kuruppu & Willie, 2015). Yet, tourism in the context of PSIDS occurs as part of other social, political, economic, cultural, and historical processes. Hence, to understand the vulnerability of tourism in an indigenous Pacific Island context governance bodies need to pay attention to these contextual processes while simultaneously considering the nature of place-based attractions in a broader sustainability setting.

Although much has been written about the potential impacts of weather and climate change (Aylen, Albertson, & Cavan, 2014; Dubois, Ceron, Gössling, & Hall, 2016; Gössling, Scott, Hall, Ceron, & Dubois, 2012; Lise & Tol, 2002; Rauken, Kelman, Jacobsen, & Hovelsrud, 2010; Rosselló & Santana-Gallego, 2014), there is an enduring gap in the assessment and examination of tourism sector vulnerability and governance within an indigenous context. This chapter examines some of the emerging alternative approaches in tourism governance and policy that are based on indigenous governance, as an attempt to increase the resilience of the tourism sector and the socio-ecological system it depends on. It aims to characterize vulnerability and adaptive capacity to climate change – two central concepts of resilience theory – from an indigenous perspective rather than from a purely economic sector-specific perspective. Furthermore, we provide a conceptual model that integrates indigenous governance and knowledge structures and values for a more resilient and inclusive tourism governance, while using a Fijian context as a case study to demonstrate the potential use of the framework.

Following this introduction, the next section summarizes some of the main debates regarding concepts such as climate adaptation, vulnerability, adaptive capacity, and resilience. The third section introduces conceptual frameworks for knowledge and governance integration for increased tourism resilience and adaptive capacity from the Pacific Islands perspective, including a Fijian case study. To conclude, the fourth section discusses some of the implications of the framework and makes recommendations for further research and policy considerations.

Defining concepts in the context of tourism resilience

The main concepts used to assess, describe, and examine the ways in which particular sectors are impacted by and can respond to climate change and sustainability issues are those of vulnerability, resilience, adaptation, and adaptive capacity. Vulnerability, resilience, and adaptation, in particular, each have their own scientific communities and, at times, pursue research in isolation from each other (Schipper & Burton, 2009). While, for example, the assessment reports produced by the Intergovernmental Panel on Climate Change (IPCC) have aimed to provide more defined understandings of these key terms, variety still exists in how they are approached and used in practice (Levina & Tirpak, 2006). In this section, we demonstrate some of this variety and highlight the need to be clear about which terms are used and how.

Vulnerability can generally be understood as the sum of interacting factors and processes which either strengthen or decrease a community's, an individual's or an institution's capacity to respond to climate change. Yet, Ensor and Berger (2009) note that vulnerability is often researched from different angles, which may stem from a focus on vulnerability reduction, resilience strengthening, or ways to build adaptive capacity. The authors differentiate between startpoint versus end-point vulnerability. Those focused on end-point vulnerability try to measure how effective a particular adaptation option is in reducing the negative impacts arising from a particular hazard event (Ensor & Berger, 2009). In contrast, those focusing on start-point vulnerability begin by trying to understand which factors are currently responsible for increasing the vulnerability of communities. The start-point vulnerability view underlines the perception that we cannot understand adaptation processes without first understanding the current context (Burton, 2009). Others, such as Warrick, Aalbersberg, Dumaru, McNaught, and Teperman (2017), define end-point vulnerability as biophysical and start-point as social vulnerability. Preston and Stafford-Smith (2009), on the other hand, make a distinction between whether vulnerability is the sum of climate–society interaction or whether it emerges in the end due to current system structure.

Resilience, like vulnerability, is another concept which is often understood and used differently across disciplines, including in tourism (see Becken, 2013; Espiner & Becken, 2014). In a seminal paper on vulnerability, Nelson, Adger, and Brown, (2007, p. 396) define resilience as "the amount of change a system can undergo and still retain the same function and structure while maintaining options to develop." A richer understanding of adaptation, Nelson et al. (2007) argue, is to approach it through a resilience framework. This is because socio-ecological system perspectives have the ability to increase our understanding and conceptualization of change. Moench (2009, p. 257) defines systems resilience as "the ability to adjust to shocks and variability without fundamental changes in overall system structure." In this view, resilience is used to maintain current structures rather than transform them.

Handmer and Dovers (2009) take a different approach and use a resilience typology to examine three different dimensions of resilience that drive the way institutions respond to risks. The typology, further refined for climate change by Nalau and Handmer (2015), shows clearly the boundaries of action which each type of management approach to resilience brings forth. Type I typifies a change-resisting approach that denies the existence of risk and is focused on enabling the business-as-usual management type to flourish. Type II is more accommodating of change, but only at the margins: risks are acknowledged but there is no perceived need for large-scale changes in management approaches. Type III acknowledges risks and is focused on making changes in the structures of the system in order to fare better through increased flexibility. In the climate change and sustainability context, the three types of resilience differ in whether they deny climate change (Type I), accept it and make some changes (Type II), or accept climate change as a significant driver and adjust operations accordingly (Type III) (Nalau & Handmer, 2015).

The typology is tied to the notion of adaptive capacity, which is another core concept in the adaptation literature. Adaptive capacity can be described as "the property of a system to adjust its characteristics or behaviour, in order to expand its coping range under existing climate variability, or future climate conditions" (Lim, Spanger-Siegfried, Burton, Malone, & Huqet, 2005, p. 36). Here again, several authors provide different approaches that one might take in researching adaptive capacity: one could focus on specific adaptive activity (sector-specific adaptation approaches, e.g., sea-level rise planning) or generic adaptive capacity (macro-scale improvements in education or health) (Handmer, 2009, p. 214).

Grasso (2010) makes a distinction between end-point and starting-point adaptive capacity: starting-point adaptive capacity describes the current factors that explain a system's ability to adapt, whereas end-point adaptive capacity is seen as the sum of technological adaptations to future climate impacts. Adaptive capacity centered on present-day vulnerability is "the set of resources available for adaptation, as well as the capacity to use these resources for effective adaptations" (Grasso, 2010, p. 23). Fresque-Baxter and Armitage (2012) also differentiate between subjective adaptive capacity (people's risk perceptions, perceived capacity to adapt) and objective adaptive capacity (assets, political support, human resources). The psychological dimensions relating to perceived adaptive capacity have also been recognized in tourism-related research (Becken, Lama, & Espiner, 2013; Shakeela & Becken, 2015).

This short introduction to some of the key concepts has hopefully shown that the way adaptation or vulnerability or resilience are framed has a direct impact on the way research and policy processes are carried out and what are identified as priority outcomes (Levina & Tirpak, 2006; Nalau & Handmer, 2015). Yet, many of these concepts have been criticized as being Western-oriented and based upon predominantly Western knowledge and historical conceptual constructions. This also relates to knowledge construction processes where indigenous knowledge and experiences are bypassed and not taken into account (Ford et al., 2016; Parsons & Nalau, 2016; Parsons, Nalau, & Fisher, 2017). Next, we examine several conceptual frameworks which aim to situate these concepts more closely in the Pacific Island tourism context.

Conceptual frameworks

In this section, we explore what an indigenous governance approach in a PSIDS context could mean for a resilient tourism sector and its ability to adapt to change. Many tourism destinations in SIDS are heavily reliant on particular landscapes and ecosystems, such as beaches and coral reefs, which are often under customary governance systems. This means that the destination features might not be governed by the private sector, but through a broad array of actors who need to cooperate in order to maintain the viability of the sector and its activities (Nalau et al., 2017a).

In the Pacific, traditional calendars and the way people understand and conceptualize time are based on values which render landscapes and the environment into something more than mere biophysical contexts (Mondragon, 2014). In essence, local knowledge is not just about the environment; it also relates to knowledge about the social and political contexts within which people live (Lebel, 2013). The time frames among indigenous communities can be quite different compared with those used by Western scientists and evident in prevailing worldviews (Climate and Traditional Knowledges Workgroup [CTKW], 2014). These differences need to be considered in adaptation and resilience planning from the outset.

Indeed, Kuruppu and Willie (2015) note that one of the main cultural barriers in climate adaptation is the lack of attention paid to traditional knowledge and the role that different ceremonies and cultural 'ways of being' contribute to how communities respond to environmental change. Hence, it is conceivable that "the trend in declining traditional knowledge is a barrier to [the] adaptive capacity of communities" (Kuruppu & Willie, 2015, p. 78). Next, we examine two frameworks that, it has been suggested, tie the concepts of vulnerability, resilience, and adaptive capacity closer to the Pacific context.

The Pacific Adaptive Capacity Assessment Framework

The roles of traditional knowledge and governance systems play a part in a recent initiative to contextualize adaptive capacity in the Pacific context – the Pacific Adaptive Capacity Assessment Framework (Warrick et al., 2017). The Framework builds upon seven main principles (see Figure 7.1), and seeks to establish a form of guidance to delineate what adaptive capacity consists of in the Pacific context. The aim is that eventually the Framework could be used to assess and measure such capacity in any given community. From a tourism governance perspective, Social capital (Capacity 2), Belief systems, worldviews, and values (Capacity 3) and Resources and distribution (Capacity 4) are important aspects when analyzing the decision-making processes and the extent to which a community is able to utilize the available resources. In this section, we analyze the Framework based on our experience working in the Pacific and relevant literature.

Social capital (Capacity 2) is an important part of adaptive capacity as social networks and relationships partly determine what is possible in a particular context. This relates also to governance and decision-making processes within a community – who has a say in how particular decisions are made, and how the community as a whole then functions based on these relationships and governance arrangements. However, here it should be added that, in cases where family members have migrated overseas, such as New Zealand or Australia, many Pacific communities of place, including indigenous tourism operators, also have

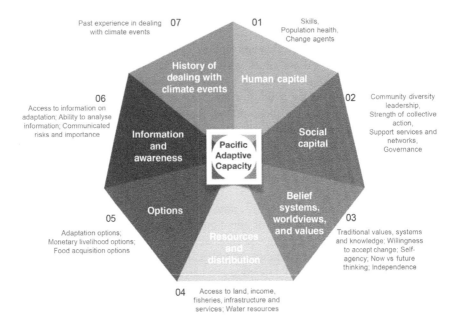

Figure 7.1 Warrick et al.'s Pacific Adaptive Capacity Assessment Framework.

Source: Adapted from Warrick et al. (2017).

social networks in other countries (Brown, 2015). What this means in terms of adaptive capacity and Social capital and, relatedly, to Resources and distribution (Capacity 4), is that solely measuring a community's capacity on the basis of geographical place (e.g., a particular village on a particular island in Fiji or Samoa) will not tell us the complete story. For example, in Samoa, a major factor in how communities and indigenous tourism operators cope with extreme events lies in the extent of remittances coming from overseas (Brown, 2015; Parsons, Brown, Nalau, & Fisher, 2018). The extended family, even if overseas, also has a say in decision-making back in the villages and communities, including decisions regarding tourism operations and investments (Brown, 2015).

The Framework does recognize the role of traditional knowledge and skills as part of adaptive capacity (Capacity 3). Yet, the Pacific region is a dynamic and historically adaptable context where missionaries, merchants, and Pacific peoples themselves have continuously reinvented and reshaped what we regard as 'the Pacific.' Hence, the context in which climate change adaptation occurs in the region is not static, but builds on rich historical, political, and cultural roots that continue to evolve over time. This means that approaches to managing change, including climate change adaptation, need to understand specific types of traditional knowledge in contexts where adaptation options are being discussed and developed (CTKW, 2014). Traditional knowledge is not fixed, however, and

changing environmental contexts also impact its accuracy; for example, changing climate can impact weather indicator species (such as the movement of particular birds before extreme events, or the flowering of plants) (Chand,
Chambers, Waiwai, Malsale, & Thompson, 2014).

Many Pacific communities have also increasingly developed a wider variety
of social networks beyond the places where they live, and hence it is rare to find
communities nowadays where traditional knowledge is the only source of
information. An important factor, therefore, is understanding the kind of
information people use to make decisions and where the information is sourced
from (Nalau, Becken, Noakes, & Mackey, 2017b; Nalau, Handmer, & Dalesa,
2017c). Understanding the variety of knowledge sources in use becomes highly
relevant for the tourism sector, particularly when there is a change towards more
extreme weather events that have the potential to seriously undermine sustainable development. Understanding and further developing information sources is
also important, as these determine whether and how people are being able to
prepare for extreme events and recover from their impacts (Nalau et al., 2017b).

Traditional indigenous knowledge is much more than just ecological knowledge about the weather and natural resource management as it also speaks to a
holistic way of living, which connects the community to its environment in a
profound, spiritual manner (Parsons, Fisher, & Nalau, 2016; Parsons et al.,
2017). Indigenous social systems are highly embedded and comprised of
complex, interconnected relationships in which indigenous knowledge plays a
key role in maintaining the functions and longevity of indigenous systems.
Indigenous knowledge, particularly in the Fijian context, is an integral part of
everyday life and is not confined to specific rituals and traditions. Instead, it
informs and facilitates all aspects of survival, which is often linked to sustaining life in a given geographical setting. As such, indigenous knowledge per-
taining to social relations, environmental custodianship, governance, and
political systems is part of the larger social and ecological order of a particular
community. Those working in indigenous contexts therefore need to consider
this broader cultural context and the range of beliefs and values held by communities, as well as the historical trajectories of power relationships (Parsons
& Nalau, 2016; Parsons et al., 2017). All of these aspects have ramifications
for how tourism operations can be governed and perceptions around concepts
such as a 'resilient tourism sector.'

While the Framework is very useful in providing specific examples of the
kinds of capacities that could be measured in the Pacific Islands context, it is
largely silent on issues such as gender. This is somewhat surprising given that
women still largely carry most of the workload and often have highly differential
access to, for example, information and decision-making processes, as well as
limited social ability to participate in tourism. Men usually control decision-
making processes and leadership positions and hence this is an increasingly
important issue that needs to be considered in the region. However, this is slowly
changing; in tourism-related communities in Fiji in particular, women are
becoming more prominent in their communities because of the entrepreneurial

success and economic independence they have gained through tourism (Movono & Dahles, 2017).

The focus of the Pacific Adaptive Capacity Assessment Framework is at the communal level; however, we suggest that it would also benefit from an indicator for the environmental quality of the resources that the community relies on. Given that the quality of the environment in a destination is often the main basis for developing and marketing an attraction (Edgell et al., 2008), this should be included in any assessment of adaptive capacity and resilience. In coastal areas, such an indicator could, for example, rank destination quality in terms of the health of coral reefs, areas of undisturbed environment (e.g., intact forest areas), fresh fish abundance/availability, and similar environmental qualities. In this way, the assessment of the adaptive capacity of the community and destination would include both social and ecological systems. Next, we explore in more detail a Fijian model which seeks to combine all of these factors.

Vanua Social and Ecological Systems and Resilience Model

The term 'vanua' refers to a sacred overarching structure which unifies multiple and interdependent components under a single, internally and externally acknowledged communal unit (Ravuvu, 1983). Seminal Fijian scholars have described the Vanua as having physical (land, sea, air), social (customs, people, religion), economic (employment, politics, wealth), and ecological (animals, birds, marine life) components which are interrelated (Nayacakalou, 1975; Ravuvu, 1983). It is therefore essential that, from the outset, studies which seek to examine resilience and adaptivity within a community setting employ research methodologies and approaches that are suited to the complex nature of indigenous societies (Movono & Dahles, 2017). The apparent restricted use of post-modernist techniques in Pacific community research has resulted in a body of knowledge that falls short of adequately delayering communities and understanding the complex embedded social and ecological constructs that influence vulnerabilities and adaptive capacities.

Research practice must also consider localized research paradigms and look to the knowledge and experience of indigenous researchers to complement the largely Western body of literature (Nabobo-Baba, 2008). Indigenous people are best placed at the center of research, in this inclusive way, to ensure that empirical pursuits are tailored specifically to match the context of a particular community. This then allows for concepts such as adaptive capacity and vulnerabilities to be researched in terms of indigenous ideologies, traditions, and social processes (Gallopin, 2006). Taking an indigenous approach to research methodology further paves the way for understanding how traditional knowledge is linked to custodianship roles and daily practices, thus giving attention to how people live. Employing a comprehensive, bottom-up research approach has significant implications for understanding localized manifestations of the various processes, relationships, and governance structures within indigenous communities. Immersion, the inclusion of indigenous methodology and local expertise, opens doors for the adequate delayering of community constructs with a focus on intricate issues relating to gender, minority groups, and communal dynamics that would otherwise be overlooked (Movono, Dahles, & Becken, 2018).

Recent studies conducted in a tourism-related community in Fiji (Movono, 2017), have shown that communities are complex social and ecological systems (SES) that have multiple elements embedded within what would normally be considered a homogeneous village. Employing Holling's (2001) SES constructs and using indigenous methodology, Movono (2017) draws attention to the links between culture, livelihoods activities, and their influence on the overall resilience of Fijian communities involved in tourism. Movono's findings show that the introduction of the tourism system at the livelihood level has created socio-cultural and economic shifts within other system elements that affect levels of community resilience.

In his study of tourism in the Coral Coast of Fiji, Movono (2017) links the construction of the Naviti Resort to the replacement of pre-existing ecological resources and specific livelihood practices attached to those resources. He argues that the construction of resorts on communally-owned land replaces specific trees, nesting grounds, and ecosystems which have a certain cultural and spiritual significance for locals. The replacement of natural resources with the physical resort structure involves the loss of specific totems and customs, traditions, and livelihood activities, as well as the traditional knowledge attached to those resources (Movono, 2017). With these change processes, resilience is affected due to a reduced diversity of knowledge and livelihood activities, which may now be centrally focused on the new tourism system. Movono's findings have provided an empirical basis for the use of the Vanua Social and Ecological Systems and Resilience Model (Figure 7.2) as a means of conceptualizing a tourism destination community as a system.

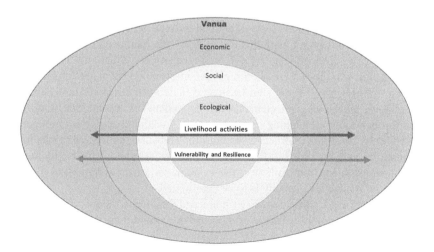

Figure 7.2 Vanua Social and Ecological Systems and Resilience Model.

Source: Adapted from Movono (2017, p. 293).

The Vanua Social and Ecological Systems and Resilience Model shows that a community consists of multiple systems or elements that influence how people in a Fijian community typically live. Within one community, there are many elements and institutions ranging from the church to communal land, each element simultaneously interacting (and being manipulated/managed) at multiple levels in order to meet an objective of the villagers. Whether it be an economic push to raise funds for a church event, or the presentation of food, mats, and money as contributions for a village member's funeral, the elements within the Vanua are 'mobilized' to meet villagers' short-term and long-term needs. These embedded elements of a Vanua are often out of view to outsiders and their importance as building blocks to successful resilient community development in the Pacific is often misunderstood.

Like other indigenous communities in the Pacific, Fijians have legally and customarily recognized social processes and political structures that not only reflect traditional patterns of social organization, but also indicate the interdependence between humans and the biosphere (Movono, 2017). The Vanua Social and Ecological Systems and Resilience Model provides a pathway for examining communities holistically, and various levels of investigation can also be conducted in terms of both starting-point adaptive capacity and end-point adaptive capacity. This is possible because the ecological and social aspects of adaptive capacity are considered within an appropriately defined complex adaptive system, with locally acknowledged social, ecological, and economic components (Holland, 2006). The Vanua Social and Ecological Systems and Resilience Model shows the multiple layers within the community and provides pathways so that a community can be examined in terms of women's empowerment, social capital, social and ecological change, vulnerabilities, and resilience.

Using ethnographic techniques based on immersion and in-depth engagement with the cohort, Movono (2017) was able to weave himself into the community and uncover its various components. These components and their interconnectivity were identified and meticulously examined through genuine engagement with the cohort, deep immersion, participation in daily life, relationship building, and gaining the trust and confidence of community members. Trust and the respect of participants was critical in yielding rich information from conversational interviews. The level of immersion facilitated understanding about how certain socio-cultural and ecological elements are dependent on one another and are linked through the wide-ranging combinations of livelihood activities employed by community members in order to sustain life. The various resource utilization combinations and options selected by community members affects, in turn, levels of vulnerability and resilience; the examination of these options is therefore essential if adaptive capacity is to be determined.

The Vanua Social and Ecological Systems and Resilience Model also captures the transitional and complex nature of indigenous communities. It pays attention, holistically, to the different elements (social, economic, ecological) and actors in the community, from influential leaders to the most marginalized, as part of an interconnected system. This holistic approach provides a clearer picture than previous studies of resource implications, political structures, and the strengths and weaknesses of the system in terms of resilience (Gallopin, 2006; Holland, 2006). In essence, managing resilience is facilitated by assessing human interaction with each other and with the biosphere; this provides a focus on the elements of the system that need to be strengthened in order to increase adaptive capacity (Holling, 2001). For instance, after experiencing 40 years of tourism, people in the Coral Coast of Fiji are now turning back to their traditional skills, reverting to fishing and farming in order to lessen their reliance on tourism income. This turn of livelihood approaches demonstrates reflexivity and growing local awareness of changes in and around the community. Researching these processes in indigenous communities highlights the adaptive nature of their systems, and ultimately a sense of managing resilience.

Indigenous society is highly reflexive, and its non-homogenous components have the potential to self-organize as it adjusts to the initial disturbances brought about by tourism. As such, a holistic approach to research is imperative in order to understand the dynamic and fluid nature of indigenous people as they respond to tourism-related change. More importantly, Movono (2017) acknowledges that tourism itself may not lead to a loss of resilience. The indigenous community's resilience can be reduced by the diminishing attention to traditional values and indigenous knowledge over the long term, but this situation could be mitigated through cultural preservation and increased awareness and retention of traditional livelihood activities, and might be recoverable with proper restoration and reinvigoration of traditions and customs (Movono, 2017). Micro-level influences such as tourism employment can stimulate profound changes and adjustments in the overall system, leading to increasing wealth and affluence, but also to a decline in traditional activities which can be detrimental to food security and traditional indigenous knowledge. Therefore, with a tailored approach to research, indigenous communities can be examined as complex adaptive systems rather than being regarded as homogeneous and mere spectators in the tourism development process.

Discussion and conclusion

In this chapter we have examined concepts related to social and environmental changes such as adaptive capacity (Ensor & Berger, 2009; Warrick, 2011), resilience (Handmer & Dovers, 2009; Nalau & Handmer, 2015) and vulnerability (Nelson et al., 2007) and considered how they could be better situated in a regional context such as the Pacific. We have also presented examples from the Pacific region where several recent frameworks (Movono, 2017; Warrick et al., 2017) were used to situate such concepts into a culturally differentiated context that makes them more relevant within the region. Such frameworks are well placed to provide alternative approaches to understanding how tourism is governed, the extent of adaptive capacity in tourism systems, and the way associated policies are developed in indigenous contexts.

These frameworks may also help us to move from a perspective that indigenous communities are 'impacted' upon by tourism, to one in which locals are seen as active agents who play an essential part in creating their own future

(Movono et al., 2018). For example, the Vanua Social and Ecological Systems and Resilience Model starts with a focus on culture and its links to livelihoods and examines how these interact with tourism activities and the tourism sector overall (Movono, 2017). Using the framework to understand historic development and the status quo then helps in transitioning from a less-than-perfect system to one that integrates tourism as one of several sustainable livelihoods that are embedded within the socio-cultural context of local communities. Particular attention needs to be paid to how natural resources are governed, how (and by whom) decisions are made, where investment flows are coming from, and who the beneficiaries are. These types of analyses then help determine the extent to which international tourism is boosting or decreasing communities' adaptive capacities in a particular locale (Movono & Dahles, 2017).

In the Pacific Islands context, governance is a very diverse concept given that there are several stakeholder groups who can claim ownership of particular assets and landscapes (Parsons et al., 1918). For tourism resilience and governance this means that while a resort might physically reside in a particular location and own activities within the resort area the perceived ownership of the land often still remains with indigenous communities, regardless of their signing land sale documentation with the resort owner (Brown, 2015). Hence, when thinking about what makes a Pacific Island destination resilient, one cannot consider concepts such as 'adaptive capacity' or 'vulnerability' without truly understanding the myriad social networks and groups that all inhabit the same physical space (Movono, 2017; Parsons et al., 1918). As such, a consideration of indigenous communities as complex adaptive systems and their appropriate examination, taking into account social networks and groups as mentioned above, becomes relevant. Ultimately, this also raises the question of what exactly is encapsulated in the notion of 'resilient tourism' – the tourism assets and key stakeholders (e.g., hotels) or the wider communities and environments in which they operate and that they depend on?

International tourism is now, more than ever, a complex phenomenon given that it relies on international aviation and other forms of resource consumption to bring consumers to the attractions. This is particularly problematic in Pacific Island nations such as Fiji, Vanuatu, and Samoa, where a growing informal sector relies on international tourism arrivals. Yet, as has been seen with Cyclone Pam in Vanuatu in 2015, extreme events can bring the whole industry to a shutdown due to one single event, with long-term consequences for destination image and recovery of the sector (Nalau et al., 2017c). In the context of climate change, this means that destination resilience is a combination of the efforts in the formal and informal sectors to understand the risks that are impacting tourism (Becken, 2013). Product diversification can increase the resilience of the sector, particularly in places where other impacts – such as coral bleaching – may eventually make some sites unviable for particular types of tourism.

The vulnerability of tourism infrastructure also needs to be considered given the projected impacts of climate change (Nalau et al., 2017a; Shakeela & Becken, 2015). In the Pacific, as in many island destinations, much of this infrastructure has been built directly on the beach or adjacent to beaches. Although hard infrastructure solutions (e.g., seawalls) remain popular and quick solutions to issues such as coastal erosion, storm surges, and flooding that affect the tourism sector, alternative options are emerging – for example, ecosystem-based adaptation (EbA) strategies. EbA focuses on using ecosystems in helping communities to adapt to climate change (Munang et al., 2013), such as using coastal forest buffer zones and re-vegetation to protect hotel infrastructure and coastal villages (Mustelin et al., 2010). Such approaches are seen as increasing the resilience and adaptive capacity of both ecosystems and humans, and they can also boost attractiveness while providing storm protection and improving sand retention on beaches. Resilient tourism governance is likely to combine a diversity of options and stakeholders in the management of adverse impacts in a manner which secures business continuity and the distribution of benefits (Movono, 2017; Movono & Dahles, 2017).

There are also global frameworks, such as the Global Sustainable Tourism Dashboard (http://tourismdashboard.org), which could be scaled to regional, country, and community levels and enable a better understanding and tracking of the sustainability of the tourism sector on the ground. This could help decision-makers and policy-makers to start building a better understanding of the sustainability and resilience of a tourism destination and the destination community. Of course, in the Pacific context some of these indicators might have to be tailored to local indigenous contexts, but along with existing work and the refinement of frameworks, this will be an excellent area of future research and policy work.

Acknowledgments

Dr Nalau's contribution was supported by a grant from a private charitable trust.

References

Adger, W.N., & Barnett, J. (2009). Four reasons for concern about adaptation to climate change. *Environment and Planning A, 41*(12), 2800–2805.

Aylen, J., Albertson, K., & Cavan, G. (2014). The impact of weather and climate on tourist demand: The case of Chester Zoo. *Climatic Change, 127*(2), 183–197.

Becken, S. (2013). Developing a framework for assessing resilience of tourism sub-systems to climatic factors. *Annals of Tourism Research, 43*, 506–528.

Becken, S., Lama, A., & Espiner, S. (2013). The cultural context of climate change impacts: Perceptions among community members in the Annapurna Conservation Area, Nepal. *Environmental Development, 8*, 22–37.

Becken, S., Mahon, R., Rennie, H., & Shakeela, A. (2014). The Tourism Disaster Vulnerability Framework: An application to tourism in small island destinations. *Natural Hazards, 71*(1), 955–972.

Brown, C. (2015). *An exploration of climate change adaptation strategies of accommodation providers in Samoa* (Unpublished master's thesis). University of Auckland, New Zealand

Burton, I. (2009). Climate change and the adaptation deficit. In E.L.F. Schipper & I. Burton (Eds.), *The Earthscan reader on adaptation to climate change* (pp. 89–95). London: Earthscan.

Chand, S.S., Chambers, L.E., Waiwai, M., Malsale, P., & Thompson, E. (2014). Indigenous knowledge for environmental prediction in the Pacific Island countries. *Weather, Climate and Society*, *6*(4), 445–450.

Climate and Traditional Knowledges Workgroup. (2014). *Guidelines for considering traditional knowledges in climate change initiatives*. Retreived from https://climatetkw. wordpress.com/about/.

Dubois, G., Ceron, J.-P., Gössling, S., & Hall, C.M. (2016). Weather preferences of French tourists: Lessons for climate change impact assessment. *Climatic Change, 136*(2), 339–351.

Edgell, D.L., Allen, M., Smith, G., & Swanson, J.R. (2008). *Tourism policy and planning: Yesterday, today and tomorrow*. Oxford: Elsevier.

Ensor, J., & Berger, R. (2009). Community-based adaptation and culture in theory and practice. In N. Adger, I. Lorenzoni, & K.L. O'Brien (Eds.), *Adapting to climate change: Thresholds, values, governance* (pp. 227–254). Cambridge, UK: Cambridge University Press.

Espiner, S., & Becken, S. (2014). Tourist towns on the edge: Conceptualising vulnerability and resilience in a protected area tourism system. *Journal of Sustainable Tourism, 22*(4), 646–665.

Ford, J.D., Cameron, L., Rubis, J., Maillet, M., Nakashima, D., Willox, A.C., & Pearce, T. (2016). Including indigenous knowledge and experience in IPCC assessment reports. *Nature Climate Change, 6*(4), 349–353.

Fresque-Baxter, J.A., & Armitage, D. (2012). Place identity and climate change adaptation: A synthesis and framework for understanding. *Wiley Interdisciplinary Reviews: Climate Change, 3*(3), 251–266.

Gallopin, C.G. (2006). Linkages between vulnerability, resilience, and adaptive capacity. *Global Environmental Change, 16*, 293–303.

Grasso, M. (2010). *Justice in funding adaptation under the international climate change regime*. Dordrecht: Springer.

Gössling, S., Scott, D., Hall, C.M., Ceron, J.-P., & Dubois, G. (2012). Consumer behaviour and demand response of tourists to climate change. *Annals of Tourism Research, 39*(1), 36–58.

Handmer, J.W. (2009). Adaptive capacity: What does it mean in the context of natural hazards? In E.L.F. Schipper & I. Burton (Eds.), *The Earthscan reader on adaptation to climate change* (pp. 213–227). London: Earthscan.

Handmer, J.W., & Dovers, S. (2009). A typology of resilience: Rethinking institutions for sustainable development. In E.L.F. Schipper & I. Burton (Eds.), *The Earthscan reader on adaptation to climate change* (pp. 187–210). London; Earthscan.

Hay, J.E., Forbes, D.L., & Mimura, N. (2013). Understanding and managing global change in small islands. *Sustainability Science, 8*(3), 303–308.

Holland, J. (2006). Studying complex adaptive systems. *Journal of System Science & Complexity, 19*(1), 1–8.

Holling, C.S. (2001). Understanding the complexity of economic, ecological and social systems. *Ecosystems, 4*(5), 390–405.

Jeuring, J., & Becken, S. (2013). Tourists and severe weather – An exploration of the role of "Locus of Responsibility" in protective behaviour decisions. *Tourism Management, 37*, 193–202.

Johnston, A., Johnston, M., Stewart, E., Dawson, J., & Lemelin, H. (2012). Perspectives of decision makers and regulators on climate change and adaptation in expedition cruise ship tourism in Nunavut. *The Northern Review, 35*, 69–95.

Kuruppu, N., & Willie, R. (2015). Barriers to reducing climate enhanced disaster risks in Least Developed Country-Small Islands through anticipatory adaptation. *Weather and Climate Extremes, 7*, 72–83.

Lebel, L. (2013). Local knowledge and adaptation to climate change in natural resource-based societies of the Asia-Pacific. *Mitigation and Adaptation Strategies for Global Change, 18*(7), 1057–1076.

Levina, E., & Tirpak, D. (2006). *Key adaptation concepts and terms* (OECD/IEA Project for the Annex I Expert Group on the UNFCCC). Paris: Organisation for Economic Co-operation and Development.

Lim, B., Spanger-Siegfried, E., Burton, I., Malone, E.L., & Huq, S. (2005). *Adaptation policy frameworks for climate change: Developing strategies, policies, and measures.* New York: Cambridge University Press.

Lise, W., & Tol, R S.J. (2002). Impact of climate on tourist demand. *Climatic Change, 55*(4), 429–449.

Matzarakis, A. (2006). Weather- and climate-related information for tourism. *Tourism and Hospitality Planning & Development, 3*(2), 99–115.

Moench, M. (2009). Adapting to climate change and the risks associated with natural hazards: Methods for moving from concepts to action. In E.L.F. Schipper & I. Burton (Eds.), *The Earthscan reader on adaptation to climate change* (pp. 249–280). London: Earthscan.

Mondragon, C. (2014, June 4–7). *Te hurihuri o te Ao: Cycles of change – Traditional calendars for informing climate change policies.* Background paper presented at International Experts Meeting sponsored and organized by Climate Frontlines, UNESCO Small Islands and Indigenous Knowledge Section Division of Science Policy and Capacity-Building, and New Zealand National Commission for UNESCO, Auckland, New Zealand.

Movono, A. (2017). Conceptualizing destinations as a Vanua: An examination of the evolution and resilience of a Fijian social and ecological system. In J. Cheer & A. Lew (Eds.), *Understanding tourism resilience: Adapting to environmental change* (pp. 304–320). London: Routledge.

Movono, A., & Dahles, H. (2017). Female empowerment and tourism: A focus on businesses in a Fijian village. *Asia Pacific Journal of Tourism Research, 22*(6), 681–692.

Movono, A., Dahles, H., & Becken, S. (2018). Fijian culture and the environment: A focus on the ecological and social interconnectedness of tourism development. *Journal of Sustainable Tourism, 26*(3), 451–469.

Munang, R., Thiaw, I., Alverson, K., Mumba, M., Liu, J., & Rivington, M. (2013). Climate change and ecosystem-based adaptation: A new pragmatic approach to buffering climate change impacts. *Current Opinion in Environmental Sustainability, 5*(1), 67–71.

Mustelin, J., Klein, R., Assaid, B., Sitari, T., Khamis, M., Mzee, A., & Haji, T. (2010). Understanding current and future vulnerability in coastal settings: Community perceptions and preferences for adaptation in Zanzibar, Tanzania. *Population & Environment, 31*(5), 371–398.

Nabobo-Baba, U. (2008). Decolonising framings in Pacific research: Indigenous Fijian Vanua research framework as an organic response. *AlterNative: An International Journal of Indigenous Peoples, 4*(2), 140–154.

Nalau, J., Becken, S., Noakes, S., & Mackey, B. (2017b). Mapping tourism stakeholders' weather and climate information-seeking behavior in Fiji. *Weather, Climate, and Society, 9*(3), 377–391.

Nalau, J., & Handmer, J. (2015). When is transformation a viable policy alternative? *Environmental Science & Policy, 54*, 349–356.

Nalau, J., Handmer, J., & Dalesa, M. (2017c). The role and capacity of government in a climate crisis: Cyclone Pam in Vanuatu. In W. Leal Filho (Ed.), *Climate change adaptation in Pacific countries: Fostering resilience and improving the quality of life* (pp. 151–161). Berlin: Springer.

Nalau, J., Schliephack, J., & Becken, S. (2017a). Sustainable tourism growth: Tanna Island, Vanuatu. In World Tourism Organization (UNWTO) and Griffith University, *Managing growth and sustainable tourism governance in Asia and the Pacific* (pp. 118–126). Madrid: UNWTO.

Nayacakalou, R.R. (1975). *Leadership in Fiji*. Oxford: Oxford Unversity Press.

Nelson, D.R., Adger, W.N., & Brown, K. (2007). Adaptation to environmental change: Contributions of a resilience framework. *Annual Review of Environment and Resources, 32*, 395–419.

Nurse, L.A., McLean, R.F., Agard, J., Briguglio, L.P., Duvat-Magnan, V., Pelesikoti, N., ... Webb, A. (2014). Small islands. In V.R. Barros, C.B. Field, D.J. Dokken, M.D. Mastrandrea, K.J. Mach, T.E. Bilir, ... L.L. White (Eds.), *Climate change 2014: Impacts, adaptation, and vulnerability. Part B: Regional aspects. Contribution of Working Group II to the Fifth Assessment Report of the Intergovernmental Panel on Climate Change* (pp. 1613–1654). Cambridge, UK: Cambridge University Press.

Parsons, M., Brown, C., Nalau, J., & Fisher, K. (2018). Assessing adaptive capacity and adaptation: Insights from Samoan tourism operators. *Climate and Development, 10*(7), 644–663.

Parsons, M., Fisher, K., & Nalau, J. (2016). Alternative approaches to co-design: Insights from indigenous/academic research collaborations. *Current Opinion in Environmental Sustainability, 20*, 99–105.

Parsons, M., & Nalau, J. (2016). Historical analogies as tools in understanding transformation. *Global Environmental Change, 38*, 82–96.

Parsons, M., Nalau, J., & Fisher, K. (2017). Alternative perspectives on sustainability: Indigenous knowledge and methodologies. *Challenges in Sustainability, 5*(1), 7–14.

Preston, B., & Stafford-Smith, M. (2009). *Framing vulnerability and adaptive capacity assessment: Discussion paper* (CSIRO Climate Adaptation Flagship Working Paper No. 2). Canberra: Commonwealth Scientific and Industrial Research Organisation.

Rauken, T., Kelman, I., Jacobsen, J.K., & Hovelsrud, G.K. (2010). Who can stop the rain? Perceptions of summer weather effects among small tourism businesses. *Anatolia, 21*(2), 289–304.

Ravuvu, A. (1983). *The Fijian way of life*. Suva, Fiji: Institute of Pacific Studies of the University of the South Pacific.

Rosselló, J., & Santana-Gallego, M. (2014). Recent trends in international tourist climate preferences: A revised picture for climatic change scenarios. *Climatic Change, 124*(1), 119–132.

Schipper, E.L.F., & Burton, I. (2009). Understanding adaptation: Origins, concepts, practice and policy. In E.L.F. Schipper & I. Burton (Eds.), *The Earthscan reader on adaptation to climate change* (pp. 1–8). London: Earthscan.

Scott, D., & Lemieux, C. (2010). Weather and climate information for tourism. *Procedia Environmental Sciences, 1*, 146–183.

Shakeela, A., & Becken, S. (2015). Understanding tourism leaders' perceptions of risks from climate change: An assessment of policy-making processes in the Maldives using the social amplification of risk framework (SARF). *Journal of Sustainable Tourism, 23*(1), 65–84.

South Pacific Tourism Organisation. (n.d.). *Quarterly review of tourism 2013–2014.* Retrieved from http://spto.org/resources/rtrc.

Uyarra, A.M.C., Cote, I.M., Gill, J.A., Tinch, R.R., Viner, D., & Watkinson, A.R., (2005). Island-specific preferences of tourists for environmental features: Implications of climate change for tourism-dependent states. *Environmental Conservation, 32*(1), 11–19.

Warrick, O. (2011). *Local voices, local choices? Vulnerability to climate change and community-based adaptation in rural Vanuatu* (Unpublished doctoral dissertation). Department of Geography, The University of Waikato, New Zealand.

Warrick, O., Aalbersberg, W., Dumaru, P., McNaught, R., & Teperman, K. (2017). The "Pacific Adaptive Capacity Analysis Framework": Guiding the assessment of adaptive capacity in Pacific island communities. *Regional Environmental Change, 17*, 1039–1051.

Whitford, M., & Ruhanen, L. (2016). Indigenous tourism research, past and present: Where to from here. *Journal of Sustainable Tourism, 24*(8), 1080–1099.

World Meteorological Organization, United Nations Environmental Programme, & World Tourism Organization. (2008). *Climate change and tourism – Responding to global challenges.* Madrid: World Tourism Organization and United Nations Environment Programme.

Yu, G., Schwartz, Z., & Walsh, J.E. (2009). A weather-resolving index for assessing the impact of climate change on tourism related climate resources. *Climatic Change, 95*(3–4), 551–573.

8 Post-disaster recovery, tourism, and heritage conservation

Insights from the impacts of Nepal's 2015 earthquake in Kathmandu Valley

Sanjay K. Nepal and Bishnu Devkota

Introduction

Globally, disasters and related physical, economic, and societal damages are increasing steadily, and have doubled each decade since the early 1960s (Pelling, 2003). 'Significant' disasters have reached 500–800 events annually, and losses from natural disasters now average around US$250 billion/year (United Nations International Strategy for Disaster Reduction [UNISDR], 2015), surpassing the global total of all foreign aid spending. Tourism destinations in particular have been identified as highly vulnerable to disasters (Biggs, Hall, & Stoeckl, 2012), and a number of these have been significantly impacted by disasters. Most recently, in 2017, several Caribbean island destinations and the state of Florida in the US experienced enormous destruction in the aftermath of Hurricane Irma. Later that year a major earthquake impacted Iran and Iraq.

Disasters result in significant disruption and impacts on human, social, economic, cultural, political, and physical systems (El-Masri & Tipple, 1997). Because of this, a disaster can be defined as a "serious disruption of the functioning of a community or a society involving widespread human, material, economic or environmental losses and impacts, which exceeds the ability of the affected community or society to cope using its own resources" (UNISDR, 2009). While this definition recognizes that disasters can overwhelm communities, it should also be acknowledged that impacted communities might still retain significant resources and capital with which to facilitate response and recovery, including cultural and social capital. This is particularly true among communities that have had a long tradition of collective action, mutual interdependence, and social cohesion due to cultural ties and values.

The 2015 Nepal earthquake and subsequent major aftershocks brought unprecedented devastation in Nepal as it killed nearly 9,000 people, injured another 22,491, and damaged 510,929 built structures in central Nepal (Government of Nepal, 2015). The earthquake resulted in the loss of nearly half of the country's gross domestic product (GDP) and affected nearly one-third of the national population (Stanton, 2015). It also turned into rubble many of the ancient monuments and historical buildings protected as UNESCO World Heritage Sites in Kathmandu valley, some of them dating back to the fifth century AD (United

Nations Educational, Scientific and Cultural Organization [UNESCO], n.d.). Media around the world mourned the great loss of these heritage sites, which defined Nepal's ancient civilization. For the growing tourism industry in Nepal, the sites were very important; as many as 800 foreign visitors would visit each site per day during peak seasons before the earthquake (Rai & Kaiman, 2015).

The purpose of this chapter is two-fold. First, it documents the impact of the 2015 earthquake on three UNESCO World Heritage Sites in Nepal's Kathmandu Valley. Second, it examines community responses to post-disaster rescue and recovery efforts specific to cultural heritage within the three World Heritage Sites. Additionally, it examines linkages between heritage conservation, international tourism, and sustenance of culture and livelihoods, as perceived by local communities. The focus of this study is on local communities resident in and around the three palace squares of Kathmandu, Bhaktapur, and Patan.

Post-disaster recovery and tourism

Disaster recovery encompasses the process of rebuilding, reconstructing and repairing the damages (both tangible and intangible) associated with a disaster and returning the affected areas to a functional condition (Coppola, 2007), although it has been recognized that communities rarely return to their pre-disaster state (Alesch, 2004; Paton, 2006). Disaster response and longer-term recovery processes usually require considerable resources, and involve a variety of stakeholders and actors in efforts to rebuild long-term economic and social development (Coppola, 2007). Because of this, the disaster response and recovery period is often the most complex and least well-understood phase of the disaster cycle (Coppola, 2007; Lloyd-Jones, 2006), and there is still a lack of assessment and studies on the long-term impacts and processes of recovery (Edgington, 2010).

Current thinking on recovery is that support-driven, people-centered reconstruction and rehabilitation that incorporates the local social, cultural, and economic context should be promoted (Schilderman, 2010; Tierney & Oliver-Smith, 2012). Furthermore, since the Indian Ocean tsunami in 2004, the recovery phase has been viewed as a time for renewal and improvement on pre-existing conditions, often incorporating tourism as a strategy to achieve community vulnerability reduction (Clinton, 2006). Popularly referred to as "build back better" (Clinton, 2006), this approach to recovery builds on Mileti's (1999) "sustainable hazards mitigation" paradigm, the United Nations Development Programme's (UNDP) "sustainable recovery framework" (United Nations Development Programme [UNDP], n.d.), and McEntire's (2001) "invulnerable development approach."

Globally, tourism is an important economic industry, although it is also highly vulnerable to the impacts of disasters (Cassedy, 1992; Loperena, 2017; Mair, Ritchie, & Walters, 2016). There is ample evidence of the negative impacts of disasters on tourism-related activities, including: devastation of tourism infrastructure (Ichinosawa, 2006); destruction of heritage sites (Ghimire, 2015);

economic losses associated with reduced tourism levels (Kim & Marcouiller, 2015); reduction in the number of tourists due to risk-induced shift in tourists' perception of the destination, sometimes over long periods of time (Hystad & Keller, 2008; Ichinosawa, 2006); and reduced spending by tourists (Ghimire, 2015). Some research has been conducted on post-disaster tourism recovery, although this often focuses on strategies to return tourism revenue and total tourist numbers to pre-disaster levels (Mair et al., 2016). Recent calls to move beyond the 'business as usual' understanding of tourism and disaster recovery have been made in order to develop a more nuanced understanding of the inter-sections between tourism and post-disaster recovery that incorporates thinking from the hazards/disasters literature (Gurtner, 2016; Mulligan, Ahmed, Shaw, Mercer, & Nadarajah, 2012; Robinson & Jarvie, 2008).

More recently, some disaster-affected regions have been highlighted as tourism destinations through the somewhat pejorative term 'disaster tourism,' also known as 'dark tourism' (Miller, Gonzalez, & Hutter, 2017). Much of the research associated with disaster tourism focuses on tourists and their motivation for attending such sites (Buda & Shim, 2015; Isaac & Cakmak, 2014); tourists' experience at such sites (Yankovska & Hannam, 2014); or local communities' perceptions of disaster tourism (Wright & Sharpley, 2018). Furthermore, most of this research focuses on tourism related to historical conflicts (e.g., Nazi concen-tration camps) or environmental devastation (e.g., Chernobyl), with limited studies on the short-term tourism that may develop in the post-disaster context, the processes that lead to such tourism, and the impact this has on recovery.

Considering the impact of disasters on the tourism industry, the fact that research has focused mainly on the negative impacts on tourism is surprising. There have been limited studies on the long-term impacts of disasters on the tourism industry, and on how tourism can impact the recovery process (Hystad & Keller, 2008). Also, the interconnections between cultural and social capital and tourism within the context of disaster recovery have yet to be explored. This chapter aims to contribute to the understanding of how local communities see these interconnections, particularly the interdependence between tourism, heri-tage, and livelihood.

Methods

This study employs qualitative methods and is based on data collected in Kath-mandu Valley two months after the April 2015 earthquake had occurred. The main part of the fieldwork, conducted between June and August 2015, consisted of 33 semi-structured interviews with local residents living in and around the three palace squares. As the field visit took place when the trauma of the disaster was still very recent, and local residents were busy in post-disaster recovery, purposive sampling followed by snowball sampling was preferred in light of local sensitivities. The interviews were complemented by field observations and photographic documentation, the results of which are not included in this chapter but reported elsewhere (see Devkota, 2016). Prior to arriving at the study site, formal approval for the research was obtained from the Office of Research Ethics at the University of Waterloo in Canada. The empirical section of this chapter is complemented by news reports and articles published in national and international newspapers and magazines regarding local people's responses to the earthquake. Similarly, government reports, notices and announcements were obtained from the official websites of numerous Ministries of the Nepal Government and the Nepal Police.

The empirical part of this study was conducted in the pre-dominantly Newar communities surrounding the three *Durbar* squares (ancient royal palace complexes), namely, Hanumandhoka (Kathmandu), Patan (Lalitpur) and Bhaktapur within Kathmandu Valley. The *Durbar* squares were selected as the sites of study because they have collectively preserved the most significant historical and cultural landmarks of Nepal, and are the principal tourist destinations of the valley. These squares, formerly royal residences of the three city states of Kathmandu Valley before they were surrendered to modern Nepal, evolved as centers of trade, culture, and civilization that Newars cultivated over millennia. Of the 126 ethnic groups in Nepal, Newars are the sixth largest, comprising 5 percent of the national population (Government of Nepal, 2015). The Newars are a culturally and historically rich ethnic group, distinct among all others in Nepal, and they are the original inhabitants of Kathmandu Valley. Thus, the majority of Newars are concentrated in and around the valley. They are often considered as being more educated, urban, and generally more advanced socio-economically than other ethnic groups in Nepal. Trade and business, sculpting, woodcarving, agriculture, and the civil service are their major occupations.

Study participants were initially identified, purposively, both through the researchers' existing local connections and through a post-earthquake content review of daily editions of national newspapers and magazines including *The Kathmandu Post*, *The Republica*, *Kantipur*, *Nepali Times*, and *Himal South Asian*. The pool of initial participants was then built upon using snowball sampling. Those who voluntarily agreed to participate and were over 18 years of age were recruited for interviews. Since the timing of the fieldwork coincided with restoration and rehabilitation efforts, and for the vast majority of residents in the valley life had not returned to normality, only those who voluntarily agreed to participate were interviewed. The respondents ($n=33$) ranged in age from 21 to 96, with 60 percent between 40 and 60 years of age. The majority were well-educated, with 85 percent having an undergraduate degree or higher. The majority of the respondents were male ($n=28/33$); this gender bias was unavoidable as most female respondents were not available for interview due to the timing of the fieldwork and the sensitivity of the topic. The respondents represented all walks of life: community leaders, business people, club/non-governmental organization members, priests, professors, municipality workers, civil servants, housewives, engineers, and students.

A consent statement was formally signed with each respondent. The interview time and location was agreed according to respondents' convenience; while most interviews were conducted at participants' places of work, several were carried out at public locations that were private enough to have a conversation (e.g., a café). All interviews were conducted in the Nepali language and audio recorded with participants' consent and later translated into English. Although the Newars primarily speak Nepal Bhasa (commonly referred to as Newari), they use Nepali for formal communication and when speaking to a non-Newar. The semi-structured interview questions were relevant to gathering demographic characteristics of the respondents, their pre-existing knowledge and awareness of the earthquake, and their responses in the immediate aftermath of the earthquake with specific reference to their family and community as well as what facilitated them to cope with the disaster before the arrival of any external, formal assistance. The interviews were reviewed immediately after completion to look for emerging themes that could provide further insights in upcoming interviews. Generally, the interviews lasted from 20 minutes to two hours. Interviews were ended when no new information emerged from the participant's narrative. All interviews were translated into English. The scripts were then coded, categorized, and organized into common themes. Due to the sensitivity of the subject-matter, for the purpose of this chapter most interviews are summarized to present a generalized perspective instead of using direct quotes.

Effect of the earthquake on tourism

Tourism in Nepal started in the early 1960s, with the opening of the first private tourist agency in 1964. The Ministry of Tourism was established 14 years after that and Nepal Tourism Board (NTB), a public–private partnership, came into existence in 1998. Tourism in Nepal is heavily dependent on its natural and cultural resources. For example, 23 percent of the country's territory is designated as protected areas where there is much nature-based tourism. Similarly, its high mountains – eight of the world's top ten mountains above 8,000 meters are in Nepal – are premier destinations for adventure trekking and mountaineering. There are ten UNESCO World Heritage Sites – eight cultural and two natural sites – which offer a diverse mix of unique natural and cultural experiences to international visitors.

From a tourism perspective, it should be noted that the 2015 earthquake could not have occurred at a worse time. After almost a decade of stagnation and decline in tourist arrivals, tourism was gradually gaining momentum. Tourist arrivals in Nepal are still below one million, and this figure dramatically reduced in the aftermath of the earthquake (see Figure 8.1). The severe decline in tourist arrivals significantly impacted the tourism industry, which was recovering from a decade-long Maoist insurgency and a series of political upheavals after 1996 (Nepal, 2010). The Royal massacre of 2001 and the revolution of 2006 effectively ended the 240-year-long monarchy in Nepal, turning the country into a republic in December 2007. Political upheavals since then, with frequent shutdowns and street protests, adversely affected the development and growth of tourism.

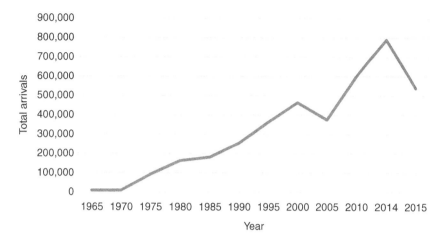

Figure 8.1 Tourist arrivals in Nepal.
Data source: Government of Nepal (2016, pp. 12–13).

The April 2015 earthquake hit the tourism industry hard, as it seriously compromised the tourism infrastructure and significantly destroyed heritage monuments in Kathmandu Valley. It is important to note that tourism is the major generator of foreign currency in Nepal as it comprises 8.2 percent of GDP, and is a source of livelihood for 7 percent of the country's population (World Travel and Tourism Council [WTTC], 2015). The earthquake and subsequent major aftershocks brought unprecedented devastation in Nepal (Government of Nepal, 2015). Within Kathmandu Valley, 1,725 people were killed, 11,046 were injured, and at least 66,780 residents were displaced (Nepal Police, 2015). The earthquake also caused significant damage to 833 government buildings, 473 school buildings, 185 health facilities, and 152,988 private houses (Nepal Police 2015).

Immediately following the earthquake, tourist arrivals sharply dipped, the popular Everest climbing season was cancelled for the whole year, hotel occupancy remained almost zero, and many people who worked in the tourism sector became unemployed. The earthquake and its aftermath was widely covered by all major international media outlets, thus further discouraging potential visitors to travel to Nepal amidst the chaos, risk, and insecurity brought about by the disaster. Travel advice from most of the tourist originating countries deterred tourists from visiting Nepal. Six months post-disaster (October 2015), tourist arrivals remained 46 percent down compared with before the disaster with only 300,325 tourists visiting Nepal, plunging hotel occupancy to an all-time low at or below 20 percent (Prasain, 2015). During this time, the average length of stay also dropped from 12 to six days and jobs in the tourism sector decreased by 25 percent (Prasain, 2015). According to the government of Nepal's *Post disaster needs assessment* report, the tourism sector lost around US$765 million, most of which was due to the losses of tourism businesses after the disaster (Government of Nepal, 2015).

Heritage tourism in Kathmandu Valley

Nepal's ancient civilization originated and developed in Kathmandu Valley. Kathmandu, the capital of Nepal, is a 667 km^2 valley that lies in three of Nepal's 75 administrative districts – Kathmandu, Lalitpur, and Bhaktapur – and has three vibrant cities with identical names (Devkota, Doberstein, & Nepal, 2016). Most of the extraordinary built heritage of Kathmandu was constructed by the Malla kings between the thirteenth and eighteenth centuries. The centers of these cities have ancient, architecturally wonderful palace squares made by the ancestors of Kathmandu's indigenous Newar inhabitants. Thomas Bell (2014, pp. 121–122) describes the development of the palace squares of Kathmandu in his narrative:

> In each city centre stood a palace. On their exterior, the palaces were decorated like temples, with stone lions at the door and gods and goddesses on the timbers. The [Malla] kings filled the plazas beyond the palace wall with temples of the high, pure Hindu gods who rule in heaven. Within, they built towering shrines to their private goddesses Taleju, whose secret worship offered them power in this world. More palace courtyards spread but to accommodate their priests. Her secret Mantra was passed from father to son on the king's deathbed, to validate the succession and to give the new ruler control of her power. So, a forest of pagoda roofs was raised over the centres of Patan, Kathmandu and Bhaktapur. Masterpieces of timber and fired earth accumulated through the joint proceeds of jealousy, trade, and debasing the coinage [of the rulers].

Kathmandu's ancient history is reflected in its rich heritage of traditional arts, architecture, and culture. Owing to its outstanding, unmatched cultural richness, UNESCO placed seven cultural sites from Kathmandu on the World Heritage list in 1979 and later designated the Kathmandu Valley as a World Heritage Site. Numerous historic monuments, temples, stupas, legends, and the living heritage of indigenous Newar communities make Kathmandu a popular destination for visitors from within and outside the country (Devkota et al., 2016).

Kathmandu is significant from a tourism perspective, as it is the only entry point to Nepal by air. Most tourists arrive at Kathmandu before heading elsewhere. Kathmandu's three *Durbar* squares (palace courtyards), Hanumandhoka, Patan, and Bhaktapur were significant for local businesses and trans-Himalayan traders in the past, and they are equally important now due to tourism. Prior to the earthquake, it is estimated that as many as 800 foreign visitors would visit these sites during the tourist seasons (March–May and October–December) (Rai & Kaiman, 2015). The entry fee levied on foreign visitors to Kathmandu's UNESCO World Heritage Sites, especially the three palace squares, is utilized for heritage conservation and community welfare activities. Local hotels, souvenir shops, guides, tour operators, taxi drivers, and street vendors among others directly rely on tourists for their livelihoods. Alongside this, the indirect benefits that spill over to people who are not involved in tourism is equally important. Many of the monuments in these squares, which were rebuilt after two major catastrophic earthquakes in 1833 and 1934, again turned into rubble due to the 7.8 magnitude earthquake on 25 April 2015 (UNESCO, n.d.).

Kathmandu's UNESCO World Heritage Sites are not just tourism attractions; they are also focal points for the daily religious, spiritual, and cultural practices of local people who live in and around these sites. The combination of the tangible architectural grandeur of the monuments, combined with intangible heritage expressed through religious and cultural practices, offers a unique experience for foreign visitors. International tourism has been a source of much needed conservation funds for these aging monuments as well as providing a livelihood for many people living in the surrounding areas. The economic significance of these ancient heritage sites cannot be overstated. For instance, almost one million US dollars of the revenue generated in a year in Bhaktapur Durbar Square comes from the US$15.00 entrance fee a foreign visitor pays to enter the site. Many local residents benefit directly from tourism as tour guides, street vendors, and owners or employees of souvenir shops, restaurants, and hotels. Entrance fees are utilized primarily to protect the monuments and also help to keep the streets clean, maintain architecturally significant private dwellings in the area, and subsidize day care centers, health posts, and colleges. During an interview, a souvenir shop owner near Nyatapola Temple in Bhaktapur stated:

> Perhaps, we can survive when they [monuments] are there; if they are not there, we will be people without culture and art. Our culture is our survival, it is feeding us, it is doing all things to us. They are hugely important to us.

In another interview, a local historian commented, "These heritage monuments are hens that lay golden eggs for us due to their significance for tourism."

After the earthquake, many Western countries declared Nepal unsafe for travel. This had an adverse impact on the local communities, particularly those directly employed in the tourism industry. Some of respondents stated that the lack of tourists at such a critical time was a double blow – not only have the monuments gone, but so have the tourists. With the destruction of heritage monuments and no tourist activity, another earthquake had occurred in their lives. From the street vendor to the owners of large hotels and restaurants, all faced an economic crisis. The realization that heritage and tourism are strongly linked motivated people further to actively engage in safeguarding the damaged monuments, and in the safekeeping of artifacts retrieved from the rubble.

Recovery of artifacts and reconstruction concerns

Despite the recurring threats of aftershocks and the destruction left by the earthquake, as reported by respondents, local residents were acutely aware of the importance of securing artifacts buried in the rubble. While the search and rescue of people buried in the debris was ongoing, community members also began searching for and retrieving valuable artifacts. They guarded premises, retrieved useful artifacts, and created a safe storage space for and detailed inventory of items that were salvaged. Some respondents in Patan Durbar Square stated that local youths protected the Durbar premises day and night for three days, until the local police arrived to offer protection. Similarly, in Bhaktapur, concerned that artifacts might end up in the wrong hands and be smuggled away, local residents secured everything from the debris of the collapsed temples. The residents knew that if those artifacts were not retrieved or secured from the pile of rubble, they could be stolen or permanently damaged, thus hampering reconstruction efforts in the future.

Community consultations on heritage reconstruction were initiated soon after the first earthquake, even though the scale of destruction was far beyond the management capacity of the communities. While the elders were engaged in discussing future reconstruction efforts, young people began a campaign of public awareness through art and songs about the importance of reclaiming their heritage. The discussion on reconstruction focused on incorporating modern earthquake resistant design elements without compromising authenticity in architectural details. Many respondents stressed the need to combine traditional wisdom with modern technology. They were concerned to make the inner restoration and construction of monuments more disaster resistant, as altering the outer appearance of the monuments was out of the question. The majority of respondents expressed the view that there was a wide consensus among local residents to fuse modern technology with traditional techniques because almost all the recent reconstructions carried out in the palace squares had survived the earthquake. Kathmandu Valley Preservation Trust, a local non-government heritage conservation organization, had renovated parts of Mul Chowk and Sundari Chowk in Patan, reinforcing traditional structures with modern earthquake resistant technology. Similarly, a German project had done the same for the last 15 years in Bhaktapur. These recent renovations proved that it was possible to preserve traditional appearance while reinforcing core structural strength using modern technology. Local communities looked forward to replicating these models in heritage reconstruction. The cost of reconstruction is quite high, and often carried out with financial help from foreign governments. Many respondents stated that local communities did not want to depend solely on traditional restoration techniques as that would mean their efforts would be of no value in the event of a future earthquake of similar magnitude. As for the reconstruction fund, which may require millions of dollars, they believed the heritage sites could self-sustain if the money generated from tourism is utilized primarily for heritage renewal. Rather than mourning what they lost in the earthquake, communities focused on hope and opportunity. In fact, the history of Kathmandu's heritage monuments is the history of revival after each destructive earthquake in the past.

Future perspectives in the aftermath of the earthquake

Despite unprecedented losses, respondents perceived the earthquake as a catalyst for renewal and rebuilding using earthquake resistant technology. They expressed the opinion that the ancestral cultural heritage had been an asset to the world community, and that the present condition of the monuments was the result of resilient restoration and reconstruction efforts carried out by the community generation after generation. Respondents also expressed the view that a communal spirit and cooperative attitudes were inherent characteristics that had been passed on to them from their ancestors. Citing recent earthquakes in Haiti and Gujrat in India, one respondent (the owner of a tourist souvenir shop) stated:

> This [earthquake] has brought the community together. I think there is a future for a prosperous Nepal – Nepal with its art, culture, and architecture will rise again. People have come thus far due to renewal and revival, so we need to take it [the earthquake] positively. [An] earthquake is a natural thing. It brings development as well with it. Our monuments fell – our skills are not dead. We have skills. We can make thousands of such monuments again. I am hopeful. People here are equally hopeful. The earthquake has provided us a great lesson this time. This has provided opportunity too.

Several respondents indicated that feelings and apprehensions about losses will positively inspire them to care for their heritage and cultural practices. For those who had not taken their traditions and culture seriously, the earthquake had opened their eyes to its importance. Fear of losing their cultural traditions prompted respondents to remain strong and resolute. Some stated that local devotees were happy to visit the shrines even though they were exposed to natural elements as the temples around the shrines lay in ruins. For instance, Kasthamandapa and Maju Dega in Kathmandu, Char Narayan and Laxmi Narayan Temple in Patan, and Vatsala and Phasi Dega in Bhaktapur were completely destroyed and their shrines were out in the open, but devotees still visited the temple premises for prayers and offerings and showed reverence to the deities on a daily basis. During the field visit to Patan Durbar Square's Krishna Mandir temple, one of the authors observed a group of devotees singing prayers and hymns with utter disregard for the 'Danger Zone' signpost that had been erected by the municipality office. Upon further enquiries, some of the devotees mentioned that their hymns would help to heal the community's emotional and psychological scars; they were willing to take the risk even if they had to perform in the so-called 'danger zone.'

Many respondents considered the suffering brought about by the earthquake as transitory and hoped for a better future. In the immediate aftermath, several influential international media including CNN, the BBC, and the New York Times showed a series of before and after images of Kathmandu's heritage monuments. International journalists reported directly from Kathmandu, eulogizing the historical significance of the lost and damaged heritage. The extent of the publicity around the world about Nepal's precious monuments was unprecedented, even though it was primarily related to the destruction brought about by the earthquake. Some respondents held the view that, whether good or bad, there was useful exposure about Nepal among the international community. One respondent suggested that this disaster-related publicity was a "sort of blessing in disguise." Several respondents also asserted that although the earthquake was inauspicious, the message that there is a country called Nepal – where Buddha was born, where Mount Everest lies, and where much cultural and historical heritage remains – was also spread simultaneously. Although it was not desirable, respondents believed that the publicity Nepal and its heritage received globally will eventually be good for the country's tourism industry once things return to normal. As for the revival of tourism, respondents were hopeful that it would recover in about a year's time. However, visitor arrivals from overseas have not, to date, reached pre-earthquake numbers.

Conclusions

This chapter examined the effects of the 2015 earthquake in Nepal on its UNESCO World Heritage Sites in Kathmandu Valley. It also focused on community responses to heritage protection and renewal in the immediate aftermath of the earthquake. The study was based on fieldwork conducted two months after the earthquake, and as such it provides a preliminary assessment of community responses to heritage protection and tourism prospects. Findings suggest local communities in and around the three palace squares have remained resolute as they seek opportunities for heritage restoration and reconstruction. They were cognizant of the strong linkages between heritage conservation, tourism, and livelihoods. The actions and responses of the local communities in the immediate aftermath of the earthquake indicate a positive outlook for heritage reconstruction and tourism revival.

Based on this study it is rather difficult to evaluate community resilience, which requires a longer-term assessment of disaster impacts (Walsh, 2007). However, the findings indicate that communities in Kathmandu Valley are steadfast in their resolution to restore and renew their culture and heritage. For example, exactly two years after the earthquake, community members gathered to commemorate the fateful event at the premises of Kasthamandapa, the oldest wooden pavilion in the valley from which the name Kathmandu is derived. Kasthamandapa, located in Kathmandu Durbar Square, was totally obliterated by the earthquake. Local members of the Rebuild Kasahamandapa initiative held a ceremony during which they made a promise to reclaim the rebuilding process of Kasthamandapa with local fervor and ownership, making it a spiritual awakening of the present generation to hand down the heritage monument to the future generation (Pradhananga, 2017). This indicates a strong sense of resilience and responsibility among locals in the stewardship of heritage reconstruction, as had been carried in the past by their ancestors. The earthquake put to test local knowledge, skills, perseverance, and community spirit. Rising from the rubble, local communities exhibited considerable emotional and psychological strength, and a collective capacity to face adversity with courage, pride, and responsibility.

Many tourism destinations have experienced frequent and sudden onset natural and human-induced disasters, as they are often located in vulnerable locations such as coastal areas, mountainous regions, and densely populated cities (Ritchie, 2008). Following the earthquake, Nepal's tourism industry suffered unprecedented losses. However, despite the losses, respondents in this study believed that the earthquake also put into focus the grandeur of the monuments in the eyes of the outside world, a sort of 'blessing in disguise' for Nepal's destination marketing and promotion. Respondents not only believed in a positive outlook for their own future livelihoods, but also considered tourism critical to heritage renewal. Post-disaster community actions and behavior have been very positive towards the reconstruction of heritage monuments and the revival of associated intangible cultural practices. Local communities around the heritage sites have begun consultations on heritage reconstruction, and are considering a blend of traditional and modern restoration techniques. Many commented that the ancient monuments could self-sustain their reconstruction and maintenance through earnings from tourism. This, perhaps, suggests that the community is aware of transitioning to a post-disaster tourism renewal (Tucker, Shelton, & Bae, 2017). Furthermore, communities took the earthquake as a warning, and saw it as an opportunity to rebuild and renew. Scholars have noted that positive outlook during a period of catastrophe contributes to disaster response in a positive way, by providing the energy to rebuild and renew lives, revise dreams, and help establish positive legacies for future generations (Walsh, 2007). Studies on disaster afflicted tourism destinations such as Bangkok after the 2011 flood, New Orleans after Hurricane Katrina in 2005, and San Francisco following the earthquake in 1989 have found that these destinations recovered rapidly, restoring businesses back to normal in a short period of time and with a high degree of resilience (Durocher, 1994; Ghaderi, Mat Som, & Henderson, 2015). Tourism industry stakeholders in Nepal also hope that visitor arrivals will soon return to pre-earthquake levels and continue to rise thereafter.

Pottorff and Neal (1994) contend that effective planning and mitigation measures can reposition tourism destinations in a post-disaster period. A comprehensive tourism revival approach should integrate initiatives of national government, airline companies, foreign tour operators, local tourism business owners, media, and other related organizations. Previous studies have shown that recovery of a tourism destination depends on the level of destruction, the efficiency of tourism stakeholders in bringing their facilities back into service, and appropriate marketing techniques that assure the readiness of the destination to provide tourist services (Durocher, 1994). As disasters produce long-lasting positive and negative images, the "expectation of returning the destination to a situation that exactly replicates the pre-disaster equilibrium" may be difficult in some cases because negative stigmas remain unavoidable (Faulkner & Vikulov, 2001, p. 344). Notwithstanding the 2015 earthquake, the main drivers of risk and vulnerability for tourism in Nepal are induced by socio-economic instability, political instability, a politicized and cumbersome bureaucracy, unequal service delivery, corruption, and an ill-equipped workforce (Lama, 2010). The earthquake has exacerbated these problems, which need to be addressed adequately as the country gears up for a new era of post-disaster tourism. In the context of Kathmandu Valley, and Nepal as a whole, tourism and heritage are intertwined with local tradition, culture, and livelihood, as this study has shown. Current and future efforts directed on disaster mitigation and reconstruction at heritage tourism destinations in Nepal must therefore consider these interconnections and interdependencies.

References

Alesch, D.J. (2004, January 19). *Complex urban systems and extreme events: Towards a theory of disaster recovery. Proceedings of the 1st international conference on urban disaster reduction*, Kobe, Japan.

Bell, T. (2014). *Kathmandu*. New Delhi: Random House.

Biggs, D., Hall, C.M., & Stoeckl, N. (2012). The resilience of formal and informal tourism enterprises to disasters: Reef tourism in Phuket, Thailand. *Journal of Sustainable Tourism, 20*(5), 645–665.

Buda, D.M., & Shim, D. (2015). Desiring the dark: "A taste for the unusual" in North Korean tourism? *Current Issues in Tourism, 18*(1), 1–6.

Cassedy, K. (1992). Preparedness in the face of crisis: An examination of crisis management planning in the travel and tourism industry. *World Travel and Tourism Review, 2*, 169–174.

Clinton, W. (2006). *Lessons learned from tsunami recovery: Key propositions for building back better* (A report by the United Nations Secretary-General's Special Envoy for Tsunami Recovery). New York, NY: Office of the UN Secretary-General's Special Envoy for Tsunami Recovery.

Coppola, D.P. (2007). *Introduction to international disaster management*. Burlington, MA: Elsevier.

Devkota, B.P. (2016). *Revival from rubble: Community resilience at UNSECO World Heritage Sites in Kathmandu after 2015 Earthquake* (Unpublished master's thesis). University of Waterloo, Canada.

Devkota, B.P., Doberstein, B., & Nepal, S.K. (2016). Social capital and natural disaster: Local responses to 2015 earthquake in Kathmandu. *International Journal of Mass Emergencies and Disasters, 34*(3), 439–466.

Durocher, J. (1994). Recovery marketing: What to do after a natural disaster. *The Cornell Hotel and Restaurant Administration Quarterly, 35*(2), 66–71.

Edgington, D.W. (2010). *Reconstructing Kobe: The geography of crisis and opportunity*. Vancouver: UBC Press.

El-Masri, S., & Tipple, G. (1997). Urbanisation, poverty and natural disasters: Vulnerability of settlements in developing countries. In A. Awotona (Ed.), *Reconstruction after disaster: Issues and practices* (pp. 1–12). Aldershot, UK: Ashgate.

Faulkner, B., & Vikulov, S. (2001). Katherine, washed out one day, back on track the next: A post-mortem of a tourism disaster. *Tourism Management, 22*(4), 331–344.

Ghaderi, Z., Mat Som, A.P., & Henderson, J.C. (2015). When disaster strikes: The Thai floods of 2011 and tourism industry response and resilience. *Asia Pacific Journal of Tourism Research, 20*(4), 399–415.

Ghimire, H.L. (2015). Disaster management and post-quake impact on tourism in Nepal. *Journal of Tourism and Hospitality, 7*, 37–57.

Government of Nepal. (2015). *Nepal earthquake 2015: Post disaster needs assessment.* Kathmandu: Government of Nepal, National Planning Commission.

Government of Nepal. (2016). *Nepal tourism statistics 2015.* Kathmandu: Ministry of Culture, Tourism and Civil Aviation.

Gurtner, Y. (2016). Returning to paradise: Investigating issues of tourism crisis and disaster recovery on the island of Bali. *Journal of Hospitality and Tourism Management, 28*, 11–19.

Hystad, P.W., & Keller, P.C. (2008). Towards a destination tourism disaster management framework: Long-term lessons from a forest fire disaster. *Tourism Management, 29*(1), 151–162.

Ichinosawa, J. (2006). Reputational disaster in Phuket: The secondary impact of the tsunami on inbound tourism. *Disaster Prevention and Management, 15*(1), 111–123.

Isaac, R.K., & Cakmak, E. (2014). Understanding visitor's motivation at sites of death and disaster: The case of former transit camp Westerbork, the Netherlands. *Current Issues in Tourism, 17*(2), 164–179.

Kim, H., & Marcouiller, D.W. (2015). Considering disaster vulnerability and resiliency: The case of hurricane effects on tourism-based economies. *The Annals of Regional Science, 54*(3), 945–971.

Lama, A.K. (2010). *Vulnerability of nature based tourism to climate change: Stakeholders' perceptions of and response to climate change in the lower Mustang Region of the Annapurna conservation area* (Unpublished doctoral dissertation). Lincoln University, New Zealand.

Lloyd-Jones, T. (2006). *Mind the gap! Post-disaster reconstruction and the transition from humanitarian relief* (Summary Report for the Royal Institution of Chartered Surveyors by the Max Lock Centre). London: University of Westminster.

Loperena, C.A. (2017). Honduras is open for business: Extractivist tourism as sustainable development in the wake of disaster? *Journal of Sustainable Tourism, 25*(5), 618–633.

McEntire, D. (2001). Triggering agents, vulnerability and disaster reduction: Towards a holistic paradigm. *Disaster Prevention and Mitigation, 10*(3), 189–196.

Mair, J., Ritchie, B.W., & Walters, G. (2016). Towards a research agenda for post-disaster and post-crisis recovery strategies for tourist destinations: A narrative review. *Current Issues in Tourism, 19*(1), 1–26.

Mileti, D. (1999). *Disasters by design: A reassessment of natural hazards in the United States.* Washington, DC: Joseph Henry Press.

Miller, D.S., Gonzalez, C., & Hutter, M. (2017). Phoenix tourism within dark tourism: Rebirth, rebuilding and rebranding of tourist destinations following disasters. *Worldwide Hospitality and Tourism Themes, 9*(2), 196–215.

Mulligan, M., Ahmed, I., Shaw, J., Mercer, D., & Nadarajah, Y. (2012). Lessons for long-term social recovery following the 2004 tsunami: Community, livelihoods, tourism and housing. *Environmental Hazards, 11*(1), 38–51.

Nepal, S.K. (2010). Tourism and political change in Nepal. In R.W. Butler & W. Suntikul (Eds.), *Tourism and political change* (pp. 147–159). Oxford: Butterworth-Heinemann.

Nepal Police. (2015). *Great earthquake, 2015: Details of human casualties of districts within the valley.* Kathmandu: Nepal Police.

Paton, D. (2006). Disaster resilience: Building capacity to co-exist with natural hazards. In D. Paton & D. Johnston (Eds.), *Disaster resilience: An integrated approach.* Springfield, IL: Charles C. Thomas Publisher.

Pelling, M. (2003). *The vulnerability of cities: Natural disasters and social resilience.* London: Earthscan.

Pottorff, S.M., & Neal, D.D.M. (1994). Marketing implications for post-disaster tourism destinations. *Journal of Travel & Tourism Marketing, 3*(1), 115–122.

Pradhananga, S.B. (2017, April 26) With heritage reconstruction shuttering, locals seize initiative for Kasthamandap rebuild. Retrieved from http://kathmandupost.ekantipur.com/news/2017-04-26/locals-seize-kasthamandap-rebuild-initiative.html.

Prasain, S. (2015, November 11). Arrivals drop by half as disasters take their toll. *The Kathmandu Post.* Retrieved from http://kathmandupost.ekantipur.com.

Rai, B., & Kaiman, J. (2015, May 23). Ancient temples, key to Nepal tourism, suffer severe quake damage. *Los Angeles Times.* Retrieved from www.latimes.com.

Ritchie, B. (2008). Tourism disaster planning and management: From response and recovery to reduction and readiness. *Current Issues in Tourism, 11*(4), 315–348.

Robinson, L., & Jarvie, J.K. (2008). Post-disaster community tourism recovery: The tsunami and Arugam Bay, Sri Lanka. *Disasters, 32*(4), 631–645.

Schilderman, T. (2010). Putting people at the centre of reconstruction. In M. Lyons, T. Schilderman, & C. Boano (Eds.), *Building back better: Delivering people-centred housing reconstruction at scale* (pp. 7–38). Rugby, UK: Practical Action Publishing.

Stanton, J. (2015, May 20). Nepal slowly begins to rebuild: Before and after pictures reveal the full extent of the damage wreaked across the country by giant earthquakes. *The Daily Mail.* Retrieved from www.dailymail.co.uk.

Tierney, K., & Oliver-Smith, A. (2012). Social dimensions of disaster recovery. *International Journal of Mass Emergencies and Disasters, 30*(2), 123–146.

Tsai, C.H., Wu, T.C., Wall, G., & Linliu, S.C. (2016). Perceptions of tourism impacts and community resilience to natural disasters. *Tourism Geographies, 18*(2), 152–173.

Tucker, H., Shelton, E.J., & Bae, H. (2017). Post-disaster tourism: Towards a tourism of transition. *Tourist Studies, 17*(3), 306–327.

United Nations Development Programme (UNDP). (n.d.). *Post-disaster recovery guidelines.* New York: Bureau for Crisis Prevention and Recovery Disaster Reduction Unit, UNDP.

United Nations Educational, Scientific and Cultural Organization (UNESCO). (n.d.). Kathmandu Valley. Retrieved from http://whc.unesco.org/en/list/121.

United Nations International Strategy for Disaster Reduction (UNISDR). (2009). *UNISDR terminology on disaster risk reduction.* Retrieved from www.unisdr.org/we/inform/terminology.

United Nations International Strategy for Disaster Reduction (UNISDR). (2015). *GAR: Global assessment report on disaster risk reduction.* Geneva: UNISDR.

Walsh, F. (2007). Traumatic loss and major disasters: Strengthening family and community resilience. *Family Process, 46*(2), 207–227.

World Travel and Tourism Council (WTTC). (2015). *Travel and tourism economic impact, 2015.* Nepal: WTTC.

Wright, D., & Sharpley, R. (2018). Local community perceptions of disaster tourism: The case of L'Aquila, Italy. *Current Issues in Tourism, 21*(14), 1569–1585.

Yankovska, G., & Hannam, K. (2014). Dark and toxic tourism in the Chernobyl exclusion zone. *Current Issues in Tourism, 17*(10), 929–939.

9 Working towards resilience

Collective agency in a tourism destination in the Swiss Alps

Tina Haisch

Introduction

In the social sciences, resilience describes the ability of regional economies to respond and adapt to crises and disturbances (Bristow & Healy, 2013; Pendall, Foster, & Cowell, 2010; Simmie & Martin, 2010). Closely linked to the resilience debate is the notion of a system's vulnerability (Gallopín, 2006), often conceptualized as pre-shock sensitivity towards natural disasters resulting, for example, from climate change, and especially assigned to marginalized groups in a population (Adger, 2009; Voss, 2008). Both attributes of a system, vulnerability and resilience, are distributed unequally across space. With regard to the recent world economic crisis, diversified urban regions have more or less managed to overcome job losses and GDP decline while peripheral communities are still having to deal with the consequences of restructuring processes and austerity (Haisch, 2018).

While some studies have described, in theoretical terms, the ability of regional economies to adapt to change and to transform (see Martin & Sunley, 2014), there is still a need to further elaborate the meaning and the potential added value of the concept of economic resilience to explain the development of regions and municipalities, mainly from a long-term perspective (Boschma, 2014; Martin, 2011). Several studies have investigated types of regions which are able to resist or 'bounce back' after crises (Davies, 2011; Simmie & Martin, 2010); however, literature that aims to understand processes of human agency that lead to adaptation and resilience building within a region is rare. Studies using macro-economic approaches are often limited to the analysis of post-crises developments such as employment changes or post-recession growth, or highlight policy programs that might contribute to the recovery of regional economies (see Davies, 2011; Martin, 2011).

This chapter sheds light on the role of governance in collective human agency in adaptation processes in Grindelwald, a mountain tourism destination in the Swiss Alps. This municipality, on the one hand, is highly dependent on the protection of its natural assets and facing financial restrictions due to depopulation; yet, on the other hand, it needs new amenities to attract tourists and residents and to meet and compete with global market demand.

Tourism communities in the Swiss Alps are facing three major stressors: first, the effects of climate change (Adger, 2009); second, the world economic crisis, together with a strong Swiss currency, is threatening the tourism and construction sectors (Marvel & Johnson, 1997); and third, ongoing depopulation (Bätzing, Perlik, & Dekleva, 1996) is leading to an erosion of tax revenues.

The chapter is structured as follows: first, a brief overview of resilience and complex systems is given, followed by a discussion on human agency. The case study is then introduced and methods and data collection are described. The results of the case study are subsequently presented and the chapter ends with a discussion and conclusion.

Resilience and complex systems

Complex systems exist in different fields of natural sciences, such as chemistry (molecular reactions), physics, biology (the human brain), but also in engineering (machines), economics (markets), and today's super-computers (Watson). In addition, societies can be regarded as complex systems. Complex systems are distinct from simple systems not only in terms of the quantitative number of elements that compose the system, but also – and primarily – because of their complex *behavioral mechanisms* (Haken, 2006).

In general, complex systems are described as non-linear, non-reducible to their components, unpredictable, and with multiple feedbacks, allowing a system to self-organize (Folke, 2006; Heylighen, 2012). There is no absolute definition of self-organization, but a "self-organizing system may be characterized by global, coordinated activity arising spontaneously from local interactions between the system's components or 'agents'" (Heylighen, 2012, p. 120). Thus, we do not need to "understand the behavior of individual parts, but rather their orchestration" (Haken, 2006, p. 6) and also how this orchestration leads to adaptation from a shorter-term and adaptability from a longer-term perspective (Boschma, 2014). Orchestration can also be seen as *governance of complex system components or agents* (Ostrom, 2010). With regard to societies, governance is a form of regional self-control, a reaction to deficiencies and a supplement to market-based and public guidance. It occurs in situations where the interplay between private, state, and municipal actors is needed in order to solve problems (Fürst, 2010).

Accordingly, the literature on resilience from a social sciences perspective highlights networks, institutions, and industrial knowledge bases as bearers of regional resilience (Boschma, 2014; Martin, 2011). In this chapter, emphasis is placed on the behavioral complex processes that occur between different elements of a system that, in the end, lead to collective human agency. As such, human agency and behavioral approaches to decision-making become relevant to understanding how change is produced in networks and institutions, by whom, and to what end (Bristow & Healy, 2013; Strauss, 2007).

Human agency, self-reliance, and self-organization

By including human agency in the resilience debate (Bristow & Healy, 2013), the limitations of Simmie and Martin's (2010) more deterministic adaptive cycle model – for example, in terms of the ability of humans to "break" these "cycles" – become visible (Davoudi, 2012, p. 305). In order to be able to break a cycle or to pursue a new and adjusted development path, interventions of human actions are necessary. Human agency can, according to social-cognitive theory, roughly be divided into three different types (Bandura, 2000, p. 75):

1   *Personal or individual agency*: Associated with cognitive, motivational, and choice processes that refer to the self-reliance of individuals, firms, organizations, etc. (Davoudi, 2012).
2   *Proxy agency*: People try to get other people (with more expertise or influence) to act on their behalf. This form of agency occurs in a context of change or uncertainty stemming, for example, from institutional complexity or expected high responsibilities.
3   *Collective agency*: Collective power of people or societies to reach a certain aim or produce desired outcomes based on: (i) shared beliefs, shared knowledge and skills and (ii) emergent social processes associated with interactive, synergetic, and cooperative dynamics of transactions.

A tourism municipality, with diverse actors pursuing different interests and agendas, can be described as a complex socio-economic system, where different agency types occur in all possible combinations during processes of adaptation and reorganization. Thus, a socio-economic system is an emergent system in the sense that it shows systemic characteristics that cannot be explained by the sum of individual attributes of the system components (Stephan, 1999). In respect of community resilience, collective agency is needed to push a system beyond its boundaries. When human agency is incorporated into the 'Adaptive Cycle Model' (Figure 9.1), collective agency plays a major role in the '*reorganization and restructuring phase*,' where the window of opportunity for change is wide open and the potential of accumulated resources available to the system is high.

Connectedness between different system members in the reorganization phase is low but increases with the attempts of different actors to effect fundamental change. In the '*exploitation phase*,' collective agency becomes less important; networks are stable and interactions frequent. Creativity and emergent social processes are declining. Collective agency is again seen to be more important at the end of the '*conservation phase*' and very important during the '*decline and release phase*.' In this phase resilience is low, and thus creativity and collective emergent processes are becoming more relevant.

Based on the theoretical considerations, the social and economic resilience of regions arises through processes of *collective agency* that occur in times of uncertainty, as in the reorganization and restructuring phase or in the decline and release phase. Whereas individual agency is mainly dependent on personal

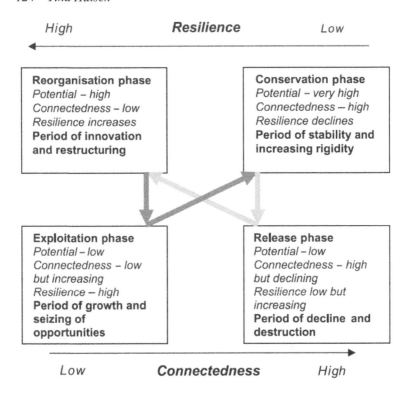

Figure 9.1 Adaptive Cycle Model.

Source: Simmie and Martin (2010, p. 33), with permission.

concerns, *collective agency* depends more on shared beliefs and knowledge that occurs through participation, communication, and sense making, resulting in collective emergent processes that are decisive for community adaptability. *Learning* is seen to be a result of several adaptation cycles. Community resilience cannot be detached from the global, national, or regional context. The extent to which other, higher levels influence the community depends, for example, on trade linkages, dependency on external financial sources, or decentralization.

Collective agency and resilience in Grindelwald

The tourism community of Grindelwald with a population today of around 3,800 inhabitants is located in the Bernese Oberland region of Switzerland. Over the past 100 years, Grindelwald has become a very famous tourism resort in the region due to its beautiful landscape, high mountains (Eiger, Jungfrau, Mönch), glaciers and lakes. The natural setting has been crucial for the development of primarily winter tourism, and hence the community is dependent on an undamaged landscape, stable snow coverage, and high quality tourism infrastructure.

The cultural landscape is a common resource that is preserved by various mountain farmer cooperatives. Grindelwald is seen as a community that, over the last decades, has found a balance between the economy, society and the environment (Wiesmann, 2001). Two mission statements, published in 1987 and 2013, laid the foundation for this balance by determining guidelines for a sustainable handling of resources and regional development in general. Another reason for the sustainable use of resources is the long-existing regulations of the mountain farmer cooperatives (*Bergschaften*); these are powerful with long-established rights and significant financial assets, but at the same time they are adaptable to change. They have successfully managed to adjust to changing environmental, economic, and social conditions over several hundred years while not losing sight of their most important aims – protecting the environment and ecosystem in the community to enable sustainable farming (Tiefenbach & Mordasini, 2006). A formal institution dating back to the year 1404, the '*Taleignungsbrief*,' defined alpine pastures as commons for sustainable use, managed by the mountain farmer cooperatives.

Method and data collection

For the analysis, a case study of Grindelwald, a Swiss mountain resort community that currently faces severe crises and shocks, was undertaken. At the first stage, semi-structured telephone interviews with 11 different actors were conducted. They were chosen on the basis of their belonging to one of the three most important industry sectors within the region (construction, finance, and tourism), as well as their commitment to environmental organizations or their role as community officials. The interviews took between 45–60 minutes. Interviewees were asked to name and describe the stressors they are facing in order to reveal their individual perceptions. They also described their individual and collective adaptation strategies.

At the second stage, the results from the initial interviews were combined with another ten face-to-face interviews with professionals from the tourism industry (hotel owners, CEOs, and communication professionals from local cable car companies), the construction sector, representatives from mountain farmer and water cooperatives, engineers, land owners, and the mayor of Grindelwald. They all played a crucial role in adaptation processes introduced in the examples below. Additionally, informal talks and discussions with local residents at official events were undertaken, to reveal their perceptions with regard to adaptation strategies. Media (newspaper articles, web pages) and official documents provided by the community were also analyzed.

Data from the telephone interviews, the face-to-face interviews and the media and document sources were analyzed using a software program for qualitative data analysis (QDA). Categories from the interview guidelines were integrated into the software and successively complemented by going through the empirical material and combining deductive and inductive practices. Categories are tools for the classification of phenomena with the ability to build sub-categories (Kuckartz, 2010, p. 62). Both have been defined with regard to perceived actual stressors and different forms of agency (individual, proxy, and collective agency) directed towards adaptation.

Shocks, stressors, and disturbances in Grindelwald

The first economic transformation of the community took place at the end of the nineteenth century, when it turned from being a purely agricultural society into one with an emerging tourism sector. Today, approximately 75 percent of the workforce is employed in the tourism sector. After 2008, during the economic crisis, the Swiss currency rose compared to other currencies and vacations in Switzerland became more expensive resulting in a decline of 20 percent in overnight stays from 2005 to 2012 (Swiss Federal Statistics Office, 2013). Almost all economic actors such as banks, the tourism industry, and the real estate sector perceive the strong Swiss Franc as an acute threat (Table 9.1).

Table 9.1 Perceived crises and stressors by actors in Grindelwald

Actors	Perceived actor-specific shocks, crises, threats, and challenges
Mountain railways	• Economic crisis and strong currency: decline of mainly foreign guests in winter tourism due to cheaper vacations elsewhere • Climate change: insecurity of snow and corresponding high investments in snow security • Vague and long-term weather forecasts
Hotels	• Economic crisis and strong currency: decline of mainly foreign guests in winter tourism due to cheaper vacations elsewhere • Climate change: insecurity of snow
Banks	• Economic crisis and strong currency • Vote on second homes: unpredictable future due to law insecurities • Insecure development of land prices
Construction sector	• Vote on second homes: reduction of building contracts and no compensation through
Real estate sector	• Economic crisis and strong currency • Vote on second homes: unpredictable future due to law insecurities; customers are anxious
Community government	• Sudden threats resulting from climate change (erosion, flooding, etc.) • Decisions taken elsewhere • Unpredictable decisions made by a 'silent majority' within the community • Slow burns: depopulation, change of population structure (young people moving away)
Environmental organizations	• Destruction of nature due to the building of skiing and sports infrastructure

Source: Results from inquiry in 2013 ($n=11$).

A further major problem in Grindelwald is *depopulation* accompanied by a higher proportion of older people, a decreasing number of school classes, and a loss of municipal tax income.

Additionally, in March 2012, Swiss people decided in a national vote that communities in which more than 20 percent of homes are second homes would no longer allowed to build additional second homes, in order to stop sprawl in mountain tourism communities. This restriction is an acute threat for the construction and real estate sectors which, in the long-term, will decline significantly. Another likely effect is that the possibility of farmers working part-time in construction will also diminish.

Grindelwald also faces significant environmental threats as it is one of the communities most affected by climate change in the Berner Oberland region. This is due to glacier melting that has been occurring over the last 100 years, but has accelerated in recent years resulting in slope instability and potential flooding from glacier lakes.

Currently, Grindelwald is going through a second economic transformation from a tourism economy to a more experience-based economy (see Pine & Gilmore, 1998). The most significant expression of this transformation is the building of a modern mountain railway directly at the top of a glacier (*V-Bahn*), along with several new types of accommodation focusing on wellbeing and luxury, new and joint marketing of various communities in the region, and a new mountain biking trail system, canyoning, and bungee jumping.

Working towards community resilience

Dense relationships as the basis for emergent social processes

Despite individual perceptions of threats and shocks leading to individual agency, it is the community as a whole that must ultimately decide on common strategies and the implementation of specific projects or institutional change. Collective agency becomes necessary also with respect to the high degree of interdependencies between different actor groups in a community such as Grindelwald, in which tourism, mountain agriculture, and construction are today highly interwoven (Figure 9.2). While tourism needs agriculture to support landscape preservation, farmers need the tourism industry to compensate for income deficits. Thus, many farmers have part-time jobs in the service sector.

On this basis, a shock or stressor affects several actors in the community, whether directly or indirectly. As one community official stated in an interview:

> Basically, we are all affected [by the restriction on building second homes], including the municipal administration, but also tourism and the whole construction sector and consequently all the businesses; also, private people who are, for example, searching for an apartment or who rent an apartment. You cannot find anybody who is not affected.

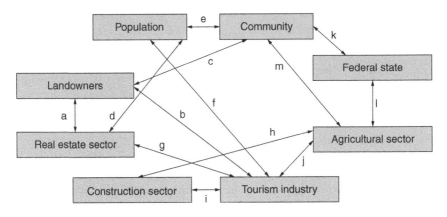

a Competitive regarding second homes
b Grindelwald as destination
c Control of usage, building application/sanitation
d Financing and purchase of real estate
e EWAP, building applications
f Jobs
g Purchasing potential of tourists, LEX Koller

h Second job
i Purchasing potential of tourists
j Landscape preservation, seond job
k Laws, loss of competences
l Subsidies,landscape maintenance
m Stabilization

Figure 9.2 Interdependencies between different actors in Grindelwald.

Source: Author's field research.

In general, the community is well organized when it comes to acute shocks such as the interruption of electricity supply or transport infrastructure. In contrast, slow, creeping processes such as demographic restructuring or the decline in overnight stays are major challenges and demand collective agency strategies.

Shared perceptions and collective agency

On the basis of these strong and intense interdependencies, collective agency and self-organization is needed in times of crisis to find a means to future regional economic development that aims to make the region more resilient to shocks and disturbances. In the following discussion, three projects are introduced as responses to recent stressors, namely, the tunnel project, the renewal of the village center, and a new mountain railway. The negotiation process in the mountain railway project (*V-Bahn*) could be followed and documented as it currently evolves, whereas the processes in respect of the two other projects (rebuilding of the village center and the tunnel project) have been reconstructed using respondents' recall of events and archival material.

Tunnel project

As a response to a melting glacier and the danger of sudden flooding in 2005, affected actors and communities, the water corporations, the canton, and the federal state collectively worked out a plan to build a tunnel for water drainage that would prevent Grindelwald from further flooding. The tunnel was successfully completed in 2009 through a collaborative process among a number of communities and financed by several landowners who were potentially affected, as well as by all three state tiers (federal state, canton, and communities).

The successful and efficient pro-active planning was based on *past experiences and learning*. In the winter of 1999–2000 Grindelwald was cut off from the outside world for several weeks, due to massive snowfall. Hundreds of people were evacuated from the mountains, the streets were blocked due to avalanches, and groceries were flown in by helicopter. The situation demonstrated the organizational capacities and social interaction between different tiers (community, canton, and federal state) in the face of acute crisis.

The tunnel project was completed very quickly (in four years) and without major resistance due to the *shared perceptions* of several actors including landowners, riverside residents, and the tourism industry. In addition, the *provision of information and knowledge* for the population was extensive: a webpage was launched by the project group which provided information on the plan and actual progress; several information events were organized in the communities and also in the nearby center of Interlaken; media conferences provided the latest news about the project and a text warning system in case of flooding was implemented. During the building phase of the tunnel, the involvement of landowners was guaranteed through a corporation ('*Schwellenkorporation*'), which is in charge of flood control in the affected communities. With the power to decide and the financial means, the corporation (re)acted very quickly, cooperating also with the canton and the federal state. The community took the lead in coordinating all the actors involved. Thus, social interactions, and the resulting mutual trust between the actors and organizations, were intense. Financial resources were provided by all three state levels: communities (landowners), canton, and federal state. The corporation was also supported by an expert group (geologists, engineers, civil engineers, etc.). In summary, citizen involvement, optimal resource allocation, and organizational capabilities all played a crucial role. Finally, the slim administrative process due to longstanding and good personal contacts with the canton was seen as a factor in successful implementation. Furthermore, in "crucial moments of decision making, the solidarity with the mountain areas in the canton and the federal state is very high due to a deep and long-term knowledge and relationship" (interview with community official).

Renewal of the village center (EIGER+)

As a response to the ongoing depopulation, the community decided to renew Grindelwald's village center and presented the EIGER+ project to the local population in March 2010. The project involved the rejuvenation of squares and streets in a specific area of the village center, including an underground car park, more shopping facilities, and additional space for pedestrians, at a total cost of 4.9 million Swiss Francs. The plan was to be achieved through a private partnership between a bank (Berner Kantonalbank), an insurance company (Schweizerische Mobiliar Asset Management AG), and a non-local construction firm (Losinger Marazzi AG), with the community paying for the underground car park.

The provision of knowledge and information in this adaptation project was low and the perceived negative effects on the population high – for example, high municipal costs, loss of free parking lots, a big supermarket threatening smaller shops, construction noise, and the high costs of running the underground car park. As a result, in November 2011, the residents of Grindelwald rejected the project in an official vote.

However, in order to find a common solution for the municipality and to counterbalance depopulation, several events were organized where citizens could exchange thoughts, concerns, and ideas. In the following months, cost reduction strategies for the community were intensively discussed between the various actors that led to savings compared to the original plan. Furthermore, a high level of participation by the population in the planning process was secured. In a second public vote in August 2012, the project was accepted.

*New mountain railway (*V-Bahn*)*

The building of a new mountain railway (*V-Bahn*) is a joint investment project by two mountain railway companies (Grindelwald Männlichen and Jungfraubahn) costing over 200 million Swiss Francs. The aim is to raise passenger capacity, shorten the travel time from the valley to the top of the mountain, and provide a unique experience for passengers.

The first plan in 2009 was to build a new railway (*Y-Bahn*) running between the valley (Grindelwald Grund) and two different peaks (Kleine Scheidegg and Männlichen). This plan, developed by Canadian planning consultant Paul Mathews, would have affected and quite severely damaged parts of the protected hill moor ecosystem around the community. In addition, affected actors such as the mountain agriculture cooperatives (*Bergschaften*) and other landowners perceived that there had been insufficient participation in the planning process. Moreover, the timing of the dissemination of the information was criticized. A member of a mountain farmer cooperative stated in an interview: "The public has been informed before we as landowners have been informed and as a result, a lot of trust got lost. It will take a long time until trust will come back."

Furthermore, environmental organizations and the Swiss Alpine Club were deeply concerned because of ecological and aesthetic factors. In a second attempt, in 2013, the mountain railways, together with architects and the community, developed a more ecologically compatible railway line (*V-Bahn*), connecting Grindelwald and the Eiger glacier but not disturbing protected hill moors. The directly affected actors, the two mountain farmer cooperatives (*Bergschaft Wärgista* and *Bergschaft Itramen*), other landowners, environmental organizations, and the inhabitants of the community were involved in the planning process. However, the mountain farmer cooperatives perceived their participation as insufficient and too late (parts of the railway would be built on their land). The cooperatives have, for example, been excluded from the reconnaissance of the affected area and the mountain railway company communicated that there is no 'plan B' for the railway, putting the landowners under extreme pressure. A member of a mountain farmer cooperative stated: "This project upsets the whole village. Nobody knows what he or she can say in front of the other one. It really splits the population."

Evidently, it is the manner of communication, leading to participation and the way in which social interactions are framed, that makes a difference in collective agency processes. A representative from a mountain railway company stated in an interview: "We must be aware of the image we [the mountain railway company] have. People in Grindelwald don't allow for arrogant behavior, and on that basis, we have to carefully think about what is possible and what is not."

Due to perceived exclusion as well as deficient and contemptuous communication, the mountain cooperatives declined the investment plans after an internal discussion and vote in October 2014. Further reasons given were the significant increase in tourism inflow coupled with the expected impact on and change to the landscape, as well as financial concerns. Nevertheless, on October 26, 2014, the building of the new glacier express was accepted at a community assembly. The voters were able to cast their votes anonymously, which was perceived as a precondition and as trust building. Preceding the vote, the mountain railway company investors announced an annual fund of over 200,000 Swiss Francs in response to an appeal by a local entrepreneur who asked for a compensation payment in order to initiate further sustainable projects. In addition, the mountain railway is now planned to be completely removable should future generations have other plans for the municipality.

Discussion and conclusion

This chapter has addressed the concept of governance in regional socio-economic adaptation processes from an evolutionary perspective. The findings call for the integration of *human agency* in concepts of regional adaptation processes and resiliency (Bristow & Healy, 2013). While individual agency plays a role in short-term adaptation, collective agency is important for longer-term adaptation and resiliency.

Swiss tourism communities now have to deal with several stressors, such as the threat of flooding, decreasing overnight stays, pressures of economic transformation, and depopulation. While differing individual aims, needs, and political agendas exist, it is the community or region and their members as a whole that have to find solutions for adaptation and future development. On this basis, manifold negotiation processes have to take place until common strategies for future development paths can be agreed upon.

In the case study presented of Grindelwald, three factors most relevant for regional adaptability from a longer-term perspective were revealed. First, there were shared concerns and perceptions regarding the expected impact and consequences of actual threats. Second, agreed informal values, such as the sustainable use of resources, developed in the past and published in two mission statements (1982 and 2014), are important vehicles in the framing of adaptation processes. Third, institutions such as norms and formal regulations – e.g., the '*Taleignungsbrief*' of the mountain farmer cooperatives, dating back to 1404 and regulating the sustainable use of alp pastures – are of utmost importance in counterbalancing the overexploitation of natural resources and various interests (see Matarrita-Cascante & Trejos, 2013).

From a more general perspective, successful *collective agency* in terms of finding a common strategy is fundamentally dependent on social interaction and communication over time, leading to citizen involvement and participation. With each 'round of negotiation,' learning and emergent behavior occurs, leading to a better mutual understanding and sense making of the respective other. In the end, resilient solutions are found if collective open assemblies or informal discussion rounds allow for participation. Communication and participation might thus be the most important vehicles to mediate between sometimes conflicting agendas and to include or exclude actors from the decision-making process. As a representative of a mountain railway company observed in an interview:

> Transparent communication is essential to convince people: the art of communication, the right timing. People should not get the sense that we force them into something like the new railway. Visualization is extremely important, to show what is planned and what it will look like, to serve different stakeholders, and inform directly affected actors first, also employees.

As such, governance of state (community officials) and non-state (mountain railway companies, landowners, population, etc.) actors plays a crucial role in framing these processes of collective human agency. Furthermore, formal institutions (e.g., the *Taleignungsbrief*) and informal institutions that shape the mindset of various actors over decades (e.g., mission statements) play a substantial part in the governance of resource dependent tourism communities, their wellbeing, and their resilience.

Acknowledgment

This work was supported by a UniBE Initiator Grant.

References

Adger, W.N. (2009). Social capital, collective action, and adaptation to climate change. *Economic Geography, 79*(4), 387–404.

Bätzing, W., Perlik, M., & Dekleva, M. (1996). Urbanization and depopulation in the Alps. *Mountain Research and Development, 16*(4), 335–350.

Bandura, A. (2000). Exercise of human agency through collective efficacy. *Current Directions in Psychological Science, 9*(3), 75–78.

Boschma, R. (2014). Towards an evolutionary perspective on regional resilience. *Regional Studies, 49*(5), 733–751.

Bristow, G., & Healy, A. (2013). Regional resilience: An agency perspective. *Regional Studies, 48*(5), 923–935.

Davies, S. (2011). Regional resilience in the 2008–2010 downturn: Comparative evidence from European countries. *Cambridge Journal of Regions, Economy and Society, 4*(3), 369–382.

Davoudi, S. (2012). Resilience: A bridging concept or a dead end? *Planning Theory & Practice, 13*(2), 299–307.

Folke, C. (2006). Resilience: The emergence of a perspective for social–ecological systems analyses. *Global Environmental Change, 16*(3), 253–267.

Fürst, D. (2010). Regional governance. In A. Benz & N. Dose (Eds.), *Governance – Regieren in komplexen Regelsystemen. Eine Einführung* (pp. 49–68). Wiesbaden: VS Verlag für Sozialwissenschaften.

Gallopín, G.C. (2006). Linkages between vulnerability, resilience, and adaptive capacity. *Global Environmental Change, 16*(3), 293–303.

Haisch, T. (2018). Interplay between ecological and economic resilience and sustainability and the role of institutions: Evidence from two resource-based communities in the Swiss Alps. *Resilience, 6*(3), 215–229.

Haken, H. (2006). *Information and self-organization: A macroscopic approach to complex systems.* Berlin: Springer.

Heylighen, F. (2012). Self-organization in communicating groups: The emergence of coordination, shared references and collective intelligence. In Á. Massip-Bonet & A. Bastardas-Boada (Eds.), *Complexity perspectives on language, communication and society* (pp. 117–149). Berlin: Springer.

Kuckartz, U. (2010). *Einführung in die computergestützte Analyse qualitativer Daten.* Wiesbaden:VS Verlag für Sozialwissenschaften/GWV Fachverlage GmbH.

Martin, R. (2011). Regional economic resilience, hysteresis and recessionary shocks. *Journal of Economic Geography, 12*(1), 1–32.

Martin, R., & Sunley, P. (2014). On the notion of regional economic resilience: Conceptualization and explanation. *Journal of Economic Geography, 15*(1), 1–42.

Marvel, W.M., & Johnson, C.B. (1997). A crisis of currency or creativity? Problems and prospects for the Swiss hotel industry. *International Journal of Hospitality Management, 16*(3), 279–288.

Matarrita-Cascante, D., & Trejos, B. (2013). Community resilience in resource-dependent communities: A comparative case study. *Environment and Planning A, 45*(6), 1387–1402.

Ostrom, E. (2010). Beyond markets and states: Polycentric governance of complex economic systems. *American Economic Review, 100*(3), 641–672.

Pendall, R., Foster, K., & Cowell, M. (2010). Resilience and regions: Building understanding of the metaphor. *Cambridge Journal of Regions, Economy and Society, 3*(1), 71–84.

Pine, B.J., & Gilmore, J.H. (1998). Welcome to the experience economy. *Harvard Business Review, 76*, 97–105.

Simmie, J., & Martin, R. (2010). The economic resilience of regions: Towards an evolutionary approach. *Cambridge Journal of Regions, Economy and Society, 3*(1), 27–43.

Stephan, A. (1999). *Emergenz. Von der unvorhersagbarkeit zur selbstorganisation.* Dresden: Dresden University Press.

Strauss, K. (2007). Re-engaging with rationality in economic geography: Behavioural approaches and the importance of context in decision-making. *Journal of Economic Geography, 8*(2), 137–156.

Swiss Federal Statistics Office. (2013). HESTA, Beherbergungsstatistik, Bundesamt für Statistik 2013.

Tiefenbach, M., & Mordasini, A.G. (2006). *Bergschaften in Grindelwald.* Grindelwald, Switzerland: Sutter Druck AG.

Voss, M. (2008). The vulnerable can't speak. An integrative vulnerability approach to disaster and climate change research. *Behemoth: A Journal on Civilisation, 1*(3), 39–56.

Wiesmann, U. (2001). Umwelt, landwirtschaft und tourismus im berggebiet – konfliktbearbeitung im leitbild "Grindelwald 2000." In G. Mader, W.-D. Eberwein, & R.V. Vogt (Eds.), *Schriftenreihe des Österreichischen Studienzentrums für Frieden und Konfliktlösung* (pp. 237–249). Münster: Agenda Verlag.

10 Resort retail resilience

The contested spaces of retailing in Whistler, Canada

Sarah Wongkee and Alison M. Gill

Introduction

Retailing is an important component of the resort attraction mix and the economic stability of resorts. However, the experience of tourists and residents is also impacted by the quality of a resort's natural and built environments. As Timothy (2005, p. 115) observes, "managing places, venues, shoppers, employees, and destination community members" is challenging, and maintaining the appropriate balance among these components is key to the long-term resilience of a resort. The concept of resilience can be a useful approach for understanding retail systems as change is an inherent condition of the retail system (Dolega & Celinska-Janowicz, 2015), and a resilience approach provides a method for identifying weaknesses and strengths in the system. Understanding the resilience of a retail system facilitates the design of successful policy and planning interventions (Cachinho, 2014; Singleton, Dolega, Riddlesden, & Longley, 2016; Wrigley & Dolega, 2011). Although there are increasing numbers of resilience studies focused on retail systems, several gaps remain in understanding the dynamics of system components (Dolega & Celinska-Janowicz, 2015), especially in resort settings.

In this chapter we examine the complex and contested spaces of retailing in the mountain resort community of Whistler, British Columbia, Canada. The overall objective of this research was to gain an insight into the factors that influence the resilience and vulnerability of the retail sector in a resort environment. The research involved a multi-method approach to interpreting local stakeholder perceptions, predominantly those of business owners and operators. The method included the analysis of empirical data from key informant interviews and an online survey, as well as secondary sources such as official community documents and local media reports. To guide the research design and frame the findings a Destination Retail Resilience Framework (DRRF) was developed. This was based on an adaptation of Calgaro, Lloyd, and Dominey-Howes' (2014) broader model of resilience and vulnerability in tourism destinations to more specifically address issues relevant to the resort retailing sector. In this chapter the focus of the discussion is on core elements of the resilience model, notably vulnerability and its component elements of exposure and sensitivity.

The chapter begins by presenting a brief overview of the literature on resort retailing and resilience, including an elaboration of Calgaro et al.'s (2014) Destination Sustainability Framework. A summary of the study site including the evolution of Whistler's retail sector is then presented and the research methods explained. After the findings of the study have been presented, the subsequent discussion section addresses a key objective of this chapter – that of identifying the components of resilience in the contested retail spaces of the resort. The chapter concludes by highlighting key elements of overall resort resilience that decision-makers should consider in the management of the retail sector.

Tourism retailing and resilience

In contemporary society the retail landscape is continually adapting to changing conditions. Over the past couple of decades, the retail sector has experienced increasingly globalized markets, rapid advances in technology, and shifting economic conditions, as well as frequent changes in consumer preferences and behavior (Dolega & Celinska-Janowicz, 2015; Kärrholm, Nylund, Prieto, & Fuente, 2014). The constantly shifting environment has driven individual retailers to adjust their methods to remain competitive and prevent stagnation and decline (Fernandes & Chamusca, 2014). Successful retailers are adapting in innovative ways, including incorporating different types of goods and services, with a focus on creating customer experiences (Mehmetoglu & Engen, 2011; Pine & Gilmore, 2000); introducing sustainable practices (Jones, Comfort, Hillier, & Eastwood, 2005); altering the shopping environment (Cachinho, 2014); or creating entirely new business models (Cachinho, 2014; Kärrholm et al., 2014; Ozuduru, Varol, & Ercoskun, 2014).

Retailing within resort destinations is susceptible to additional changes, which retailers are required to understand and to which they must adapt to remain competitive. Resort retailers are affected by tourism trends, variable exchange rates, the costs of transportation, airport security protocols, and conditions in visitors' home countries including political volatility, domestic taxation, and customs (Calgaro et al., 2014). In destinations that rely on the quality of the natural environment for competitive advantage, the structures and operations of the retail system need to conform to shifts in local ecological conditions (Strickland-Munro, Allison, & Moore, 2010). For example, changing climatic conditions may affect seasonal visitation patterns and activities. In order to anticipate and prepare for these potential shifting conditions, understanding the factors that influence a retailer's ability to respond to change is pertinent (Bec, McLennan, & Moyle, 2015). Without adequate understanding, continuous shocks and stressors challenge the viability of many retail establishments. Individual business failure is natural in a healthy retail sector; however, widespread inability to adapt may eventually destabilize the sector and affect the systems that rely on it (Cachinho, 2014). In resort environments, the retail sector shapes the overall destination vibrancy and image (Kemperman, Borgers, & Timmermans, 2009;

Kim & Littrell, 2001) and its resilience is integral to the overall success and performance of the destination.

Researchers increasingly use resilience and the related concepts of vulnerability and adaptive capacity to understand the dynamics of complex adaptive systems, including tourism (Biggs, 2011; Biggs, Hall, & Stoeckl, 2012) and retail systems (Cachinho, 2014). Resilience is a theoretical approach that originated in ecological studies and is now used in multiple disciplines to guide thinking related to how social–ecological systems respond to change and adversity (Adger, 2000; Bec et al., 2015; Folke et al., 2010). Within the field of tourism, researchers use resilience concepts to investigate how resorts may respond and cope with sudden shocks and gradual changes. Studies examine systems in the face of natural disasters, economic crashes, and climate change, as well as shifts in consumer preferences and the gradual deterioration of the physical environment (e.g., Biggs et al., 2012; Calgaro et al., 2014; Larsen, Calgaro, & Thomalla, 2011; Strickland-Munro et al., 2010). Examining the factors that influence resilience leads to a thorough understanding of a system's strengths, weaknesses, and opportunities for improvement (Calgaro et al., 2014; Clark et al., 2000; Pelling, 2003; Turner et al., 2003). Systems that are resilient can take advantage of opportunities for innovation and development (Folke, 2006), while in vulnerable systems even small disturbances can have severe consequences (Adger, 2006).

A few resilience frameworks have been proposed in the context of tourism communities. Calgaro and Lloyd (2008) adapted Turner et al.'s (2003) sustainability framework to examine a tourism-based community after the 2004 Indian Ocean tsunami. They conceptualize vulnerability as a function of exposure, sensitivity, and resilience. Tsao and Ni (2016) also presented a framework that integrates resilience and vulnerability concepts with Gunderson and Holling's (2002) adaptive cycle. They applied the framework to understand how communities respond to disasters and argued that in a tourism environment the adaptive cycle becomes more rapid.

The research presented in this chapter (Wongkee, 2016) adapted the Destination Sustainability Framework developed by Calgaro et al. (2014) to the resort retailing context. The Destination Sustainability Framework incorporates traditional resilience concepts to guide the identification and analysis of factors that influence destination vulnerability and resilience. It builds on previous frameworks in the sustainability and human–environment discourse, including Gunderson and Holling's (2002) adaptive cycle, Polsky, Neff, and Yarnal's (2007) vulnerability scoping diagram, and Turner et al.'s (2003) vulnerability framework. The framework also builds on tourism-specific models, particularly the previous work of Calgaro and Lloyd (2008). It includes the influence of shocks or stressors, the interconnected dimensions of vulnerability and resilience, feedback loops, important contextual aspects, and multiple spatial scales and timeframes. Calgaro et al.'s (2014) framework contains a systematic approach to assessing a destination's defining features, including its key stakeholders and the characteristics of the biophysical and built environment.

Case study and methods

Whistler's destination retail system

Whistler is a four-season alpine resort located in southwest British Columbia, Canada, 125 km north of Vancouver. The resort is internationally renowned for its abundance of all-season outdoor recreation opportunities, and the quality of the surrounding natural environment, including its lakes, rivers, parks, and forests. Whistler attracts a mix of over three million international and regional visitors annually and is consistently ranked as one of North America's top ski resorts (Resort Municipality of Whistler, 2016). The resort community is home to approximately 10,000 permanent residents and a nearly equal number of part-time residents including second-home owners, 2,500 seasonal and temporary residents, and a further 2,000 employees who commute to work in Whistler (Economic Partnership Initiative Committee, 2016).

For this study, the destination retail system consists of all retail outlets in the Resort Municipality of Whistler that receive most of their revenue from visitors as opposed to residents. Whistler has a well-developed retail sector with about 215 retail outlets located within the municipal boundaries and 158 stores in the prominent tourist areas. Retailers offer a broad range of products and include a mix of independently owned retail establishments and regional, national, and international chain stores (Resort Municipality of Whistler, 2012). Retailers' primary merchandise includes clothing and apparel (34 percent), recreational goods (21 per cent), grocery and convenience items (16 percent), pharmacy and health products (6 percent), liquor (5 percent), accessories (3 percent), art (4 percent), specialty foods (2 percent), gifts and souvenirs (3 percent, and other items including books, electronics, hardware, and photography (6 percent). The retail sector produces 26 percent of the local gross domestic product (C$361 million) and employs 9 percent of the workforce. In 2015, visitors accounted for 78 percent of all retail expenditure (C$593 million), with residents accounting for the remaining 22 percent (C$130 million) (Economic Partnership Initiative Committee, 2016).

Several organizations and local stakeholders are influential in shaping the destination retail system, particularly the municipal government; the mountain lift corporation, Whistler Blackcomb; the resort marketing agency, Tourism Whistler; and the local business organization, Whistler Chamber of Commerce. Although these organizations operate on a resort-wide scale and outside the retail system, their actions and linkages within the retail system are prominent in shaping its functioning, vulnerability, and resilience. The Resort Municipality is responsible for creating, implementing, and enforcing regulations, strategies, and policies that impact the retail environment at the local scale. Zoning and development bylaws shape the commercial environment and affect the physical evolution of the resort. The Municipality is also responsible for maintenance of municipal property and providing municipal services, which influences the overall character of the resort's built and natural physical environment.

Research methods

The study findings are based on a multi-method research approach, using both primary and secondary data. The primary data originates from a combination of responses to an online survey and subsequent in-depth interviews. The survey data is a subset of 24 responses from a broader online survey of local business owners and operators conducted in collaboration with the Chamber of Commerce and the Municipality that sought to identify existing challenges and opportunities to strengthen Whistler's retail sector. Subsequently, four individuals with professional and personal expertise and knowledge relevant to the resilience of Whistler's retail sector were interviewed and additional insights were obtained from engagement with a discussion group on retailing challenges. Industry reports, academic sources, local news sources, and policy documents were also employed in the triangulation of data from these various sources. The Destination Retail Resilience Framework (DRRF) (Figure 10.1) was developed to inform the investigative process and the data analysis. The framework integrates vulnerability and resilience concepts from the literature that are relevant to retail systems and builds on previous conceptual models. The DRRF draws upon Calgaro et al.'s (2014) Destination Sustainability Framework that aligns with wider debates on sustainability within human–environment systems (e.g., Turner et al., 2003). It includes additional components such as tourism-specific sensitivities, conditions, and characteristics that are specific to the destination retail system.

The DRRF is comprised of six elements that are either internal or external to the retail system. The external components are (1) shocks and stressors; and (2) scale; elements nested within the retail system are (3) vulnerability, which includes exposure and sensitivity; (4) system resilience, which includes adaptive capacity; (5) coping response; and (6) feedback loops. The model is designed to

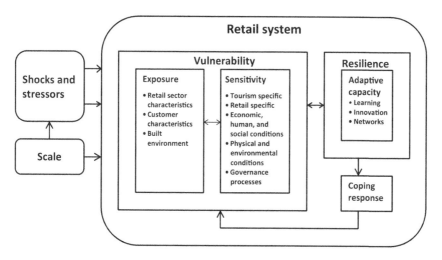

Figure 10.1 The Destination Retail Resilience Framework.

guide the investigative process and includes lists of factors that shape each of the system elements.

While resilience is place-based, the interactions between system components occur through networks that transcend local boundaries and extend to regional, national, or international scales (Calgaro et al., 2014). These spatial scales, along with time, encompass the 'scale' box, which links to the stress and stressors that threaten a destination and require it to respond. Shocks are rapid- onset events, while stressors are slow-onset events that originate from human–environment interactions. The retail system is inevitably subject to different types of disturbances in the form of shocks or stressors. Examples of shocks are terrorist attacks, natural hazards, and health epidemics, while examples of stressors are climatic changes, environmental degradation, biophysical elements, economic downturns, and changes in consumer behavior and travel trends (Calgaro et al., 2014). Shocks and stressors can happen simultaneously, and the resources required to respond depend on the severity and nature of the disturbance.

The focus of discussion in this chapter is on 'Vulnerability,' and its component parts 'Exposure' and 'Sensitivity.' 'Vulnerability' is the degree to which a system is likely to experience harm from exposure to a hazard. It is particular to the place and influenced by the specific characteristics of the retail system (Turner et al., 2003). 'Exposure' is the degree to which the retail system encounters stressors or shocks. The DRRF depicts exposure through an inventory and analysis of the retail system's defining characteristics. 'Sensitivity' is the extent to which exposure to stress will affect the retail system. This is a function of pre-existing internal conditions such as the levels of and access to accumulated capital necessary for coping with a disturbance (Turner et al., 2003). The institutions and processes that determine access to capital are particularly relevant for understanding system weaknesses, including local power dynamics, social networks, and the effectiveness of governance systems. The DRRF guides the assessment of system sensitivity through the account of tourism and retail sector sensitivities and other relevant system conditions including social, physical, economic, and governance elements.

System sensitivities may influence exposure; the double-ended arrow in Figure 10.1 represents their interconnected relationship.

A vital component of resilient systems is their capacity to adapt and respond to disturbance. This adaptive capacity is dependent on the main social and institutional relationships and processes (Armitage, 2005), including social networks, associations, and collaboration (Adger, 2000; Folke, 2006; Folke et al., 2002). Key system structures and processes that influence adaptive capacity in the resort retail sector include learning, flexibility, networks and connectivity, and innovation. Systems can respond to a disturbance with immediate and short-term coping strategies, as well as long-term adjustments and adaptation. Short-term coping responses are a function of the available capital, effectiveness of governance structures, and system preparedness, while long-term adaptation and adjustment may also involve self-organization, reflection, social learning, and taking opportunities to reorganize (Calgaro et al., 2014).

Examining shocks, stressors, and vulnerabilities in Whistler's retail system

The DRRF is employed to guide discussion of findings from the research project. The focus is on vulnerability and its two key components – exposure and sensitivity. Whistler's retail system exposure is contingent on Whistler's current position relative to threats, while its sensitivity depends on whether the retail system has the resources required to respond.

To understand some of the fundamental stressors surrounding the current debate within the resort community on growth and changing retail spaces, one needs to consider the fundamental principles upon which the resort was founded in 1975. It was comprehensively planned, anchored by an alpine-themed, pedestrian commercial village center. Foundational development and management principles included: a focus on human scale with a 'sense of place'; establishing a critical mass of carefully selected independent retail tenants in the village; and limiting and managing growth.

As an alpine resort destination, Whistler has experienced a wide range of shocks and stressors, including changing economic conditions, unfavourable weather conditions, shifts in travel behavior, natural disasters, and competition with other mountain resorts (Whistler Blackcomb Holdings Inc., 2015). Rapid growth of the resort in the 1990s brought significant changes to the retail landscape. New commercial development doubled the size of the commercial center during this decade and, with a rapidly growing resident population, retail outlets developed outside the resort village core. Some were alarmed by the first intrusion of a chain operation – McDonald's – and the first 'corporate' retailing engagement by Intrawest (the mountain operators).

Subsequently, in the 2000s, the resort underwent a series of disturbances resulting from the 2008–2009 economic recession and the successful bid to co-host the 2010 Winter Olympic and Paralympic Games. The designation of Whistler as host resort for the 2010 Olympics attracted national and international chain store operators. Furthermore, the economic recession resulted in corporate change of the mountain operation with Intrawest being sold to a publicly traded company, 'Whistler Blackcomb Holdings,' in 2010. Most importantly for the retail sector, Whistler Blackcomb, as part of a large-scale expansion and diversification plan, aggressively acquired many local independent retail businesses. In 2016 Whistler Blackcomb was sold to a US company, Colorado-based Vail Resorts Inc., which intends to pursue the expansion plans.

Exposure challenges for Whistler's independent and small business operators

Complex adaptive systems are continually subject to diverse types of change that can occur simultaneously. Consequently, systems can be exposed to multiple disturbances simultaneously. In the context of a retail system, exposure to disturbances depends on: (1) the structure and nature of the retail sector; (2) the characteristics of its customers; and (3) the built and natural physical environment. Based on the results of survey and interview data, Table 10.1 summarizes the factors that shape Whistler's destination retail system's exposure to disturbance.

In this study, local business owners and operators were especially concerned that if local stakeholders do not intervene in some way, independent retailers will continue to struggle to compete while chain stores and Whistler Blackcomb dominate. Whistler Blackcomb owns and operates 18 retail outlets in Whistler and has identified the retail sector as an opportunity for future corporate growth and development (Whistler Blackcomb Holdings Inc., 2015). Retailers believe that the current conditions create challenges for independent and small businesses that lack the capacity to adapt. The combination of high rents, local power dynamics, and competition with chain stores is discouraging new businesses from entering the market, while also threatening existing independent businesses. Following Whistler Blackcomb's purchase of a locally owned sporting goods store in December 2014 (Whistler Blackcomb Holdings Inc., 2015), local

Table 10.1 Summary of factors that shape Whistler's destination retail system's exposure to disturbances

Condition area	Relevant condition	Findings
Retail sector characteristics	Structure (size, prices, merchandize type)	• Mix of ownership structure, with Whistler Blackcomb as a major player • Moderate diversity in merchandize offered and price • High levels of local competition for some types of retail (apparel and sportswear)
	Networks	• Existing business associations and networks (Whistler Association of Retail Merchants, Tourism Whistler, Whistler Chamber of Commerce)
Customer characteristics	Demographics	• Combination of destination and regional visitors and residents • Destination visitors are the highest spenders • Core markets are Canada, US, Australia, and the UK • Seasonal differences
	Purchase behavior	• Customer service is critical • Seasonal differences (lower priced items in summer vs winter)
Built environment	Development patterns	• Master-planned resort • Pedestrian focused with high levels of activity along the village walkway • Free and pay parking designated locations
	Public spaces	• Many outdoor attractive public spaces

Source: Wongkee (2016).

media reported community anxieties that retail in Whistler is moving to the "generic" (Taylor, 2014). There is a general perception that the current trajectory is continuing and that the conditions are creating barriers and challenges for small businesses so that the number of unique independent retail outlets will continue to decrease, which will in turn have a detrimental effect on the overall retail environment and ultimately the customer experience.

The following quotations from interviews with local retailers capture their perspectives:

> Tourists need and want to see a mix of shops that are unique and not cookie cutter [chain stores] or the same as their local mall.
>
> (Interview, local retailer, 2015)

> Whistler Blackcomb recently bought one of my favourite stores and I am pretty sad about that … but of course, you can't blame them for selling when Whistler Blackcomb is offering to pay that much.
>
> (Interview, local retailer, 2015)

> Whistler Blackcomb owns all the ski stores and bike stores in the village. Even though they have different names, they have the same flavour.
>
> (Interview, local retailer, 2015)

These views echo the well-established views of retail experts – as Matheusik (1996 p. 68) observes, "Maintaining the right mix in a dynamic consumer climate is perhaps the most significant challenge faced by resort and tourism community developers, planners and retailers worldwide."

These concerns are not new: local stakeholders shared similar views a decade earlier, when Thomas Consultants produced the *Whistler sustainable retail study background report* (Thomas Consultants Inc., 2006). Eighteen stakeholders were interviewed for the study, including resort managers, local associations, private companies, development companies, property owners, and retail tenants. In 2006, stakeholders' main concerns related to the performance of the retail sector included rent affordability, availability of retail space, operational costs, and retail sector evolution. The report stated that Whistler's market dynamics, including lease rates and demand for space, favored national tenants, and the cost structure in Whistler caused many local unique businesses to fail (Thomas Consultants Inc., 2006). There is concern that since this report was produced, there appears to have been relatively little progress in addressing the concerns of smaller, local retail operators. In the present study, several business owners expressed concerns with the current trajectory that favors external corporate retail chains.

Sensitivity to disturbance

Sensitivity is the degree to which a system is affected after being exposed to shocks or stressors. Local power dynamics, social networks, and the effectiveness of governance systems are particularly significant, as they influence the distribution, access, and use of resources, which are necessary for the system to cope and respond to a disturbance (Turner et al., 2003). Table 10.2 serves as an organizational frame of reference for highlighting key sensitivities to disturbance in Whistler's destination retail system.

In recent years, to address issues of seasonality, Whistler has focused on increasing the number of year-round activities available, pre-selling vacation packages and hosting several festivals and events between peak winter and summer seasons. Tourism Whistler is the destination marketing organization that coordinates resort-wide marketing activities, in partnership with the Whistler Chamber of Commerce, Whistler Blackcomb, the major branded hotels, and other local stakeholders. Tourism Whistler also partners with regional and national tourism organizations – such as Tourism Vancouver, Destination BC, and Destination Canada – to coordinate marketing activities.

A municipal government committee, the Economic Partnership Initiative Committee (2013), made a number of recommendations including strategies to grow visitor markets and segments, support reinvestment and development, diversify resort products, improve the guest experience, and enhance key partnerships. The

Table 10.2 Examples of elements of tourism system conditions that influence system sensitivity to disturbances

System condition	Element that influences system sensitivity to disturbances
Tourism-specific sensitivities	• Tourism seasonality • Markets and marketing strategies • Destination history and positioning • Destination image sensitivity
Human and social capital	• Knowledge of risk (traditional/historical response to part shocks and stressors that aid preparedness) • Skills that enable greater employment flexibility • Labor capacity • Networks and connectedness • Group membership • Relationships and levels of trust and reciprocity
Economic capital	• Livelihood portfolios • Accumulation of liquid and fixed assets • Credit histories and insurance • Employment opportunities • Business stability and access to welfare safety nets
Physical capital	• Access to resources • Biophysical carrying capacity • Access to infrastructure and communication systems • Transport links between tourist markets and destinations
Governance processes	• Formal and informal governance structures • Laws, policies, and rights • Tourism business networks

Source: Wongkee (2016), adapted from Calgaro et al. (2014).

Municipality is supporting the development of initiatives that diversify Whistler's resort products. In line with this objective, Whistler Blackcomb announced the Renaissance project to develop activities that are not dependent on weather conditions. However, shortly after this announcement Whistler Blackcomb was purchased by Vail Resorts Inc., which decided to replace the Renaissance proposal with their own development plan. Furthermore, building on the momentum of the Olympic Games, the Municipality created a 'Festivals, Events, and Animation' program to attract additional visitors through the promotion of spectator and participatory events (Resort Municipality of Whistler, 2012). However, some retail owners and operators are concerned that an increase in the number of festival tourists might be detrimental to the resort, by changing visitor demographics and reducing average tourist expenditure in retail outlets.

While Whistler's retail system does not currently have a coordinated resort-wide retail strategy, business owners and operators have indicated an interest in developing one. The performance of Whistler's retail sector relies on the collective actions of its individual retailers, real estate agents, property owners, and other local actors. The plans of Tourism Whistler, Whistler Chamber of Commerce, and Whistler Blackcomb have a significant bearing on local conditions and can influence retail-specific sensitivities.

Thomas Consultants Inc.'s (2007) *Whistler sustainable retail study findings & recommendations* reported a similar interest in developing a retail vision and the final report recommended several strategic initiatives. Specific recommendations included working with landlords "to devise a rental strategy to offer variable rental rates by season," creating a "distinct zoning/precinct strategy for key retail nodes throughout the Village," and developing "a recruitment and leasing strategy for targeting tenants deemed compatible with the optimal merchandise mix of each specific node" (Thomas Consultants Inc., 2007, p. 12). To date, there appears to have been a limited response to these recommendations.

A significant sensitivity is Whistler's heavy reliance on temporary foreign workers to fill positions in hospitality and retail (Barrett, 2013). Although international staff may increase the brand awareness of Whistler and contribute to the overall atmosphere in the resort (Whistler Blackcomb Holdings Inc., 2015), reliance on temporary foreign workers enhances its sensitivity to changes in Canadian immigration policies. Canada's temporary foreign worker program allows Canadian employers to hire foreign workers to fill positions where labor needs cannot be met by Canadian citizens and permanent residents (Government of Canada, 2016). In 2015, CBC News reported that although tourism visits in Whistler were high, a lack of foreign labor supply negatively affected businesses. Local businesses stated that the shortage of foreign workers in Whistler resulted in overwhelming demands on existing employees and some businesses closed (CBC News, 2015).

In 2015, stores reduced their operating hours or closed entirely due to lack of staff. Inadequate staffing affects service quality and brand image (Dupuis, 2015). The labor challenges are indicative of the systems' sensitivity to changes in labor supply. The current conditions in Whistler are of particular concern due to the characteristics of the village's customers, and the role customer service has in tourist satisfaction and purchase behavior. Hiring temporary foreign workers encourages a seasonal rotation of staff as employees have a limited period of time during which they can work. The constant staff turnover requires a continuous process of recruiting and training staff. High employee turnover affects staffing needs as well as employee morale.

The physical elements of a retail venue are essential components of the retail experience (Kemperman et al., 2009). Store layout, atmosphere, and ease of moving around influence customer experience (Dabholkar, Thorpe, & Rentz, 1996). The limited availability of commercial space is another physical condition within the retail system that increases sensitivity to change. Whistler's growth management policies and zoning bylaws restrict the amount of retail space available. Commercial spaces available for rent are often in locations with low levels of pedestrian traffic and are inappropriate relative to the needs of small independent retailers (interview with retail operator, 2015). The limited space available creates challenges for the sector to adapt to changing conditions. For example, in 2013, when a fire damaged the Tyndall Stone Lodge, commercial tenants had limited options for alternative locations to re-open their stores (French, 2013).

Having a limited ability to alter the physical store reduces retailer ability to adapt or adjust in response to change. In respect of challenges with visibility, access, and pedestrian traffic, retailers often felt restricted in their capacity to improve conditions. Limitations include local bylaws, which inhibit activities that alter the physical appearance of the village, or the structure of current rental agreements, which can be significant barriers to making alterations or substantial investments. For example, a local business owner created a set of stairs to provide better access to the store, which improved pedestrian traffic and sales significantly (Atkinson, 2013). Although the retailer owned the space, the process to acquire the necessary approvals and conduct the work took several years and involved the Municipality, two building strata companies, and timeshare owners (Atkinson, 2013). In 2012, the Municipality recognized the challenges associated with the process of making alterations and has since streamlined the procedures and published a retail streetscape guide to assist businesses in creating diverse and interesting storefronts (Resort Municipality of Whistler, 2012).

Governance is generally understood as "the values, rules and laws, as well as the institutions and processes (i.e. policy-making, discursive debates, negotiations, mediation, elections, referendums, public consultations, protests, etc.) through which public and private stakeholders seek to achieve common objectives and make decisions" (Sheppard, 2015, p. 10). Effective governance and management structures are integral components of resilient tourism systems (Larsen et al., 2011). Although the retail sector is subject to regulations and policies at the provincial, national, and international scales, only those relating to the local destination environment are discussed here.

Retailers expressed concern about the power differences between system actors. In Whistler, the Resort Municipality of Whistler, Whistler Chamber of

Commerce, Tourism Whistler, and Whistler Blackcomb are the four organizations that are particularly influential in shaping the local environment. Although all retailers are members of Tourism Whistler and the majority are members of the Chamber of Commerce, many retailers perceive their interests are not adequately considered. As observed earlier, the main target of retailer frustration is Whistler Blackcomb. During the interviews, many small retailers observed that Whistler Blackcomb has the loudest voice and better relationships with property owners and suppliers. They believe that the company has acquired an unofficial 'right of first refusal' with respect to rental agreements for properties with expiring leases and exclusivity with respect to selling specific brands. Whistler Blackcomb also has two appointed representatives on the board of directors of Tourism Whistler and regularly collaborates with the Chamber of Commerce and the Municipality on many initiatives. Retailer frustrations are exacerbated by recent Whistler Blackcomb acquisitions of local retail companies and an increase in their market share. The recent creation of the Whistler Association of Retailers and Merchants is an attempt to create a stronger voice for the retail sector in Whistler. Local retailers and merchants created the association in 2014 and it remains a new organization with an evolving role. The association has a degree of legitimacy in the resort as the Association's monthly meetings to discuss sector-specific issues are reported by Tourism Whistler (Tourism Whistler, 2015).

The Municipality's suite of plans, strategies, policies, and bylaws shape the local retail environment and determine the regulatory framework in which retailers operate. Of particular relevance to retailers, the Municipality is responsible for zoning and planning for development, building codes, and maintaining municipal services and infrastructure. There are specific bylaws that regulate the exterior design of buildings within designated commercial zones in Whistler. The Whistler Village Design Guidelines encourage developers to maintain the existing mountain village character, including its pedestrian orientation, availability of open space amenities, and consistent landscaping, architectural features, and color scheme. Guidelines support consistency and quality of form and character of development and the protection of the natural environment. The current development approval process is perceived by some retailers as a barrier for business investment in physical improvements.

Conclusions

The focus of this chapter has been on examining core elements of vulnerability, notably, exposure and sensitivity in Whistler's resort retail system. The research methods introduce a conceptual framework, grounded in the literature, that can be adapted and used as a heuristic device in examining resilience in other destination retail systems. Using the DRRF to guide the analysis, the study identified the factors that local business owners and operators perceived as influential to the functioning of Whistler's destination retail system and explored how these factors influenced the retail system's vulnerability and resilience to shocks and stressors. Conceptual frameworks that recognize the vulnerability of socio-ecological systems can help us to understand which system components are vulnerable to shocks and disturbances, and provide insights into how resilient and adaptable communities can be created (Turner et al., 2003).

For retail systems in resort environments, understanding the elements that shape their vulnerability and resilience is critical to anticipate change and design practical solutions that build resilient systems. The study findings reveal potential linkages between Whistler's current conditions and its vulnerabilities, including the retail sector composition in terms of merchandise diversity and ownership type, trends in customer markets, and local labor conditions. The results reveal the complex interdependencies within the resort's retail sector and offer insights into the resilience of the sector in the face of increasing external growth stresses and potential contestation with community and environmental priorities. At the heart of this debate is the contested resort landscape of corporate retail establishments versus small, independently-owned businesses and the influence of this on resort resilience and sense of place. Whistler retailers recognize the importance to visitor experience of a pedestrian streetscape and an intimate scale that creates local ambience and social engagement; but concerns were expressed by a number of retailers that the carefully planned and controlled 'sense of place' that has characterized Whistler is being lost, and that the feel and experience of the village is becoming 'homogenized.' This concern is related to attaining the critical retail mix. Local independent retailers reinforce a sense of community and authenticity but often feel powerless in decision-making when competing with larger corporate retailers. However, some might argue that national and international specialty brand anchor-stores contribute to resilience by providing traffic and economic stability for local operators. Beyond the retail sector, non-retail 'staging' of amenities, events, and activities that animate, energize, and attract visitors and locals also contribute to a sense of place that in turn helps support retail activity, especially in shoulder seasons. However, some retailers are concerned that these events may distract customers away from retail outlets.

In conclusion, it is evident that the resort retailing system presents a complex landscape with contested spaces. Understanding the vulnerabilities to the resilience of this system are necessary precursors to policy and planning intervention. In Whistler's case, there are strong social networks including the Whistler Chamber of Commerce and Tourism Whistler, together with the recently created Whistler Association of Retailers and Merchants. Although previous retail studies in Whistler have not resulted in any significant policy interventions, learning continues with various further studies and research. The findings of this study indicate areas for further investigation; for example, aspects of adaptive capacity such as learning, innovation, and knowledge sharing. Ultimately it is the collective capacity for collaboration, effective decision-making, and governance that influences the effectiveness of responses to stressors.

References

Adger, W.N. (2000). Social and ecological resilience: Are they related? *Progress in Human Geography*, *24*(3), 347–364.

Adger, W.N. (2006). Vulnerability. *Global Environmental Change*, *16*, 268–281.

Armitage, D. (2005). Adaptive capacity and community-based natural resource management. *Environmental Management*, *35*(6), 703–715.

Atkinson, C. (2013, August 1). Whistler Village 3.0 takes change to the streets. *Pique News Magazine*. Retrieved from www.piquenewsmagazine.com.

Barrett, B. (2013, May 9). Changes to temporary foreign worker program bad for business, says Whistler Chamber. *Whistler Question*. Retrieved from www.whistlerquestion.com.

Barrett, B. (2016, April 22). Rainbow Plaza set to open in June. *Pique News Magazine*. Retrieved from www.piquenewsmagazine.com.

Bec, A., McLennan, C., & Moyle, B.D. (2015). Community resilience to long-term tourism decline and rejuvenation: A literature review and conceptual model. *Current Issues in Tourism*, *19*(5), 431–457.

Biggs, D. (2011). Understanding resilience in a vulnerable industry: The case of reef tourism in Australia. *Ecology and Society*, *16*(1), 30 [online]. Retrieved from www.ecologyandsociety.org/vol.16/iss1/art30/.

Biggs, D., Hall, C.M., & Stoeckl, N. (2012). The resilience of formal and informal tourism enterprises to disasters: Reef tourism in Phuket, Thailand. *Journal of Sustainable Tourism*, *20*(5), 645–665.

Cachinho, H. (2014). Consumerscapes and the resilience assessment of urban retail systems. *Cities*, *36*, 131–144.

Calgaro, E., & Lloyd, K. (2008). Sun, sea, sand and tsunami: Examining disaster vulnerability in the tourism community of Khao Lak, Thailand. *Singapore Journal of Tropical Geography*, *29*, 288–306.

Calgaro, E., Lloyd, K., & Dominey-Howes, D. (2014). From vulnerability to transformation: A framework for assessing the vulnerability and resilience of tourism destinations. *Journal of Sustainable Tourism*, *11*(3), 341–360.

CBC News (2015, August 14). Whistler tourism soars, but crackdown on foreign labour hurts business. Retrieved from www.cbc.ca.

Clark, W.C., Jaeger, J., Corell, R., Kasperson, R., McCarthy, J.J., Cash, D., … Levy, M.A. (2000, May 22–25). Assessing vulnerability to global environmental risks. In *Report of the workshop on vulnerability to global environmental change: Challenges for research, assessment and decision making*, Warrenton, VA. Cambridge, MA: Belfer Center for Science and International Affairs, Environment and Natural Resources Program, Kennedy School of Government, Harvard University.

Dabholkar, P.A., Thorpe, D.I., & Rentz, J.O. (1996). A measure of service quality for retail stores: Scale development and validation. *Journal of the Academy of Marketing Science*, *24*(1), 3–16.

Dolega, L., & Celinska-Janowicz, D. (2015). Retail resilience: A theoretical framework for understanding town centre dynamics. *Studia Regionalne I Lokalne*, *60*(2), 8–31.

Dupuis, B. (2015, August 13). "Dismal" staffing struggles worsen in Whistler. *Pique News Magazine*. Retrieved from www.piquenewsmagazine.com.

Economic Partnership Initiative Committee (2013). *Economic partnership initiative: Summary of key findings report*. Whistler, BC: Resort Municipality of Whistler.

Economic Partnership Initiative Committee (2016). *2016 update summary of key findings & economic planning report*. Whistler, BC: Resort Municipality of Whistler.

Erkip, F., Kızılgün, Ö., & Akinci, G.M. (2014). Retailers' resilience strategies and their impacts on urban spaces in Turkey. *Cities*, *36*, 112–120.

Espiner, S., & Becken, S. (2015). Tourist towns on the edge: Conceptualising vulnerability and resilience in a protected area tourism system. *Journal of Sustainable Tourism*, *22*(4), 646–665.

Fernandes, J R., & Chamusca, P. (2014). Urban policies, planning and retail resilience. *Cities*, *36*, 170–177.

Folke, C. (2006). Resilience: The emergence of a perspective for social–ecological systems analyses. *Global Environmental Change*, *16*, 253–267.

Folke, C., Carpenter, S., Elmqvist, T., Gunderson, L., Holling, C.S., & Walker, B. (2002). Resilience and sustainable development: Building adaptive capacity in a world of transformations. *Ambio*, *31*(5), 437–440.

Folke, C., Carpenter, S.R., Walker, B., Scheffer, M., Chapin, T., & Rockström, J. (2010). Resilience thinking: Integrating resilience, adaptability and transformability. *Ecology and Society*, *15*(4) [online]. Retrieved from http://doi.org/10.1038/nnano.2011.191.

French, J. (2013, November 30). Tyndall Stone tenants finding new spaces. *Pique News Magazine*. Retrieved from www.piquenewsmagazine.com.

French, J. (2014, June 5). Whistler retailers form new association. *Pique News Magazine*. Retrieved from www.piquenewsmagazine.com.

Government of Canada. (2016). Fact sheet – Temporary foreign worker program. Retrieved from www.cic.gc.ca/english/resources/publications/employers/temp-foreign-worker-program.asp.

Gunderson, L.H., & Holling, C.S. (2002). *Panarchy: Understanding transformations in human and natural systems*. Washington, DC: Island Press.

Jones, P., Comfort, D., Hillier, D., & Eastwood, I. (2005). Retailers and sustainable development in the UK. *International Journal of Retail & Distribution Management*, *33*(3), 207–214.

Kaltcheva, V.D., & Weitz, B.A. (2006). When should a retailer create an exciting store environment? *Journal of Marketing*, *70*(1), 107–118.

Kärrholm, M., Nylund, K., Prieto, P., & Fuente, D. (2014). Spatial resilience and urban planning: Addressing the interdependence of urban retail areas. *Cities*, *36*, 121–130.

Kemperman, A.D.A.M., Borgers, A.W.J., & Timmermans, H.J.P. (2009). Tourist shopping behavior in a historic downtown area. *Tourism Management*, *30*(2), 208–218.

Kim, S., & Littrell, M.A. (2001). Souvenir buying intentions for self versus others. *Annals of the Association of American Geographers*, *28*(3), 638–657.

Larsen, R.K., Calgaro, E., & Thomalla, F. (2011). Governing resilience building in Thailand's tourism-dependent coastal communities: Conceptualising stakeholder agency in social–ecological systems. *Global Environmental Change*, *21*(2), 481–491.

Matheusik, M. (1996). Resort retailing: Finding the right mix. *Urban Land*, *55*(August), 68–72.

Mehmetoglu, M., & Engen, M. (2011). Pine and Gilmore's concept of experience economy and its dimensions: An empirical examination in tourism. *Journal of Quality Assurance in Hospitality & Tourism*, *12*(4), 237–255.

Ozuduru, B.H., Varol, C., & Ercoskun, O.Y. (2014). Do shopping centers abate the resilience of shopping streets? The co-existence of both shopping venues in Ankara, Turkey. *Cities*, *36*, 145–157.

Pelling, M. (2003). *The vulnerability of cities: Natural disasters and social resilience*. London: Routledge.

Pine II, J.B., & Gilmore, J.H. (2000). Satisfaction, sacrifice, surprise. *Strategy & Leadership*, *28*(1) 18–23.

Pique News Magazine (2016, September 23). Whistler Blackcomb named no. 1 resort for third year in a row. Retrieved from www.piquenewsmagazine.com/whistler/whistler-backcomb-voted-no-1-resort-for-third-year-in-a-row/Content?oid=2804851.

Polsky, C., Neff, R., & Yarnal, B. (2007). Building comparable global change vulnerability assessments: The vulnerability scoping diagram. *Global Environmental Change*, *17*, 472–485.

Resort Municipality of Whistler (2012, May 15). Whistler retail strategy council update. Presentation to the Committee of the Whole, Resort Municipality of Whistler, BC.

Resort Municipality of Whistler (2016). Whistler visitation. Retrieved from: www. whistler.ca/municipal-gov/community-monitoring/whistler-facts-and-figures/whistler-visitation.

Sheppard, V.A. (2015). *Factors nurturing resilience in resort destination governance* (Unpublished doctoral dissertation). Simon Fraser University, Burnaby, BC, Canada.

Singleton, A.D., Dolega, L., Riddlesden, D., & Longley, P.A. (2016). Measuring the spatial vulnerability of retail centres to online consumption through a framework of e-resilience. *Geoforum*, *69*, 5–18.

Skerratt, S. (2013). Enhancing the analysis of rural community resilience: Evidence from community land ownership. *Journal of Rural Studies*, *31*, 36–46.

Strickland-Munro, J.K., Allison, H.E., & Moore, S.A. (2010). Using resilience concepts to investigate the impacts of protected area tourism on communities. *Annals of Tourism Research*, *37*(2), 499–519.

Strickland-Munro, J., & Moore, S. (2014). Exploring the impacts of protected area tourism on local communities using a resilience approach. *Koedoe*, *56*(2), 1–11.

Swarbrooke, J., & Horner, S. (2007). *Consumer behaviour in tourism* (2nd ed.). Amsterdam: Elsevier.

Taylor, A. (2014, December 18). WB grabs another slice of retail/rental pie: Sale of Summit Sports opens up competition questions. *Pique News Magazine*. Retrieved from www.piquenewsmagazine.com.

Thomas Consultants Inc. (2006). *Whistler sustainable retail study background report*. Whistler, BC: Resort Municipality of Whistler.

Thomas Consultants Inc. (2007). *Whistler sustainable retail study findings & recommendations*. Whistler, BC: Resort Municipality of Whistler.

Timothy, D.J. (2005). *Shopping tourism, retailing, and leisure*. Buffalo, NY: Channel View Publications.

Tourism Whistler. (2015). *Tourism Whistler annual report 2015*. Whistler, BC: Tourism Whistler.

Tsao, C., & Ni, C. (2016). Vulnerability, resilience, and the adaptive cycle in a crisis-prone tourism community. *Tourism Geographies*, *18*(1), 80–105.

Turner II, B.L., Kasperson, R.E., Matson, P.A., McCarthy, J.J., Corell, R.W., Christensen, L., … Schiller, A. (2003). A framework for vulnerability analysis in sustainability science. *Proceedings of the National Academy of Sciences of the United States of America*, *100*(14), 8074–8079.

Turner, L.W., & Reisinger, Y. (2001). Shopping satisfaction for domestic tourists. *Journal of Retailing and Consumer Services*, *8*(1), 15–27.

Whistler Blackcomb Holdings Inc. (2015). *Management's discussion and analysis for the three months ended December 31, 2014 and 2013*. Whistler, BC: Resort Municipality of Whistler.

Wongkee, S. (2016). *Understanding resilience in a vulnerable industry: A case of retailing in a mountain resort community* (Unpublished master's thesis). Simon Fraser University, Burnaby, BC, Canada.

Wrigley, N., & Dolega, L. (2011). Resilience, fragility, and adaptation: New evidence on the performance of UK high streets during global economic crisis and its policy implications. *Environment and Planning A, 43*, 2337–2363.

11 Examining social–ecological resilience

Using content analysis to assess changes in public perceptions of the synergetic interactions between tourism development and landscape protection

Jasper Heslinga, Peter Groote, and Frank Vanclay

Introduction

Tourism destinations constantly need to adapt to socio-economic and environmental changes (Davidson, 2010; Lew, 2014). Resilience thinking has recently emerged as a concept for understanding how to cope with these changes (Biggs, 2011; Espiner & Becken, 2014; Imperiale & Vanclay, 2016; Lew, 2014; Luthe & Wyss, 2014). Resilience thinking may contribute to better decision making regarding the management of the interactions between tourism and landscape. In the academic scholarship on tourism, resilience has been primarily discussed as a theoretical concept, and its application in empirical research lags behind the conceptual discussion (Lew, 2014). This chapter addresses this gap by providing an empirical application of the concept of resilience to the Island of Terschelling in the Wadden Sea region of the Northern Netherlands, a tourism destination experiencing changing social–ecological conditions.

In this chapter, resilience is examined from the perspective of the institutional context. While the institutional context consists of both formal (e.g., rules and regulations) and informal (e.g., cultural values and norms) aspects (Alexander, 2005; Cumming, Cumming, & Redman, 2006; Pahl-Wostl, 2009), the focus in this chapter is on the informal aspects. A brief synopsis of the key constructs of resilience, social–ecological systems, and institutions precedes discussion of the empirical study. We examine the institutional context by analyzing changes in public thinking about the interactions between tourism development and landscape protection. The current institutional context of Terschelling reflects the trajectories of the island's past path dependencies, which will, in turn, also influence future development plans.

We use content analysis as a method to analyze the informal aspects of the institutional context. Content analysis can assist in analyzing the changing dynamics over a long time period. We argue that institutional ways of thinking are reflected in all forms of publication, and institutions are also influenced by public opinion. Because the informal context is intangible, it is difficult to measure. To get an indication of the informal institutional context, and arguably a proxy for it, we analyzed newspaper articles dealing with the interactions between tourism development and landscape protection for the period 1945 to 2015. To gain extra information about the situation and to cross-validate the data, our content analysis was supported by key informant interviews with local experts and other stakeholders. We specifically considered the case of the Island of Terschelling (Province of Friesland) in the Wadden Sea region of the northern Netherlands.

Tourism and landscape can interact in multiple ways (Liburd & Becken, 2017; Terkenli, 2004). The emphasis in the institutional context can vary over time between nature protection, socio-economic development, or on the synergies between them (Heslinga, Groote, & Vanclay, 2017). In this chapter, we are particularly interested in the synergetic interactions and how they emerged over time. Synergies can be described as situations in which the interactions between elements of a system catalytically combine in ways that result in a greater sum-total outcome than would have been achieved otherwise, with benefits across the full range of social, economic, and ecological dimensions (Persha, Agrawal, & Chhatre, 2011).

We believe that synergies hold promise for resilience thinking in tourism destinations because they relate directly to the feedback mechanisms in social–ecological systems in which the interactions between tourism and landscape take place. For a tourism destination to increase its resilience, a balance between nature protection and socio-economic development is desirable (Heslinga et al., 2017). This means that a destination should not just be managed for the sake of nature protection (which can be socially undesirable) or for socio-economic development (which would be ecologically undesirable) but should be managed for the sake of both. The idea of synergies offers potential for better understanding and management of tourism–landscape interactions. To discover whether synergies are considered in public thinking and how they have changed over time, we conducted a content analysis of newspaper articles between 1945 and 2015. We argue that this approach reveals the informal aspects of the institutional context.

Synergies, social–ecological systems, institutions, and resilience

Tourism destinations are facing environmental and social changes (Davidson, 2010; Lew, 2014). To deal with these changes, there is an ongoing need to address the ecological, economic, and social–cultural aspects of tourism (Wesley & Pforr, 2010). Policy makers adapt to these changes by making interventions. Understanding the institutional context in which these decisions and interventions have been made helps policy makers and planners make better future decisions (Alexander, 2005) and can help build the resilience of the destination.

Tourism destinations tend to experience conflicting goals – the protection of nature versus socio-economic development. However, the promise of synergies means that these goals do not necessarily have to be in conflict. For example, nature-based tourism is not just a socio-economic activity that provides income and other benefits to local communities (Libosada, 2009); it also plays an important role in facilitating the understanding of natural heritage, and in gaining public support and raising funds for conservation (Libosada, 2009; McCool & Spenceley, 2014). Nevertheless, tourism may also have negative impacts on the landscape (Buckley, 2011; Saarinen, 2006) and on the host communities (King, Pizam, & Milman, 1993; Liu et al., 2007; McCombes, Vanclay, & Evers, 2015). In this chapter, we look at the synergetic interactions between tourism development and landscape protection.

To help identify these synergetic interactions, we use a social–ecological systems (SES) perspective, which presumes an integrated system of human society and ecosystems, with reciprocal feedback loops and interdependencies (Berkes, 2007). This means that tourism development and landscape protection are not seen as separate social and ecological entities; they are part of a coupled social–ecological system. In SES theory, institutions play an important role in managing the social–ecological interactions within the system (Anderies, Janssen, & Ostrom, 2004; Brondizio, Ostrom, & Young, 2009; Ostrom, 2009; Ostrom & Cox, 2010). They are the central component linking social and ecological systems (Adger, 2000). As institutions are often path-dependent, a contextual and long-term approach to institutional development is needed. This is also reflected in SES thinking where the exploration of historical (long-term) relationships between society and the environment is important for understanding the current institutional context (González, Montes, Rodriguez, & Tapia, 2008; Parra & Moulaert, 2016).

Institutions can be defined as "systems of established and prevalent social rules that structure social interactions" (Hodgson, 2006, p. 2). They consist of formal aspects (e.g., rules and regulations) and informal aspects (e.g., cultural values and norms) (Alexander, 2005; Cumming et al., 2006; Pahl-Wostl, 2009). Formal institutions are openly codified, in the sense that the social rules are established and communicated through channels that are widely accepted as official. Informal institutions are socially shared rules that are created, communicated, and enforced outside of the officially sanctioned channels (Helmke & Levitsky, 2004). Because we are interested in the way people think about how tourism and landscape interactions have been changing over time, our focus lies on the informal institutional aspects.

Resilience is a key concept in SES thinking; it implies that a system is able to cope with changes in the present and in the future (and preferably prosper) (Folke et al., 2010; Holling, 2008; Walker, Holling, Carpenter, & Kinzig, 2004). For a tourism destination to increase its resilience, a balance between nature protection and socio-economic development is required. Tourism may have a key role in this balance, especially if the potential synergies between tourism and landscape are acknowledged (Heslinga et al., 2017). If the potential synergies between tourism and landscape are recognized, and regional development options that find a balance between tourism and landscape are selected, then tourism could provide an opportunity to increase the social–ecological resilience of a region (Buckley, 2011; Heslinga et al., 2017).

We adhere to the social–ecological (or evolutionary) view of resilience, which rejects the idea of steady states (Davoudi, Brooks, & Mehmood, 2013). The evolutionary view sees the world as complex, uncertain, and relatively unpredictable, rather than as ordered, mechanical, and reasonably predictable (Davoudi et al., 2013; Wilkinson, 2012). Carpenter, Westley, and Turner (2005) conceive of resilience not as the return to a normal or stable situation, but as the ability of systems to continuously change, adapt, and transform in response to stresses and tensions. The social–ecological system is continuously influenced by social and environmental changes. To deal with these changes and to enable the system to maintain resilience, the various formal and informal institutions within tourism destinations need to constantly adapt.

Undertaking a content analysis

Krippendorff (2013) defines content analysis as a research technique for making replicable and valid inferences from texts and other meaningful materials. Content analysis has been frequently used in the field of tourism studies, for example, as a method to analyze destination image representations (Choi, Lehto, & Morrison, 2007). An important advantage of content analysis over interviewing is that it avoids the problem of memory reconstruction by research participants (Lowenthal, 2015). This is particularly important in research that seeks to go back over time. Thus, instead of asking people to try to recollect what happened in the distant past, content analysis uses material that was actually published in the past – in other words, that was published contemporaneously with the events described in the articles. A further advantage is that, although there is still room for varying interpretations, the source material remains constant (rather than the key informant telling a different story depending on how they feel each time they are interviewed). Content analysis therefore tends to have high reliability (Krippendorff, 2013).

We undertook a content analysis of newspaper articles extracted from the online database, *De Krant van Toen* (www.dekrantvantoen.nl), which contains all the articles in major Dutch newspapers. To construct our database of articles for analysis, we started with the two major daily newspapers published in the Province of Friesland, the *Leeuwarder Courant* and the *Friesch Dagblad*. Since our interest was in the Island of Terschelling, only articles that contained the word 'Terschelling' were included in the initial selection. To further select the articles for analysis, we chose various combinations of the terms: *toerisme* (tourism), *recreatie* (recreation), *natuur* (nature), and *landschap* (landscape). The stipulated time period was 1945 to 2015, since this is the period during which tourism became strongly established in the Wadden region (Sijtsma, Broersma, Daams, Hoekstra, & Werner, 2015).

From the initial selection, some articles were excluded because they were inappropriate. First, many advertisements were removed. Second, some articles were excluded because they were published in both regional newspapers. Third, articles that were accidently selected because of the inclusion of the Dutch word '*natuurlijk*' (meaning 'naturally' or 'of course' rather than inferring nature) were removed. Finally, articles that contained some of the keywords but on examination were evidently primarily about other topics were excluded. After the process of selection and deselection, the resultant database consisted of 291 articles.

Content analysis is carried out using codes (usually in a hierarchy) to describe the content of the text (Gläser & Laudel, 2013; Krippendorff, 2013). Codes can be derived from theory (i.e., a priori coding), from the texts themselves (i.e., emergent coding), or the methods can be mixed (Drisko & Maschi, 2015). For our analysis, the overarching a priori codes were: (1) socio-economic development; (2) nature protection; and (3) synergies between socio-economic development and nature protection. A wide range of subcodes was used (see Table 11.1). The subcodes were developed by scanning the newspaper articles for any word that arguably functioned as synonyms, alternates, or flags for the concepts represented by the overarching codes. The analysis was performed using the qualitative data analysis software, ATLAS.ti (version 7.5.10). The 'Word Cruncher' function in ATLAS.ti gave the frequency and relative proportion of each code and subcode per article.

Expert interviews were conducted to critically reflect on the content analysis and to increase our understanding of the role of changing public opinion in influencing policy, and of the pivotal points in time and significant events. The experts were recruited via the lead author's network, snowballing, and through online searching. A total of eight interviews were held. The interviewees comprised a local tourism expert, a representative from a local interest group concerned with the preservation of the island, representatives from the national forest management organization, a civil servant, a former mayor, and a local historian. Prior to the interviews, the respondents were provided with a research information sheet and asked to complete an informed consent form which covered issues of anonymity, the use of the research, and their rights during and after the interview (Vanclay, Baines, & Taylor, 2013). With the permission of all respondents, the interviews were audio-recorded, and later transcribed. For the analysis of the interviews, the qualitative data software ATLAS.ti was also used.

Applying content analysis to examine tourism–landscape interactions on the Island of Terschelling

We analyzed newspaper articles about the island of Terschelling, which is part of the Dutch Wadden. The Wadden is the largest contiguous natural area of Western Europe and one of the largest tidal wetlands in the world (Kabat et al., 2012). Stretching from the northwest of the Netherlands, along the German

Table 11.1 Overview of the subcodes and variants associated with each overarching code used in the content analysis

Nature protection	Socio-economic development	Synergy
General	*General*	*Balance*
• nature	• tourism	• synergy/synergies
• landscape	• recreation	• win-win
• attractiveness/attractive	• leisure	• balance
• vulnerable/vulnerability	• economy	• harmony/harmonious
• quietness	• human/humans	
• open space	• prosperity	*Integration*
	• profit	• integral/integration/integrated
Activities		• interwoven
• protect/protection	*Activities*	• coherence/coherent
• conserve/conservation	• develop/development/developments	• sustainable/sustainability
• preserve/preservation	• growth	
	• expand/expansion	*Social*
Actors	• build/building	• collaboration/collaborative
• Staatsbosbeheer	• construct/construction	• together
• nature organizations	• initiative/initiatives	• involved/involvement
	• service/services	• aware/awareness
Objects	• mass/massively	• understanding
• fauna	• industry/industries	• respect
• flora	• investing/investment	• responsible/responsibility
• dune/dunes	• establishing/establishment	
• forest/forests		
• beach/beaches	*Actors*	
• salt marsh/salt marshes	• entrepreneur/entrepreneurs	
• polder/polders		
• bird/birds	*Objects*	
• seal/seals	• hotel/hotels	
• ban/bans	• camping/camping grounds	
• wire	• caravan/caravans	
• fence/fences	• pavilion/pavilions	
• closed area	• traffic	
	• cycle path/cycle paths	
	• hospitality industry	

Note
These are English translations of the Dutch terms.

coast and the southwestern part of Denmark, the Wadden includes an archipelago of more than 30 inhabited and many uninhabited islands that shield a tidal mudflat from the North Sea (see Figure 11.1). The area is renowned for its outstanding ecological qualities and scenic landscapes, and was listed as a UNESCO Natural World Heritage Site in 2009 (Sijtsma, Daams, Farjon, & Buijs, 2012). Because of the widespread recognition of its ecological qualities and scenic landscapes, the Wadden has become very attractive to tourists (Revier, 2013). Since the 1950s, the Wadden islands have become an increasingly popular holiday destination, and tourism has become the dominant economic activity (Sijtsma et al., 2012). The Wadden is an area where the objectives of tourism development and landscape protection coincide and potentially clash, and therefore the region is very relevant for researching tourism–landscape interactions.

How the Wadden Sea region is and/or should be managed has been under constant discussion (Kabat et al., 2012; Van der Aa, Groote, & Huigen, 2004). Managing the Wadden is complicated because the area is not a remote ecosystem that humans can be excluded from; rather, the area has been heavily influenced by human activity for centuries (Knottnerus, 2005). Nowadays, the area is used for socio-economic activities such as agriculture, energy generation, fisheries, gas extraction, mining, manufacturing, shipping, and tourism (Kabat et al., 2012). Management that contributes to tourism and landscape protection is therefore necessary.

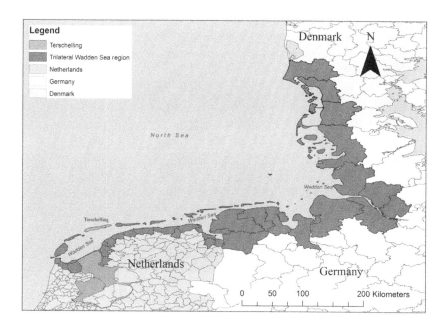

Figure 11.1 The Wadden Sea region.

Here, we specifically discuss the island of Terschelling, one of five inhabited Dutch Wadden islands. Terschelling is renowned for its biodiversity and much appreciated landscapes (Kabat et al., 2012). The island has an area of 8,616 hectares, with around 80 percent comprising dunes, forests, and salt marshes, which are highly attractive to tourists (Hoekstra, Zijlstra, Zwart, Smit-Zwanenburg, & Kok, 2009). Terschelling is an established tourist destination attracting over 400,000 visitors annually (Municipality of Terschelling, 2016; Sijtsma et al., 2015) and around 1.8 million overnight stays (Municipality of Terschelling, 2014). Historically, there have been strong interactions between tourism development and landscape protection. The island is among the most important tourism destinations in the Wadden, even though Terschelling has many highly sensitive, significant nature areas (Sijtsma et al., 2012). While tourism impacts on the landscape, the landscape is a key asset that must remain attractive if tourists are to continue visiting Terschelling in the future.

Results: what content analysis reveals about changing tourism–landscape interactions

The coding and analysis of the 291 newspaper articles for the period 1945 to 2015 resulted in a total of 4,031 coded words. Of these, almost 52 percent were classified under 'socio-economic development,' 41 percent under 'nature protection,' and 7 percent under 'synergies.' The frequency of use of the three overarching codes changed constantly, with a high annual volatility and without a clear trend. Using a three-year rolling average of the annual scores to reduce any

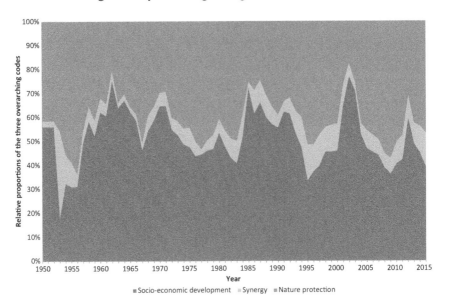

Figure 11.2 Relative proportion of the three overarching code words depicted as a rolling three-year average.

arbitrary annual fluctuation (see Figure 11.2), the relative proportions of the three categories become quite stable over time.

In the 1950s and the early 1960s, there was a significant increase in thinking in socio-economic terms, from 18 percent in 1953 to 75 percent in 1962 (see Figure 11.2). From 1962 until the end of the 1970s, socio-economic thinking decreased and nature protection gained in importance. The next turning point is visible in 1979. From then until the end of the 1980s, the emphasis shifted back to socio-economic development. From the end of the 1980s, the attention given to nature protection gained in importance again at the expense of socio-economic development. However, from the mid-1990s until the start of the twenty-first century there was again a reversal in thinking with a stronger focus on socio-economic development.

Since our interest is primarily with synergies, in Figure 11.3 we focus specifically on how the topic of 'synergy' has changed over time. Overall, there was an increase in thinking in terms of synergies. However, despite the overall increase, there was much fluctuation from year to year, and the percentage interest in synergy remains quite low.

Figure 11.4 presents an analysis of the subcodes for synergy. The five most important subcodes (i.e., most frequently used) were 'Together,' 'Involved,' 'Collaboration/collaborative,' 'Responsible/responsibility,' and 'Sustainable/ sustainability.' In Figure 11.5, the historical fluctuations of these five subcodes is given. For example, 'Sustainable' increases in frequency from the end of the 1980s and, after a decrease in 2002–2003, it again increases. We also observed that the subcode 'Together' is relatively dominant in these fluctuations over time. This analysis at the subcode level helps to determine the factors that contribute to an increase in the usage of synergies.

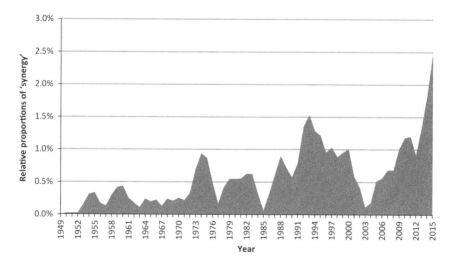

Figure 11.3 Relative proportion of 'synergy' weighted by newspaper article size (three-year rolling average).

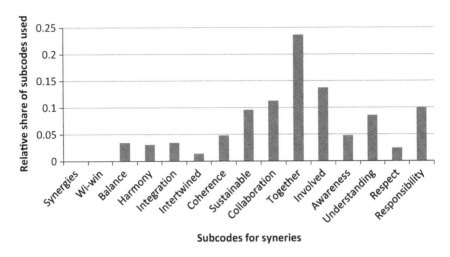

Figure 11.4 Relative share of subcodes contributing to 'synergies.'

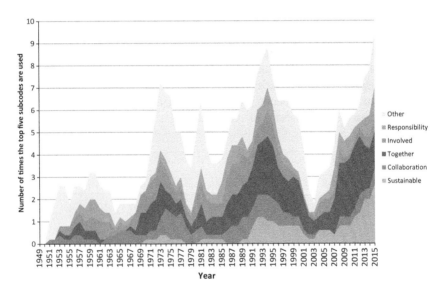

Figure 11.5 Frequency of use of the top five subcodes for synergy over time.

Discussion: what does the fluctuating public discourse mean for Terschelling?

The dominance of the code 'socio-economic development' in the 1950s is not surprising. During this time, the Netherlands was in a period of post World War II reconstruction. This period was characterized by a strong sense of the need to rebuild Dutch society and its economy. During the Nazi occupation (1940–1945), planning and policy making in The Netherlands was a centralized and top-down system and, perversely, this remained in place during the subsequent period of reconstruction and arguably still applies to some extent today (van der Cammen & de Klerk, 2012). As the socio-economic situation gradually improved and people started to have more money and leisure time, tourism developed on Terschelling, as reflected in the following newspaper extract:

> The National Forest Management Agency makes the dune area available for the expansion of the village of Terschelling-West.
>
> (*Leeuwarder Courant*, September 7, 1951)

Our interviewees stated that tourism started to grow exponentially, starting with relatively small-scale camping sites with only basic amenities. To meet the increasing demand, local residents would rent out their backyards, spare rooms, and sometimes dwellings during the summer season to gain additional income. The substantial increase in tourist arrivals during the post-war period explains the shift towards a more nature-protection oriented discourse midway through the 1960s. Local people started to realize that it might be necessary to safeguard the island's natural qualities and character. This growing concern about development resulted in the establishment of the S.O.S. Foundation (*Stichting Ons Terschellingerland*), an interest group of local inhabitants concerned with preserving the unique character of Terschelling (Interview 5; *Leeuwarder Courant*, August 27, 1962). As stated in the newspaper extract:

> S.O.S. stands up to defend the character and beauty of the island.
>
> (*Leeuwarder Courant*, August 27, 1962)

This development coincided with the establishment of another foundation, the Wadden Association (*Waddenvereniging*) in 1965. It was founded to protect the Wadden Sea from being developed as a land reclamation (polder) project. Later, the Wadden Association broadened its objectives and stressed the importance of protecting the whole of the Dutch Wadden area due to its ecological importance. 'Keep your hands off the Wadden' was their motto (Revier, 2013, p. 13).

The shift towards nature protection in the 1960s and 1970s occurred during a period of cultural revolution that witnessed a worldwide change in thinking about human influence on the environment, and was reflected in the 1972 United Nations Conference on the Human Environment in Stockholm, and in the 'Club of Rome' report, *The Limits to Growth* (Meadows, Meadows, Randers, & Behrens, 1972). On Terschelling, the shift in attention from solely economic development (largely through tourism) towards nature protection encouraged the National Forest Management Agency to intervene, as demonstrated in the following newspaper quote.

> Recreation pressure affects the dunes on Terschelling excessively: The National Forest Management Agency closes off the inner dunes by barbed wire.
>
> (*Friesch Dagblad*, September 22, 1973)

In 1974, the Municipality of Terschelling released a plan with bold policy measures such as fixing the maximum number of tourist beds (at 20,000), restricting the number of motor vehicles, and establishing land use zoning restrictions. In addition, policy measures also focussed on the quality and added value of tourism development, and attempts were made to flatten the peaks in tourism arrivals by extending the tourist season and by holding large events in off-peak and shoulder periods. Most of these measures were considered to have had a great influence in steering the development of tourism and are still valid today (Interview 2). In 1974, a Parliamentary Commission led by Mr. J.P. Mazure advised that plans for reclamation of the Wadden should be abolished and suggested protecting the whole area as a nature reserve or National Park (Kabat et al., 2012).

At the end of the 1970s and the beginning of the 1980s, there was a shift back to a more socio-economic oriented discourse again. This can be explained by the difficulties the tourism sector experienced as a result of the international economic downturn in the early 1980s, which deeply affected the Netherlands (van der Cammen & de Klerk, 2012). Terschelling was particularly affected because island tourism was sensitive to the business cycle. Tourism entrepreneurs argued at the time (the 1980s) that the municipality should create better opportunities for the tourism sector to expand and modernize. Terschelling had not been able to adapt to a changing tourism market, and innovation had stalled due to national and local government policies of the 1970s.

After a slow economic recovery during the 1980s, a reorientation towards nature protection around 1990 is visible in the data. This reorientation can be attributed to a worldwide shift towards an environmental discourse in which sustainability was a core concept. The Brundtland Report (World Commission on Environment and Development [WCED], 1987), the United Nations Conference on Environment and Development (or 'Earth Summit'), which was held in Rio de Janeiro in 1992, and its outputs (notably the Rio Declaration and Agenda 21), were important milestones at the international level. At the local level, this sustainability thinking was clearly implemented in the 1989 Landscape Policy Plan of Terschelling. The emphasis on a shift in thinking was highlighted in many quarters:

> The policy of the municipality and the attitude of the entrepreneurs on Terschelling must change in the coming years in order to ensure a good future for Terschelling.
>
> (*Leeuwarder Courant*, April 12, 1988)

The most recent period (2005–2014) can be characterized as a period of thinking in terms of synergies. The newspaper quote below is an example of the acknowledgment of synergies:

Nature and economy can go hand in hand very well.

(*Leeuwarder Courant*, June 27, 2009)

Immediately before the latest increase in synergetic thinking, the Meijer Report (2004) was published. It proposed an integrated vision for the Wadden in which sustainable protection and development should occur together, with priority given to 'nature with human co-use.' Thinking in terms of synergies, however, is not just something that has occurred recently, as is witnessed by earlier periods when attention was given to it, often followed by decline. In the beginning of the 1960s, there was an early awareness on the islands that, although tourism was an important economic activity, it must not harm the landscape. Around 1974, awareness grew that it might be necessary to curtail the growth of tourism.

In the last ten years or so, there has been a strong increase in interest in synergies. The newspaper quote below emphasizes this by stating that nature and tourism and recreation cannot be seen as detached from each other and, with stakeholder consultation, can be combined.

> It should not be forgotten that in many places recreation is possible because of the presence of nature. Nature is the very basis of recreation! This notion becomes increasingly obvious for those involved. Proper management of nature requires a lot of consultation. Practice shows that, if this is the case, many activities can be combined with each other quite well.
>
> (*Leeuwarder Courant*, April 3, 2010)

Conclusion

Our chapter contributes to resilience thinking and SES thinking, as it assists in understanding the institutional context for managing tourism–landscape interactions. We demonstrated how content analysis can be used to help understand the institutional context in which decision-making about the future takes place. The extent and arbitrary nature of the fluctuation in usage of the discourses of socio-economic development and nature protection suggests that this fluctuation is not the result of intended and deliberate policy interventions, but rather that the institutional context is constantly adapting to changing circumstances. Our analysis of the institutional context contributes to a better understanding of the mechanisms that build the resilience of social–ecological systems.

Our analysis showed that the way people think about the interactions between tourism development and landscape protection on Terschelling has been fluctuating over time. It revealed that, during the period 1945 to 2015, thinking in socio-economic terms was important in the development of tourism and landscape on the island. The way people think about nature is heavily determined by the up-and-down swings of the business cycle. This implies short-term thinking where, for example, in times of economic downturn, nature protection become less important. This seems to fit with Maslow's (1948) hierarchy of needs, with nature protection being a higher order need that will come to the forefront only when more basic needs are fulfilled. Nevertheless, we also found that thinking about nature protection was predominant at some points in our time period. It is important to note here that these changes in public thinking were often influenced by external (and often macro) triggers, when caring for nature, landscape, and the environment was brought to people's attention.

By analysing the informal historical institutional context, our analysis also shows that thinking in terms of synergies has been increasing over the last few years. Although the acknowledgment of synergies fluctuates, overall we can observe that the general trend is upwards. In our results, we found that the factors that largely determine the overall increase in synergies thinking relate to collaboration, working together, and being involved. Also, the current frequent use of the word 'sustainability' contributes to the recent increase in the number of newspaper articles coded as synergies. While synergies remain limited compared to the emphases on tourism development and nature protection, the upward trend offers promise. Synergies, however, are not a recent phenomenon. Our analysis showed that thinking about synergies also occurred in earlier times. We can conclude that a historical approach assists in understanding that synergies develop in a cyclical way and are influenced by the vagaries of time.

Our content analysis of newspaper articles has proved to be a valuable tool for identifying changes in thinking in the public discourse on tourism and landscape interactions over time. It helped identify the way people think about tourism development and landscape protection and how this has changed over time. We used content analysis of newspaper articles as a proxy for the institutional context. The added value of content analysis is that it can be done in a rigorous and transparent manner over a long timeframe. This sets content analysis apart from research methods such as interviewing, because content analysis goes beyond the availability of people to interview, and overcomes the changes in their perceptions that may occur over time. Content analysis, therefore, is helpful in understanding the historical institutional context, although subsequent interviews are helpful in validating and interpreting the data.

We have three suggestions for policy makers and planners. First, tourism development and landscape protection have potential for synergies between them. Nevertheless, policy makers need to be aware that achieving these synergies is not easy. We showed that thinking about synergies has fluctuated considerably over time. Furthermore, it is clear that it takes time for policy measures aimed at promoting synergies to become effective. Second, to gain insights into the current institutional context, it is important to take past trajectories into account and to consider how they have evolved over time. Third, knowledge that is gained from content analysis of historical newspaper articles, or similar textual materials, can be a helpful and effective tool to systematically reveal past patterns that have shaped the current situation. Ultimately, through greater awareness of the institutional context, policy makers will be able to develop policy and strategies that lead to greater resilience and sustainability.

References

Adger, W.N. (2000). Social and ecological resilience: Are they related? *Progress in Human Geography*, *24*(3), 347–364.

Alexander, E.R. (2005). Institutional transformation and planning: From institutionalization theory to institutional design. *Planning Theory*, *4*(3), 209–223.

Anderies, J., Janssen, M., & Ostrom, E. (2004). A framework to analyze the robustness of social–ecological systems from an institutional perspective. *Ecology and Society*, *9*(1), Art. 18 [online]. Retrieved from www.ecologyandsociety.org/vol.9/iss1/art18/.

Berkes, F. (2007). Understanding uncertainty and reducing vulnerability: Lessons from resilience thinking. *Natural Hazards*, *41*(2), 283–295.

Biggs, D. (2011). Understanding resilience in a vulnerable industry: The case of reef tourism in Australia. *Ecology and Society*, *16*(1), Art. 30 [online]. Retrieved from www.ecologyandsociety.org/vol.16/iss1/art30/.

Brondizio, E.S., Ostrom, E., & Young, O.R. (2009). Connectivity and the governance of multilevel social–ecological systems: The role of social capital. *Annual Review of Environment and Resources*, *34*(1), 253–278.

Buckley, R. (2011). Tourism and environment. *Annual Review of Environment and Resources*, *36*(1), 397–416.

Carpenter, S.R., Westley, F., & Turner, G. (2005). Surrogates for resilience of social–ecological systems. *Ecosystems*, *8*(8), 941–944.

Carson, R. (1962). *Silent spring*. Boston, MA: Houghton Mifflin Harcourt.

Choi, S., Lehto, X.Y., & Morrison, A.M. (2007). Destination image representation on the web: Content analysis of Macau travel related websites. *Tourism Management*, *28*(1), 118–129.

Cumming, G.S., Cumming, D.H.M., & Redman, C.L. (2006). Scale mismatches in social–ecological systems: Causes, consequences, and solutions. *Ecology and Society*, *11*(1), Art. 14 [Online]. Retrieved from www.ecologyandsociety.org/vol.11/iss1/art14/.

Davidson, D.J. (2010). The applicability of the concept of resilience to social systems: Some sources of optimism and nagging doubts. *Society and Natural Resources*, *23*(12), 1135–1149.

Davoudi, S., Brooks, E., & Mehmood, A. (2013). Evolutionary resilience and strategies for climate adaptation. *Planning Practice and Research*, *28*(3), 307–322.

Derissen, S., Quaas, M.F., & Baumgartner, S. (2011). The relationship between resilience and sustainability of ecological–economic systems. *Ecological Economics*, *70*(6), 1121–1128.

Drisko, J.W., & Maschi, T. (2015). *Content analysis*. Oxford: Oxford University Press.

Espiner, S., & Becken, S. (2014). Tourist towns on the edge: Conceptualising vulnerability and resilience in a protected area tourism system. *Journal of Sustainable Tourism*, *22*(4), 37–41.

Folke, C., Carpenter, S.R., Walker, B., Scheffer, M., Chapin, T., & Rockström, J. (2010). Resilience thinking: Integrating resilience, adaptability and transformability. *Ecology and Society*, *15*(4), Art. 20 [online]. Retrieved from www.ecologyandsociety.org/vol.15/iss4/art20/.

Gläser, J., & Laudel, G. (2013). Life with and without coding: Two methods for early-stage data analysis in qualitative research aiming at causal explanations. *Forum: Qualitative Social Research*, *14*(2), Art. 5 [online]. Retrieved from http://nbn-resolving.de/urn:nbn:de:0114-fqs130254.

González, J., Montes, C., Rodriguez, J., & Tapia, W. (2008). Rethinking the Galapagos Islands as a complex social–ecological system: Implications for conservation and management. *Ecology and Society*, *13*(2), Art. 13 [online]. Retrieved from www.ecologyandsociety.org/vol.13/iss2/art13/.

Hartman, S., & De Roo, G. (2013). Towards managing nonlinear regional development trajectories. *Environment and Planning C: Government and Policy*, *31*(3), 556–570.

Helmke, G., & Levitsky, S. (2004). Informal institutions and comparative politics: A research agenda. *Perspectives on Politics*, *2*(4), 725–740.

Heslinga, J.H., Groote, P.D., & Vanclay, F. (2017). Using a social–ecological systems perspective to understand tourism and landscape interactions in coastal areas. *Journal of Tourism Futures*, *3*(1), 23–38.

Hodgson, G.M. (2006). What are institutions? *Journal of Economic Issues*, *40*(1), 1–25.

Hoekstra, H., Zijlstra, E., Zwart, F., Smit-Zwanenburg, E., & Kok, J.P. (2009). *Een eeuw badgasten: een beeld van 100 jaar toerisme op Terschelling* [*A century of bathers: An overview of 100 years of tourism on Terschelling*]. Terschelling-West, Netherlands: Isola Arte.

Holling, C.S. (2008). Theories for sustainable futures. *Conservation Ecology*, *4*(2), Art. 7 [online]. Retrieved from www.consecol.org/vol.4/iss2/art7/.

Imperiale, A.J., & Vanclay, F. (2016). Experiencing local community resilience in action: Learning from post-disaster communities. *Journal of Rural Studies*, *47*, 204–219.

Kabat, P., Bazelmans, J., van Dijk, J., Herman, P.M.J., van Oijen, T., Pejrup, M., … Wolff, W.J. (2012). The Wadden Sea Region: Towards a science for sustainable development. *Ocean and Coastal Management*, *68*(2012), 4–17.

King, B., Pizam, A., & Milman, A. (1993). Social impacts of tourism. *Annals of Tourism Research*, *20*(4), 650–665.

Knottnerus, O.S. (2005). History of human settlement, cultural change and interference with the marine environment. *Helgoland Marine Research*, *59*(1), 2–8.

Krippendorff, K. (2013). *Content analysis: An introduction to its methodology* (3rd ed.). Thousand Oaks, CA: Sage.

Lebel, L., Anderies, J.M., Campbell, B., Folke, C., Hatfield-Dodds, S., Hughes, T P., & Wilson, J. (2006). Governance and the capacity to manage resilience in regional social–ecological systems. *Ecology and Society*, *11*(1), Art. 19 [online]. Retrieved from www.ecologyandsociety.org/vol.11/iss1/art19.

Lew, A.A. (2014). Scale, change and resilience in community tourism planning. *Tourism Geographies*, *16*(1), 14–22.

Libosada, C.M. (2009). Business or leisure? Economic development and resource protection – Concepts and practices in sustainable ecotourism. *Ocean and Coastal Management*, *52*(7), 390–394.

Liburd, J.J., & Becken, S. (2017). Values in nature conservation, tourism and UNESCO World Heritage Site stewardship. *Journal of Sustainable Tourism*, *25*(12), 1719–1735.

Liu, J., Dietz, T., Carpenter, S.R., Alberti, M., Folke, C., Moran, E., … Taylor, W.W. (2007). Complexity of coupled human and natural systems. *Science*, *317*(5844), 1513–1516.

Lowenthal, D. (2015). *The past is a foreign country – Revisited*. Cambridge, UK: Cambridge University Press.

Luthe, T., & Wyss, R. (2014). Assessing and planning resilience in tourism. *Tourism Management*, *44*, 161–163.

McCombes, L., Vanclay, F., & Evers, Y. (2015). Putting social impact assessment to the test as a method for implementing responsible tourism practice. *Environmental Impact Assessment Review*, *55*, 156–168.

McCool, S., & Spenceley, A. (2014). Tourism and protected areas: A growing nexus of challenge and opportunity. *Koedoe, 56*(2), 1–2.

Maslow, A.H. (1948). "Higher" and "lower" needs. *The Journal of Psychology: Interdisciplinary and Applied, 25*(1948), 433–436.

Meadows, D.H., Meadows, D.L., Randers, J., & Behrens, W.W. (1972). *The limits to growth: A report for the Club of Rome's project on the predicament of mankind*. New York: Universe Books.

Meijer, W., Lodders-Elfferich, P., and Hermans, L. (2004). *Ruimte voor de Wadden: eindrapport adviesgroep waddenzeebeleid* [*Space for the Wadden: Final report of the advisory group for Wadden Sea policy*].

Municipality of Terschelling (2014). *Ontwikkeling aantal overnachtingen op jaarbasis Terschelling* [*Development of annual amount of overnight stays on Terschelling*].

Municipality of Terschelling (2016). *Toeristenaantallen per jaar vanaf 1973 (inclusief EVT)* [*Amount of tourist arrivals per year from 1973 (including Eigen Vervoer Terschelling shipping company)*].

Ostrom, E. (2009). A general framework for analyzing sustainability of social–ecological systems. *Science, 325*(5939), 419–422.

Ostrom, E., & Cox, M. (2010). Moving beyond panaceas: A multi-tiered diagnostic approach for social–ecological analysis. *Environmental Conservation, 37*(4), 451–463.

Pahl-Wostl, C. (2009). A conceptual framework for analysing adaptive capacity and multi-level learning processes in resource governance regimes. *Global Environmental Change, 19*(3), 354–365.

Parra, C., & Moulaert, F. (2016). The governance of the nature–culture nexus: Lessons learned from the San Pedro de Atacama case-study. *Nature+Culture, 11*(3), 239–258.

Persha, L., Agrawal, A., & Chhatre, A. (2011). Social and ecological synergy. *Science, 331*(6024), 1606–1608.

Revier, H. (2013). Nature conservation and tourism development in the Dutch Wadden Sea region: A common future? In A. Postma, I. Yeoman, & J. Oskam (Eds.), *The future of European tourism* (pp. 177–193). Leeuwarden, Netherlands: European Tourism Futures Institute.

Saarinen, J. (2006). Traditions of sustainability in tourism studies. *Annals of Tourism Research, 33*(4), 1121–1140.

Sijtsma, F.J., Broersma, L., Daams, M.N., Hoekstra, H., & Werner, G. (2015). Tourism development in the Dutch Wadden Area: Spatial–temporal characteristics and monitoring needs. *Environmental Management and Sustainable Development, 4*(2), 217–241.

Sijtsma, F.J., Daams, M.N., Farjon, H., & Buijs, A.E. (2012). Deep feelings around a shallow coast. A spatial analysis of tourism jobs and the attractivity of nature in the Dutch Wadden area. *Ocean and Coastal Management, 68*, 138–148.

Terkenli, T.S. (2004). Tourism and landscape. In A.A. Lew, C.M. Hall, & A.M. Williams (Eds.), *A companion to tourism* (pp. 339–348). Oxford: Blackwell.

van der Aa, B.J.M., Groote, P.D., & Huigen, P.P.P. (2004). World heritage as NIBMY? The case of the Dutch part of the Wadden Sea. *Current Issues in Tourism, 7*(4–5), 291–302.

van der Cammen, H., & de Klerk, L. (2012). *The Selfmade land: Culture and evolution of urban and regional planning in the Netherlands*. Utrecht: Spectrum.

Vanclay, F., Baines, J., & Taylor, C.N. (2013). Principles for ethical research involving humans: Ethical professional practice in impact assessment Part I. *Impact Assessment and Project Appraisal, 31*(4), 243–253.

Walker, B., Holling, C.S., Carpenter, S.R., & Kinzig, A. (2004). Resilience, adaptability and transformability in social–ecological systems. *Ecology and Society*, *9*(2), Art. 5 [online]. Retrieved from www.ecologyandsociety.org/vol.9/iss2/art5/.

Wesley, A., & Pforr, C. (2010). The governance of coastal tourism: Unravelling the layers of complexity at Smiths Beach, Western Australia. *Journal of Sustainable Tourism*, *18*(6), 773–792.

Wilkinson, C. (2012). Social-ecological resilience: Insights and issues for planning theory. *Planning Theory*, *11*(2), 148–169.

Williams, S. (2009). *Tourism geography: A new synthesis* (2nd ed.). Abingdon, UK: Routledge.

World Commission on Environment and Development (WCED). (1987). *Our common future* (The Brundtland report). Oxford: Oxford University Press.

12 Revitalizing the nation

Building resilience through ecotourism in Okinawa, Japan

Sayaka Sakuma

Introduction

Standing in front of the tranquil Alps mountains in Switzerland in the Summer of 1991, a group of Japanese tourism operators and conservation advocates were bowled over by a bizarre approach to tourism. The event was covered in a major national newspaper, in an article titled 'No car and no golf: Nature Conservation Society of Japan visits Europe to learn ecotourism' (Asahi Shimbun, 1991). The Japanese group was surprised to learn that tourists visited this site in the Alps even though no cars were allowed. Even more shocking, there were no golf courses. Some of the tourism operators were deeply impressed by this visit and, on returning to Japan, advocated ecotourism as a national strategy. In the 1990s, some stakeholders sought to explore ways of developing tourism in Japan without transforming the landscape into golf courses and resort hotels. As tourism became one of the fastest growing industries in the world, the Japanese government was keen to incorporate the industry as a governance tool to support political, economic, and social stability. Today, the Abe administration repeatedly emphasizes the slogan, 'The country has no vigor without a vigorous countryside.' Various Japanese policies incorporate ecotourism to tackle the many problems confronting rural regions. In this context, many local and government leaders promote ecotourism as a sustainable approach to regional development.

Resilient destinations as a framework for sustainable tourism development

Crises are "moments of potential change" (Hall & Massey, 2010, p. 57). Events such as climate change, disasters, depopulation, and market fluctuation are examples of the variety of crises that impose both long- and short-term pressures on society. As resilience is "the capacity to buffer change, learn and develop" (Folke et al., 2002, p. 437), resilient destinations are better able to absorb social, political, and economic changes. Furthermore, the concept of resilience focuses on the connections between social and ecological systems. Efficient resilience-building enables society to adjust to adverse environmental conditions through flexibility and adaptability in the face of external pressures. Thus, the idea of resilient destinations draws attention to how tourism as a governance tool shapes a destination while responding to a wide range of crises.

For critical tourism scholars, mass tourism is linked with problems in host destinations that result from the feckless pursuit of capital accumulation. Mass tourism has often harmed the local environment by promoting uncontrolled influxes of capital and tourists (Trask, 1999). Arguing that mass tourism was always likely to become a global development strategy, Lück (2002, p. 373) writes, "it would be naïve to think that the ever growing tourism on this planet could be without mass tourism." In response to the resentment elicited by unchecked tourism, scholars have challenged how tourism management narrowly focuses on market-oriented goals. Scholars and tourism operators seek answers in various branches of the industry such as eco-, alternative, responsible, and community-based tourism. Critics view ecotourism as "mainly promoted not for the purposes of resource conservation but for marketing reasons" (Liu 2003, p. 471). They argue that ecotourism is just another avenue to expand the tourism market by introducing "the less-traveled road" (Honey, 2008, p. 443). At the same time, tourists will not stop travelling. New destinations are marketed as hidden gems, as tourists constantly share and post on social media with visual and geographical information. Ecotourism is contested yet continues to be a critical tool for mitigating the adverse impacts of tourism (Honey, 2008).

Linking the concepts of resilient destination and tourism as a tool for sustainable development, the following section examines how national and local government in Japan incorporated ecotourism as a development strategy. It further describes how crises emerged along with the rapid economic development in the country.

Building resilience through ecotourism in Japan

The path to the resort archipelago

Japan's post World War II economic growth fueled the growth of leisure industries, and tourism became an important agenda for policymakers. At the peak of Japan's so-called 'miraculous economic growth' in the 1980s, Prime Minister Yasuhiro Nakasone's administration proposed the Comprehensive Regional Resort Preparation Plan (henceforth, Resort Law) that situated resort development as a key mechanism for achieving national growth. The Resort Law paved a path for the country to designate significant areas for resort use, particularly golf courses. The Nakasone administration even touted the policy as helping to refashion Japan into a 'resort archipelago.' The plan to remodel the whole country from Hokkaido in the north to Okinawa in the south aspired to create "regions for fun, pleasure, recreation, and relaxation by bringing together local government and private enterprises" (Rimmer, 1992, p. 1608). This section discusses key features of the Resort Law that created the conditions for ecotourism to provide a symbolic departure towards a sustainable future.

The Resort Law was enacted in 1987 with three main objectives: (1) to support an affluent lifestyle for Japanese citizens; (2) to develop suburban and rural areas set apart from urban spaces; and (3) to stimulate domestic demand for leisure consumption. The first objective of promoting affluent lifestyles proved elusive given the long hours of Japanese workers. In 1985, laborers in the Japanese manufacturing industry averaged 2,168 hours of work per year compared to 1,900 hours in the US and the UK and 1,600 hours in France and western Germany (Kokudo Kōtsū Shō, 2003). Despite increasing disposable income, Japanese citizens were slow to develop more affluent habits of consumption. Long work hours and a cultural norm to avoid taking paid leave from work for vacation purposes hindered domestic tourism, as did the spiking of hotel prices during national holidays.

The second objective sought to contribute to regional development, primarily through private actors such as construction companies and developers. Government officials reasoned that since prefectures with higher dependency on public investment had less growth, investment in the private sector would help to stimulate growth (Kokudo Kōtsū Shō, 2003). To create opportunities for the private sector to participate in regional development, the government provided various incentives such as tax reduction and low-interest loans, as well as covering the costs of developing initial infrastructure such as roads and sewage systems (Funck, 1999). The Resort Law sought to stimulate development by increasing the construction of sports and recreational facilities. Furthermore, policymakers forecasted a ripple effect whereby construction would encourage additional tourism and real estate development.

Lastly, the third objective aspired to mitigate rising economic inequalities between rural and urban areas during the bubble economy. The income gap between urban and rural areas triggered population influxes into larger industrialized cities, further hampering economic conditions in rural areas. The government loosened environmental regulations and simplified administrative procedures to encourage developers to invest in potential tourism destinations (McCormack, 1991). Loosening land-use zoning restrictions enabled developers to convert forest land into resort areas. In large multiple resort facilities, investors and developers preferred to build golf courses (McCormack, 1991). The number of golf courses in Japan rose from less than 200 to over 400 during the 1960s and then to over 1,000 in the early 1970s (Yamada, 1990, p. 296). By 1990, there were 1,700 golf courses with a staggering 1,300 additional courses under construction or planned when the bubble burst (Yamada, 1990). The Resort Law facilitated a vision for the exponential growth of golf courses with little concern for adverse environmental or social impacts.

These three objectives indicate the state's active engagement in shaping the leisure industry in the countryside through massive resort developments. The Resort Law empowered prefectural governments to propose types of development, target areas, and development goals. The proposals were then reviewed by the national government. The government defined the ideal area of a resort as between 1,500 and 1,600 square kilometers with automobiles being the primary mode of transportation (Kokudo Kōtsū Shō, 2003). Prefectural government offices urged the national government to designate resort land, as each resort was expected to create an average of 5,300 new jobs. In 1991, more than four-fifths of prefectures applied for resort development, and these applications covered approximately 18 percent of Japan's total land area (Funck, 1999).

Severe environmental issues and land speculation resulted from the nationwide resort craze. Most golf courses were constructed by flattening mountains and filling valleys. In addition, golf courses were maintained through the extensive application of germicides, herbicides, and pesticides, which contaminated groundwater and dams (Yamada, 1990). A massive amount of fish was found killed or deformed in rivers and streams around golf courses, causing some to protest about the adverse impacts of golf courses on the environment (Yamada, 1990). Public opposition accompanied unrestricted development and enthusiasm waned as the prospects of the resort archipelago gave way to the broken promises of neoliberal regional development.

Five years after the Resort Law was enacted, the national government passed a bill that introduced limits and reigned in rampant resort development (Yaka, 1995). Between 2004 and 2011, the number of prefectures with schematic plans for resort development dropped from 41 to 29 and, by 2002, of approximately 9,000 planned resorts less than 2,000 were in operation (Kokudo Kōtsū Shō, 2011). As economic growth slowed, the idea of large resorts with golf courses faced serious scrutiny because of the ecological and economic costs incurred. The rise and fall of the Resort Law created the conditions in which ecotourism flourished as a sustainable alternative.

Rise of ecotourism and the Ecotourism Promotion Act

Ecotourism began in Japan in the early 1990s; the media introduced the concept in 1989, after the resort boom resulted in unsuccessful regional development. An article in the national newspaper *Asahi Shimbun* described how conservationists in Costa Rica struggled to balance ecotourism demand with nature preservation (Asahi Shimbun, 1989). The United Nations World Tourism Organization declared 2002 as International Year of Ecotourism, reflecting global concerns over natural resource management and the need to balance the use of natural resources in tourism activities. In 2004, Prime Minister Junichirō Koizumi announced Japan's intention to become a 'Tourism Nation.' Three years later, in 2007, the Japanese government enacted the Ecotourism Promotion Act, the first law defining ecotourism in Japan. The law sought to promote ecotourism activities as a strategy for economic and regional revitalization.

The Ecotourism Promotion Act frames the concept of ecotourism as a combination of experiencing and learning from unique natural environments, histories, and cultures. The official English translation of the act defines ecotourism as

> activities through which tourists receive guidance or advice from a person with knowledge on Natural Tourism Resources, come into contact with said Natural Tourism Resources, while giving consideration to the protection of

said Natural Tourism Resources, and deepen their knowledge and understanding thereof.

(Ministry of Justice, 2018)

This framework for ecotourism sought to create alternative forms of tourism from supply-driven resort development.

What did the Japanese government seek to achieve by establishing an ecotourism policy? At a basic level, the government sought to balance conservation and the use of natural resources. However, the government authorities, particularly the Ministry of the Environment (MOE), developed a broader set of goals from Japan's national ecotourism policy.

The Ministry of the Environment (MOE)

The MOE played a key role in establishing ecotourism policy by creating a framework for ecotourism. The policy aims to promote the concept and to create tour programs that provide monitoring and guidelines for balancing tourism activities with natural resource management. Between 2003 and 2004, the head of the MOE served as chairperson for the Ecotourism Promotion Meetings, at which various stakeholders worked to establish the country's first ecotourism policy. The meetings resulted in five initiatives to promote ecotourism: the creation of an Ecotourism Charter, an Ecotourism Award, Ecotourism Promotion Model Projects, a comprehensive list of ecotourism tours ('Ecotour Comprehensive'), and an Ecotourism Promotion Manual. I describe some of these approaches below.

Ecotourism Promotion Model Projects: The MOE conducted a three-year project between 2004 and 2006 by selecting 13 model project sites from 50 nationwide entries. The project identifies three categories for ecotourism: (1) activities in areas that are nature-rich (e.g., whale-watching, hiking); (2) activities in established tourism destinations with many visitors (e.g., climbing Mount Fuji); and (3) activities that utilize unique village characteristics such as its nature, culture, and local industries (e.g., harvesting farm products and cooking traditional cuisines).

Ecotourism Award: Since 2005, the MOE has made an annual Ecotourism Award to individuals, business operators, groups, and local municipalities. The aim of the award is to encourage competition among different stakeholders and the development of ecotourism networks. Award recipients often conduct research projects in addition to being tour operators. For example, 2005 Ecotourism Award recipients included tour operators that researched black bears in Nagano Prefecture and whales on Ogasawara Island. The first recipient of the award was Picchio, a tour operator that conducts hiking tours in forests that are inhabited by the Asian black bear, which the operator also studies. Picchio monitored the bears and developed a system that employed trained dogs to prevent them from encroaching on residential areas (Picchio, 2018). The second recipient of the Ecotourism Award was the Ogasawara Whale Watching Association, a tour operator that also researches humpback and sperm whales. The operator examined their distribution, migration, reproduction, and population and further developed voluntary rules for tour boats to maintain set speeds and distances from the whales (Ogasawara Whale Watching Association, 2018). Based on their studies, tour operators developed rules and guidelines to better monitor the environment and manage the impact of ecotourism. Between 2005 and 2017, the Japan Ecotourism Society announced 101 awards for tour operators nationwide (Japan Ecotourism Society, 2018).

Ecotourism Promotion Manual: The ministry developed this manual to explain the concept of ecotourism, the Ecotourism Promotion Act, and the process for becoming a designated ecotourism operator. The Ecotourism Promotion Manual consists of eight chapters designed to educate readers and facilitate ecotourism activities. The manual provides insights into topics such as strategies for promoting mutual understanding among various stakeholders, utilizing the law to help promote ecotourism activities, establishing rules for tour and natural resource management, and ensuring sustainable levels of tourism activities.

New Tourism Projects Program

While the MOE is responsible for the Ecotourism Promotion Act, the Ministry of Land, Infrastructure and Transport supports ecotourism through a number of programs including the Creation and Dissemination of New Tourism Projects Program (henceforth, New Tourism Program). Launched in 2007, the New Tourism Program promotes seemingly novel forms of tourism based on experiences for visitors that are generated through interactions with hosts. The orientation of this program departs from conventional package-based mass tourism. Ecotourism is one of five main categories of new tourism, the other categories being green tourism, cultural tourism, industrial tourism, and health tourism. The New Tourism Program features unique activities that were previously not associated with tourism such as knife-sharpening workshops and diabetes prevention tours. Between 2007 and 2009, the New Tourism Program funded 143 projects – of which 59 were ecotourism projects – to develop and monitor new tour activities (Ministry of Land, Infrastructure, Transport and Tourism, 2010). The program considers ecotourism to include activities such as farming, visiting remote islands, and hiking – a broad range that reflects the flexible definition of ecotourism.

A number of other ministries, including those that focus on agriculture and education, collaborate to promote exchange between urban and rural populations through a program titled 'Rural Area Exchange Project for Children,' which caters for school children. A central concern for the ministries is the rapid change wrought by reduced birthrates, urbanization, and the spread of information technology (Aichi and Moriyama, 2008). The government considers ecotourism to be part of a larger goal of encouraging the urban population to visit and ideally move to the countryside. A rising social problem in Japan is isolation from nature, because children live in urban environments where they cannot experience nature (Aichi and Moriyama, 2008). A lawmaker involved in creating the Ecotourism Promotion Act tells an anecdote in which a visiting urban student asked a farmer what is planted in a rice paddy. The lawmaker worries that future generations may even believe that fish exist as packaged fillet and be unaware of how fish swim in the water. Connecting ecotourism as part of a wider educational program, the law aspired to provide urban children with rural experiences that are unavailable through the internet or virtual reality devices.

Another goal of the New Tourism Program is to promote rural revitalization by bringing people to experience rural regions that are struggling with population decline and economic stagnation. The government believes that connecting concrete covered cities and mountainous farming villages furthers regional development for rural areas. These initiatives pour investment on hard infrastructure such as accommodation and educational facilities. Some programs even support the repair of abandoned houses to attract migrants. In rural communities, where the lack of workers and material resources poses a critical threat, hosting visitors is envisioned as a path for improving local livelihoods. In this manner, the government initiatives view ecotourism as a tool for socioeconomic development in the countryside. Ecotourism activities utilize the rural environment with the aim of attracting urban populations to the unique physical landscape and cultural activities of the countryside. While policymakers remain focused on the goal of encouraging urban tourists to travel to rural areas, they often overlook the impact of these programs on local politics and on ecology. Next, I examine how ecotourism plays out in unique geographical contexts, focusing on Higashi village in Okinawa Prefecture.

The case of Okinawa Prefecture

Okinawa Prefecture, known as the independent kingdom of Ryukyu until Japan annexed it in 1879, is a core resort destination in Japan today. This southernmost prefecture in Japan consists of 49 islands that are inhabited by 1.4 million people and is the country's only subtropical area. Tourism and marketing strategies often exploit Okinawa's history and culture to attract tourists. In 2002, the International Year of Ecotourism, Okinawa was chosen to host the International Conference on Ecotourism. The main theme was "the economic benefits of the ecotourism for islands or geographically isolated communities" (United Nations World Tourism Organization [UNWTO], 2018). As a remote island community, Okinawa incorporates ecotourism into local development schemes. This section introduces the case of Okinawa where a series of economic crises triggered a shift in local development strategies towards the incorporation of ecotourism as a strategy for building a more resilient economy. With the fall of investment-driven resort development, local government reassessed its resilience in the changing economy and sought to redefine the idea of development through smaller-scale and community-based tourism activities.

Although Japan experienced nationwide construction of the resort archipelago during the 1980s, construction of resorts was nothing new in Okinawa. After 27 years of US occupation following World War II, Okinawa reverted to Japanese control in 1972, which created a "new tourism frontier" (Yaka, 1993). Following reversion, the number of tourists doubled as Okinawa debuted as Japan's prime coastal resort destination. Policymakers in Okinawa saw tourism as an ideal alternative to replace the US military economy. Prefectural officials considered Okinawa to be behind national development and saw tourism as its main economic pillar. The Resort Law meshed with these goals, and the central government approved the 'Okinawa Tropical Resort Plan' in 1991, causing developers to view the entire prefecture as a tropical resort (Rimmer, 1992). The plan marked most of the southern part of Okinawa Island as core resort sites; it assigned the southern coastal region as the main area with multiple resort functions and transportation infrastructure. A "regional resort core" in the plan designated the northern part of Okinawa Island and two neighboring islands of Miyako and Yaeyama (Yaka, 1995). Under the plan the national government approved the creation of 13 golf courses, 163 tennis courts, six marinas, five sports gyms, and 30 pools (Yaka, 1995).

With the goals of reducing dependence on public finance (Yaka, 2002) and catching up with economic development in Japan, resort development seemed to promise the economic growth longed for in post-war Okinawa. Creating the tropical resort island, often referred to as 'Japan's Hawaii,' meant becoming a part of the wider tourism market in Japan. The identity of Okinawa as a Tourism Prefecture thus discursively and materially began to be marked with hotels and golf courses that paved the way for tourism development.

From hoe to oar: pineapple crisis and the rise of ecotourism in Higashi Village, Okinawa

During an interview, former village officer Sadao Yamashiro talked about the introduction of ecotourism in Higashi, Okinawa. Raising his voice, he said, "Are we going to wait till we die naturally, or will we take action?" As one of the most remote places on Okinawa Island, Higashi village took a circuitous route to develop its current reputation as a mecca of ecotourism. Political and economic crises shifted the village's industry from timber to pineapple and later to ecotourism, reflecting global and national trends. This section examines the case of Higashi village in northern Okinawa Island to illustrate how a rural village sought opportunities for development in ecotourism.

A historical Okinawan-language poem by an unknown author describes the northern area as follows: "a pitiful place with nowhere to view." The abundance of nature was depicted as nothing of value; as the poem complains, "wherever you go, there is only ocean and mountain." The forest is populated with many endemic and endangered species. Since forest-land captures rainfall, Higashi serves as the main water source for the rest of the island. Fourteen rivers run through Higashi and there are mangrove areas where the river mouths meet the ocean.

The village's population has continued to decline over recent decades and decreased by 8 percent between 2005 and 2015 (from 1,873 to 1,721) (Okinawa

Prefecture, 2016). Having 152 fewer people in a decade has far reaching impacts on the community. Furthermore, the number of school students (elementary and middle school) dropped from 335 in 1986 to 146 in 2016 (Higashi Village Government, 2016). The declining population is tied to a lack of employment opportunities that attract younger families. The gradual decline in economic opportunities casts uncertainty over Higashi's future.

Former village officer Yamashiro describes how, five decades ago, the village consisted mostly of farming and remote settlements. It lacked the basic infrastructure required to attract other industries to relocate their factories. This status as 'have-nots' led the village to continually pursue economic development. The village's main industry before World War II stood on a fragile foundation of forestry, and materials to reconstruct the island's steps that were destroyed during the Battle of Okinawa created a temporary demand for forest timber. However, after the timber market tightened, the village sought to promote pineapple production as a cash crop. The acidic Kunigami gravel soil is suitable for pineapple production. The crop is also resilient in spite of Okinawa's harsh weather conditions, such as droughts and typhoons. As the northern part of Okinawa Island is the only area covered by the red soil, the village became the largest pineapple producer in the country. The lucrative cash crop, which gave the village good fortune, was called the 'fruit of life' because it was the main agricultural product. Aside from pineapple production, in 1977 the village began a project to plant 50,000 azalea flowers on the mountainsides that were unsuitable for pineapple production due to their steep slopes. From elementary students to elders, the village mobilized to plant a future tourism attraction and the azalea park was finally completed six years later in 1983.

Although some were not convinced that visitors would come to see such flowers, Yamashiro recalled how the project brought people together while planting the seedlings, and he described the flower park as "a new dawn for interactions." The flower park became a landmark festival connecting Higashi with visitors from distant urban areas. Despite doubts concerning outside interest, Higashi experienced a rush of visitors with the launch of the azalea park. Hosting visitors suddenly became imaginable, and the success of the azalea park seemed to promise a bright future for the villagers.

Higashi was one of many rural areas that pursued tourism development as Japan was turning into a resort archipelago during the 1980s. As described above, the Resort Law launched plans to designate almost 20 percent of national land as resort land with extensive resort planning that contributed to spiraling land speculation (Okada, 2010). In Higashi, plans for large resort developments including a hotel with 300 rooms and golf courses, which were expected to bring about prolonged growth. However, the economic bubble burst and along with it the plans for developing resorts in the village. Although many in Higashi were disappointed, ironically, the village benefited by avoiding the damaging craze for resort development. Other larger municipalities with the capacity to invest in the private sector approved large resort developments, but this often led to serious financial issues. For example, Miyazaki and Hokkaido both supported rapid resort development only to suffer through many bankruptcies in the 2000s.

Another critical turning point occurred in 1990 with the General Agreement on Tariffs and Trade (GATT) Uruguay Round. Japan agreed to expand the import of many agricultural products including pineapple, signaling a threat to Higashi village's main industry. The Minister of Agriculture, Forestry, and Fisheries, as well as the Minister of State for Okinawa and Northern Territories Affairs, conducted multiple trips to Higashi with the promise that they would support the village to "survive into the twenty-first century" (interview with Yamashiro, 2017). For Yamashiro, who was an officer in the village government at the time of pineapple crisis, this was the moment to embrace a resilient course of action.

He began by allocating money from the government budget to an unexpected item, canoes. In 1994, Yamashiro used the village government budget to purchase six canoes, an unheard of expenditure for a municipal government in Okinawa. He laughed as he recalled the consequences of purchasing the canoes. His superiors sought to punish Yamashiro for such rash expenditure by reassigning him to a different position on the village Board of Education. Yamashiro was still able to resourcefully make use of the canoes by launching canoeing classes for the public – a form of public education. While he acknowledged that the village lacked the type of resources found in other parts of the island, he also perceived that the village took its environmental diversity and beauty for granted. With visitors to the village increasing, Higashi villagers began to reimagine their identity as being about more than just farming. Embracing ecotourism helped to strengthen the village's resilience because it was better able to manage the trajectory of ecotourism, unlike past experiences with resort planning and pineapple markets that were controlled by external economic factors.

The village government is currently working on a set of projects to create 'a farming village for interaction' (*kōryū-gata nōson*). Higashi village government has conducted workshops for villagers to enable them to recognize local resources on the ground, using the slogan 'Making rocks on the ground into diamonds.' This expression is intended to encourage villagers to appreciate the value of the natural resources and activities they take for granted. The villagers' everyday activities and landscape that they may not believe to be special may hold great meaning for visitors. By incorporating tourists' desire to experience rural life as a development strategy, Higashi has embarked on a path to reinvent the village as a place for environmental and cultural education.

Yamashiro played an important role as a government officer, going to study ecotourism in countries such as Australia and the US where the concept of ecotourism is already accepted as a development tool. A series of government plans, associations, and workshops sought to transform the villagers and their homes into hosts. For example, Higashi established Okinawa's first ecotourism association in 1998. The village also launched the Blue Tourism Association in 2000 to promote programs including kayak fishing, boat fishing, diving, snorkeling, stand-up paddle yoga, and other types of marine activities (Higashi Village Tour Guide, 2018). In 2005, Higashi combined various associations to become the Higashi Village Tourism Promotion Association. The village continued to utilize government subsidies to support ecotourism by building a ten-hectare mangrove park (Hirugi Park) replete with interpreter guides and guidebooks. The park was built around Gesashi Bay where Rhizophorales trees form the largest mangrove forest on the island. Tour companies provide programs such as canoeing and walking tours for visitors at the park. The Japanese government designated the mangrove as a natural monument in 1972 and, later, as Yambaru National Park in 2016.

By developing both physical tourism infrastructure and human resources, Higashi village is now as one of the largest host villages in the Okinawa Prefecture. The initiatives to utilize its natural environment for tourism have made Higashi a popular destination for Japanese students from other prefectures, who visit the village as part of the national education curriculum. Schools, mainly from urban areas such as Tokyo and Osaka, arrange for students to participate in the village's homestay program. Students who participate in the canoeing program receive an hour of orientation – learning about paddling, the vegetation, and unique species – before they finally get to experience paddling with their oars. Interpreter guides lead groups of canoes, pointing out plants and creatures in the mangrove (Okinawa Prefecture, 2001). After the village hosted its first group of school students in 1998, the number of school groups continued to increase, reaching 350 schools in 2010. Villagers, particularly farmers, began to host students at their houses after becoming authorized host families by passing legal requirements to register their house as tourist accommodation. The obligations of authorized host families include passing a fire inspection, putting in place safety precautions, and supervising visiting students. Families host four to five students for one or two nights, providing experiences such as cooking traditional dishes and farming. Host families are encouraged to attend workshops on topics such as food poisoning prevention and Okinawan traditional cuisine. The number of students staying with host families in Higashi increased from 75 in 2002 (Yamashiro, 2012) to 10,000 in 2011 (Okinawa Prefecture, 2013). Today, residents who work as hosts (e.g., tour guides, host families, workers at restaurants and small inns) receive direct profits from tourism activities, which motivates younger generations to return to or remain in their own community. The village of 'have nots' found a way to respond to a series of external crises and build internal capacity by investing in a more resilient economic foundation. Indeed, who would have thought "a village without a convenience store" (interview with Yamashiro, 2017) would become a popular site for experiencing the virtues of rural life?

Discussion

Being a 'resilient destination' does not mean that Higashi is a perfect host community. In fact, Higashi village has faced new sets of challenges since the village became known as a successful case of utilizing rural tourism as a development strategy. For example, visitors at the mangrove park drastically increased from 100 people in 1998 to 45,000 in 2000 (Okinawa Prefecture, 2001, p. 42). Tour guides and village leaders have sought to develop guidelines for balanced use and protection of the environment. Higashi now faces competition from tour groups on different parts of the island and an increasing number of visitors. Having too many visitors stretches the capacity of tour operators to instruct them on how to properly use the site and its ecosystem. Some tour guides criticize private companies for prioritizing profits at the expense of collaborative strategies to manage natural resources, a dynamic that in their words turns ecotourism into 'egotourism.'

Even though the national government tried to provide a legal framework for promoting ecotourism, the goal of using it to build resilience materialized through a haphazard process. When Higashi village received an Ecotourism Award in 2005, the village had already long understood the potential of branding its natural environment and the challenges of balancing tourism and natural resource management. In the case of Higashi village, the development of ecotourism was shaped by a group of villagers who were concerned about the village's future prospects and sought to draw on its untapped natural resources. Even though a core group of villagers helped to establish ecotourism in Higashi, they recognize that other rural regions are responding to different circumstances and may depend on attracting factories or other industries.

Rather than viewing the ecotourism industry in Higashi as an isolated occurrence, its rise in the village reflects the wider political economy of the tourism industry in Japan. The unique historical, political, and geographical contexts of the region shaped decision-making at the local level and enabled Higashi to build resilience through ongoing responses to everyday challenges. Ecotourism happened to match villagers' interests in nurturing the environment, and emerged through the village's ability to adapt. Continual trials and flexible responses led individuals to create new ways of tackling the challenges of changing socioeconomic conditions. Villagers' passion, creativity, and resilience resulted in ecotourism as a tool for revitalization to emerge.

Conclusion

This chapter laid out the historical development of ecotourism as a tool for achieving sustainable tourism in the context of Japan. The following factors enabled Higashi to develop as a resilient destination. First, the failure of large-scale resort development created the circumstances in which ecotourism could flourish. The Resort Law exemplifies the adverse consequences of massive neoliberal development schemes. The national government failed to empower local governments to manage development strategies. Furthermore, the Resort Law overlooked the importance of local contexts and the different development goals each region may hold. With the rise and fall of resort projects, ecotourism emerged as a viable strategy in some regional contexts.

Second, the Japanese government embraced ecotourism as a national strategy to promote both environmental conservation and economic development. The government employed various initiatives to connect an expanding urban population with declining rural communities. By doing so, ecotourism policy made rural regions available for urban citizens to gain authentic experiences of rural life. However, host communities have struggled to reignite their economic engine and sense of pride by hosting tourists. In the context of Japan, the Ecotourism Promotion Act attempts to achieve both rural revitalization and ecological preservation. With growing concerns over weakening regional economies, policymakers provided subsidies and promotional support for various tourism activities. However, the policy continues to overlook ecological disturbances. While the Ecotourism Promotion Act provides a framework that caters to rural revitalization, the policy is not designed to solve environmental conservation issues that vary place by place.

Lastly, the case study of Higashi village illustrates how a rural village experienced external changes that threatened the survival of its community. The case also describes how the village incorporated ecotourism to redefine its remoteness as a new resource. What urban residents once described as a piteous place to visit is now admired for its abundant nature and rich culture. Ecotourism has provided opportunities for villagers to raise questions about the sustainability of their own community. A renewed appreciation of nature enabled villagers to recognize that they had overlooked valuable resources as mere 'rocks on the ground.' The villagers employ ecotourism as a source of resiliency that strengthens their "capacity to buffer change, learn and develop" (Folke et al. 2002, p. 437). Examining the concept of resilient destinations requires an acknowledgment of geographical and temporal contexts. Instead of viewing certain forms of tourism as a panacea, we need to carefully consider the conjunctures that enable tourism to serve as a tool for a better form of development.

References

Aichi, K., & Moriyama, M. (2008). *cotsūrizumu suishin hō no kaisetsu* [*Instruction for Ecotourism Promotion Act*]. Tokyo: Gyosei.

Asahi Shimbun. (1989, June 13). kankyō hozen e saimu katagawari shizen hogo to ruiseki saimu tokushū [Nature swap for conservation].

Asahi Shimbun. (1991, September 30). kuruma wa shimedashi gorufu dame: nihon shizen hogo kyōkai ga ōshū ekotsūrizumu shisatsu [No car and no golf: Nature Conservation Society of Japan visits Europe to learn ecotourism].

Folke, C., Carpenter, S., Elmqvist, T., Gunderson, L., Holling, C.S., & Walker, B. (2002). Resilience and sustainable development: Building adaptive capacity in a world of transformations. *AMBIO: A Journal of the Human Environment, 31*(5), 437–440 [Online]. doi: 10.1579/0044-7447-31.5.437.

Funck, C. (1999). When the bubble burst: Planning and reality in Japan's resort industry. *Current Issues in Tourism, 2*, 333–353 [online]. doi: 10.1080/13683509908667860.

Hall, S., & Massey, D. (2010). Interpreting the crisis. *Soundings, 44*, 57–71 [online]. Retrieved from www.lwbooks.co.uk/sites/default/files/s44_06hall_massey.pdf.

Higashi Village Government. (2016). Higashi son sonsei yōran shiryō hen [Higashi village data book].

Higashi Village Tour Guide. (2018) (http://higashi-kanko.jp/).

Honey, M. (2008). *Ecotourism and sustainable development: Who owns paradise?* Washington, DC: Island Press.

Japan Ecotourism Society. (2018). daiikkai ecotsūrizumu taishō kekka happyō 2005 [The first Ecotourism Award results in 2005]. Retrieved from www.ecotourism.gr.jp/.

Kokudo Kōtsū Shō [Ministry of Land, Infrastructure, Transport and Tourism]. (2003). sōgō hoyō chīki no seibi. rizōto hō no konnichi teki kōsatsu [Condition of resort area: discussion on Resort Law].

Kokudo Kōtsū Shō [Ministry of Land, Infrastructure, Transport and Tourism]. (2011). sōgō hoyō chīki seibi hō ni motozuku kihon kōsō oyobi tokutei chīki [Basic planning and special regions based on Development of Comprehensive Resort Areas Act].

Liu, Z. (2003). Sustainable tourism development: A critique. *Journal of Sustainable Tourism, 11*(6), 459–475 [online]. doi: 10.1080/09669580308667216.

Lück, M. (2002). Looking into the future of ecotourism and sustainable tourism. *Current Issues in Tourism, 5*(3–4), 371–374 [online]. doi: 10.1080/13683500208667930.

McCormack, G. (1991, July–August). The price of affluence: The political economy of Japanese leisure. *New Left Review*, 1/188.

Ministry of Justice. (2018). Ordinance for Enforcement of the Ecotourism Promotion Act. Retrieved from www.japaneselawtranslation.go.jp/law/detail/?id=2615&vm=04&re=01.

Ministry of Land, Infrastructure, Transport and Tourism. (2010). sankō shiryō: nyū tsūrizumu sōshin ryūtsū sokushin zigyō ni tsuite [Prototype projects on the creation and distribution of New Tourism projects].

Ogasawara Whale Watching Association. (2018). Research and rules. Retrieved from www.owa1989.com/english.

Okada, I. (2010). rizōto hō to chīki shakai [Law on Development of Comprehensive Resort Areas and its effect on local communities]. *kenkyu kiyō, 17*, 135–143.

Okinawa Prefecture. (2001). okinawa kōhō-shi chura shima [Okinawa prefectural magazine *Chura Shima*].

Okinawa Prefecture. (2013). fukki 40 shū nen kinen jigyō uchinā chīki zukuri jirei shisaku shū [Fortieth anniversary issue on community development case studies and projects in Okinawa].

Okinawa Prefecture. (2016). heisei 27 nen kokusei chōsa sokuhō okinawa ken no jinkō setaisū [2017 national census report: Demography in Okinawa Prefecture].

Picchio. (2018). Bear conservation: Activities and goals for the conservation of the Asian black bear. Retrieved from https://picchio.co.jp/.

Rimmer, P.J. (1992). Japan's "resort archipelago": Creating regions of fun, pleasure, relaxation, and recreation. *Environment and Planning A, 24*, 1599–1625.

Trask, H.-K. (1999). *From a native daughter: Colonialism and sovereignty in Hawai'i.* Honolulu, HI: University of Hawai'i Press.

World Tourism Organization (UNWTO). (2018). International Year of Ecotourism (2002). Retrieved from http://sdt.unwto.org/en/content/international-year-ecotourism-2002.

Yaka, M. (1993). okinawa ni okeru rizōto kaihatsu (sono 1) [Resort development in Okinawa No. 1]. Hosei Daigaku Kyoyobu Kiyo [Bulletin of the Faculty of Letters, Hosei University], 87. Retrieved from http://repo.lib.hosei.ac.jp/bitstream/10114/3666/1/kyoyo87_yaka.pdf.

Yaka, M. (1995). okinawa ni okeru rizōto kaihatsu (sono 2) [Resort development in Okinawa no. 2]. Hosei Daigaku Kyoyobu Kiyo [Bulletin of the Faculty of Letters, Hosei University]. Retrieved from http://repo.lib.hosei.ac.jp/bitstream/10114/3682/1/kyoyo94_yaka.pdf.

Yaka, M. (2002). The direction of leisure industry promotion in Okinawa (Bulletin of the Faculty of Letters, Hosei University). Retrieved from http://repo.lib.hosei.ac.jp/bitstream/10114/1681/1/J-yaka.pdf.

Yamada, K. (1990). The triple evils of golf courses. *Japan Quarterly*, *37*, 291 [Online]. Retrieved from http://eres.library.manoa.hawaii.edu/login?url=https://search-proquest-com.eres.library.manoa.hawaii.edu/docview/234910584?accountid=27140.

Yamashiro, S. (2012). kōryū gata nōson ni yoru sangyō okoshi: chīsana mura no ōkina chōsen (tokushū fukki 40 nen wo koete chīki shigen no sangyō-ka ni mukau okinawa) [Development of industry by farming village: Big challenge by a small village]. *Chīki Kaihatsu*, *573*, 8–12.

Part IV
Conclusions

13 Conclusions

Challenges and opportunities in the transition towards sustainability

Alison M. Gill and Jarkko Saarinen

Introduction

The lack of progress in implementing the variously interpreted 'grand' concept of sustainability has resulted in increasing calls to divert the discourse surrounding sustainability and adopt more transitional approaches (Kemp, Loorbach, & Rotmans, 2007; Loorbach, 2010). McCool, Butler, Buckley, Weaver, and Wheeller (2013, p. 213) have questioned the saliency of the existing construct of 'sustainable tourism' to a rapidly changing twenty-first-century world and suggested "a reformulation of the concept to one of enhancing resiliency in the face of stresses and strains on communities." In this volume we have sought to contribute to the growing body of academic interest within the realm of sustainable tourism studies by conceiving resilience as a necessary component of sustainability planning and management. We have focused on issues of governance and how resilience can be built into practices of good governance that contribute to developing 'resilient destinations.' We interpret 'governance' as encompassing "the values, rules, institutions and processes through which public and private stakeholders seek to achieve common objectives and make decisions" (Gill & Williams, 2011, p. 631).

Resilience and governance strategies towards sustainability: challenges and opportunities

Given the varying research approaches applied to studies of sustainability and resilience, the earlier chapters of this book were designed to provide framing perspectives for the subsequent case studies. As Hall observes in his overview of resilience theory and tourism, "resilience has become a new buzzword in the lexicon of tourism studies" (see p. 34). However, he raises concerns regarding the inconsistent and often ambiguous use of the term. As with the term 'sustainability,' the application of the term 'resilience' across an array of disciplines has resulted in considerable "fuzziness" (Pendall, Foster, & Cowell, 2010), although some consider this lack of clarity acts to position resilience as a 'boundary object' that offers opportunities as a bridging concept to enhance discourse across disciplines. As Hall shows (see Table 3.1, p. 38), a major distinction in resilience models is between the 'engineering model,' which examines the speed of recovery following a shock to a state of equilibrium, and 'ecological resilience' that does not assume equilibrium. Most of the case studies in this volume are informed by aspects of social–ecological systems (SES) theory (Berkes & Folke, 1998; Gunderson & Holling, 2002; Holling, 1973).

Within the general framework of SES thinking, several authors adopt an 'evolutionary resilience' lens (Davoudi, 2012). This supports Lew's (2014) proposition that studies of resilience in a community tourism context should also encompass consideration of 'slow change' in order to provide a more comprehensive view of resilience. Evolutionary economic examinations of the dynamics of change are emerging across a range of social sciences disciplines. Geographers have extended these ideas to include place-based interpretations that are grounded in SES theory (e.g., Martin & Sunley, 2015; Simmie & Martin 2010). These approaches have recently been introduced into tourism studies (e.g. Brouder, Anton Clave, & Ioannides, 2017; Gill & Williams, 2014).

As Brouder and Saarinen discuss in Chapter 5, the combination of evolutionary economic geography and resilience thinking brings together environmental and regional perspectives with a focus on mechanisms of change and the agency of stakeholders. Evolutionary understanding of resilience is best represented through the panarchy model that describes the stages of the adaptive cycle (Gunderson & Holling, 2002). This depicts a system going though cyclical phases of change in structure and function, consisting of growth and exploitation; conservation; release or creative destruction; and reorganization. Viewed through an evolutionary resilience lens, the constructs of 'sustainability' and 'resilience' are seen as elements of complex adaptive systems that do not follow linear paths but have loops and stalls and readjustments of direction, with no steady state envisaged. Studies of evolutionary resilience challenge the idea of equilibrium and do not suppose a return to a previously normal state but focus on the adaptability of complex social–ecological systems to change and transform in response to stressors (Davoudi, 2012). This perspective aligns well with the understanding of transition management in sustainability planning (Loorbach, 2010; Van Assche, Beunen, & Duineveld, 2014). These phases also echo features found in Butler's (1980) early model of the destination area life-cycle model, although Butler's model was conceived as a linear and less complex process (Cochrane, 2010). Brouder and Saarinen (Chapter 5) stress the importance of viewing aspects of scope and scale in seeking to understand tourism and sustainability. This involves adopting a co-evolutionary approach that requires looking beyond the tourism sector to understand related impacts of other economic, environmental, and sociocultural systems. They argue further that destination resilience can only be understood in the context of regional evolution.

As Dredge highlights in her framing chapter on governance and resilience (Chapter 4), key considerations in resilience studies that inform the scope and nature of research relate to the key question, "What kind of resilience and for what/whom?" (see p. 60). To provide a comprehensive framework for examining resilience at a resort level, Wongkee and Gill, in their study of retail resilience (Chapter 10), adapted a broader destination resilience framework taken from Calgaro, Lloyd, and Dominey-Howes (2014), which consists of the following interrelated dimensions: scale; shocks and stressors; vulnerability – as expressed through elements of exposure and sensitivity; resilience in the form of adaptive capacity; and coping response. These dimensions offer a useful frame to synthesize and discuss the various findings from the contributions to this volume.

Scale, timeframe, type of shocks/stressors

In examining complex adaptive socio-economic systems, the issues of scale, time-frame, and type of shock are dimensions that define the scope of studies. As noted earlier Martin and Sunley (2015) observe that most resilience studies are at the local and regional level and, as Hall states, the majority of resilience research in tourism is at this level. However, he observes that "[g]iven its centrality as a framing concept in tourism studies, there is also surprisingly limited overt research on destinations" (Hall, Prayag, & Amore, 2018, p. 56). This raises the issue of what is meant by the term 'destination,' especially in the context of governance and resilience. Dredge (Chapter 4) addresses this conceptual fuzziness in terminology. In reflecting on broader conceptual issues, she adopts a non-scalar perspective on destinations, conceiving a destination not as a compartmentalized nested territorial concept but rather as sets of interconnected, networked, socio-economic practices simultaneously occurring on multiple scales. While much policy is place-based and enacted at a community and regional scale, understanding the governance of destination resilience through an SES lens requires consideration of multiple scales of complexity, with interaction between system components that are subject to regulation and policies which occur through networks that transcend regional, national, and international scales (Calgaro et al., 2014). Issues such as resilience to the impacts of climate change as discussed by Nalau, Movono, and Becken (Chapter 7) illustrate this scalar issue.

In the case studies presented in this volume, Haisch (Chapter 9), Wongkee and Gill (Chapter 10) and Sakuma (Chapter 12) address resilience at the community scale. On the other hand, Nalau, Movono, and Becken (Chapter 7), Nepal and Devkota (Chapter 8), and Heslinga, Groote, and Vanclay (Chapter 11) examine the regional scale. Although, acknowledging broader-scale policy contexts, all these studies focus on human agency and social dimensions that occur at the local scale. In seeking to uncover underlying factors in vulnerability and adaptive capacity, the timeframes examined ranged from a few months to 25 years. This may also reflect the focus on methods associated with research on human agency, which is based on interview techniques and accessible archival materials that capture memories and interpretations of past and current events. With the exception of Nepal and Devkota's contribution (Chapter 8) on the attitudes of local residents to disaster recovery efforts in the face of the shock and destruction associated with a recent major earthquake, all the other empirical studies address evolving stressors rather than sudden shocks and as such are well suited to an evolutionary resilience approach. This approach is especially appropriate for examining governance for sustainability and the capacity of traditional institutional frameworks and management processes to adapt to complex, changing, economic, environmental and political, social, demographic, and political realities.

Human agency: vulnerability and adaptive capacity

Vulnerability is the degree to which a system is likely to experience harm from exposure to a shock or stressor. This is affected by both the degree of exposure of the system to the stressor, as well as the sensitivity (the degree to which the stress will affect it). The various vulnerabilities discussed in the chapters in this volume cover a range of environmental shocks and stressors (e.g., earthquakes; the spectre of various climate change impacts; and the potential loss of conservation lands) as well as socio-economic shocks and stressors (e.g., global economic recession; labor shortages; changing market demand; national tourism policy changes; and political instability). As Wongkee and Gill observe (Chapter 10), "[u]nderstanding the vulnerabilities of the resilience of [a] system are necessary precursors to policy and planning intervention" (p. 148). Moreover, Heslinga, Groote, and Vanclay (Chapter 11) remind us of the need to historically examine and learn from the issues surrounding fluctuating attitudes and values as policies evolve. While the existence of environmental, social, and economic policies that reduce exposure and sensitivity to anticipated shocks and stressors are important institutional tools in building destination resilience, human agency also plays an important role in establishing social and cultural resilience, as demonstrated well in Sakuma's study in Japan (Chapter 12).

Adaptive capacity is dependent on the main social and institutional relationships within a destination and involves learning, innovation, and knowledge sharing (see Chapter 10). As Nepal and Devkota state (p. 106), despite exposure in Nepal to earthquakes and many social, economic, and political stability vulnerabilities,

> impacted communities may still retain significant resources and capital with which to facilitate response and recovery, including cultural and social capital. This is particularly true among communities that have had a long tradition of collective action, mutual interdependence, and social cohesion due to cultural ties and values.

The study of adaptive capacity is also central to Nalau, Movono, and Becken's work on resilience to climate change in the Pacific Islands (Chapter 7). They highlight the importance of incorporating indigenous traditional ecological knowledge and social systems into knowledge management and governance structures. In both these case studies the importance of cultural resilience is highlighted.

Sakuma's study of ecotourism development in Okinawa, Japan (Chapter 12), demonstrates the importance of human agency and adaptive capacity in developing resilience in the wake of changing national tourism policy. Although he uses a very different analytical lens associated with the contemporary geopolitics of human mobilities, Hannam (Chapter 6) also highlights the importance of cultural resilience in a tourism context.

As illustrated in Haisch's contribution on Swiss destinations (Chapter 9), collective agency plays a major role in the 'reorganization and restructuring phases' of the adaptive cycle model. She concludes that shared perceptions of threats and crises as well as shared agreements on informal values (growth-oriented or sustainable) and formal institutions enable transparent communications and lead to participation that augments the possibility of collective agency towards adaptation and resilience. Wongkee and Gill (Chapter 10) also conclude that, "ultimately, it is the collective capacity for collaboration, effective decision-making, and governance that influences the effectiveness of responses to stressors" (p. 148). Heslinga, Groote, and Vanclay (Chapter 11) reach similar conclusions: "the overall increase in synergies thinking relate[s] to collaboration, working together, and being involved" (p. 166).

Concluding remarks

In Chapter 4, Dredge challenges readers' assumptions concerning sustainability, tourism, resilience, and governance, urging them to engage in a more complex, critical, theoretically-curious, and interdisciplinary discussion around these topics. She raises the question, "*Can resilience be decoded into a framework that might assist tourism destinations to adapt and transform on their way to becoming more sustainable?*" (p. 49). Dredge presents two scenarios for critical review regarding how resilience might be framed: the Anthropocene, where seeking to address both socio-economic and ecological concerns is a major challenge; and, late modern capitalism – where, since the 1980s, neoliberalism, with its focus on capital accumulation and economic growth, reassigned nature to being in the service of capitalism. Her concerns over neoliberal regimes are echoed by Hall (Chapter 3) who notes the dangers associated with paradigm change with respect to destination management and the extent to which the notion of resilience may be used as an opportunity for the enactment of neoliberal regimes that, ironically, may only further contribute to the vulnerability of destinations to global change.

These are big topics and within the scope of this volume we have been challenged to find answers. We do, however, find common agreement among contributors that the key to advancing resilience thinking is grounded in collective human agency. This resonates with recent advances in evolutionary economic thinking associated with path creation (Garud & Karnøe 2001), and also with the findings of other recent studies on resilience and tourism destinations, such as that of Larsen, Calgaro, and Thomalla (2011) on Thailand's tsunami recovery which calls for greater recognition and integration of the role of stakeholder agency in resilience building. As Voss, Newig, Mondstadt, & Nolting (2007) observe, the challenges of steering the direction of sustainable governance lie in integrating conflicting values and dealing with risk, uncertainties, and ambivalence.

However, as Dredge (Chapter 4) and Hall (Chapter 3) both observe, transitioning towards sustainability is grounded in power and politics. As Bosselmann, Engel, & Taylor (2008) emphasize, the dominant form of governance in Western capitalist economies is representative democracy, which is not especially conducive to sustainability planning as it favours short-term gains over long-term responsibility because politicians' jobs depend on meeting the immediate needs of voters.

Walker and Salt (2006, p. 9) observe, "[t]he key to sustainability is enhancing the resilience of the social–ecological system (SES), not by optimizing isolated components of the system." They go on to say that despite recent advances in the sustainability debate, it is evident that examination through a resilience lens clearly reveals, "that we still have a way to go" (Walker & Salt, 2006, p. 9). In Chapter 4, Dredge echoes this sentiment – over a decade later. Indeed, there has been continuing debate over the concepts of both resilience and sustainability as they share similar attributes of being fuzzy, and broadly interpreted and misunderstood in diverse contexts. Although a contested construct, resilience can be perceived as an integral part of sustainability (Berkes & Ross, 2016) and a key element of pathway creation in the process of moving towards sustainable futures.

We think that sustainability is one of the most important issues currently facing the tourism sector. Indeed, the idea of sustainable development in tourism has emerged as a paradigm or way of thinking of development in tourism (Bianchi, 2004; Holden, 2003; Macbeth, 2005) and "there is increasing pressure on tourism planners, developers and managers to consider sustainability issues" (Moscardo, Konovalov, Murphy, & McGehee, 2013, p. 533). Based on its global growth, the need for the idea of sustainability in tourism is now more urgent than ever. Still, it is important to acknowledge that there is indeed a lack of progress in implementing the fuzzy and variously interpreted 'grand' concept of sustainability. However, instead of perceiving resilience and sustainability as conflicting or alternative models per se, the idea of resilience can be positioned as an integral part of sustainability and an element of pathway creation in the process of moving towards sustainable tourism. The chapters in this edited volume have focused on tourism governance and resilience issues; the contributions have aimed to offer a range of both theoretical and applied governance perspectives for resilient destinations that address various transformations in the policy and practice of tourism in the transition towards sustainability.

References

Berkes, F., & Folke, C (Eds.). (1998). *Linking social and ecological systems*. Cambridge, UK: Cambridge University Press.

Berkes, B., & Ross, H. (2016). Panarchy and community resilience: Sustainability science and policy implications. *Environmental Science and Policy, 61*, 185–193.

Bianchi, R. (2004). Tourism restructuring and the politics of sustainability: A critical view from the European periphery (the Canary Islands). *Journal of Sustainable Tourism, 12*, 495–529.

Bosselmann, K., Engel, R., & Taylor, P. (2008). *Governance for sustainability: Issues, challenges, successes.* Gland, Switzerland: IUCN.

Brouder, P., Anton Clave, S., Gill, A.M., & Ioannides, D. (Eds.). (2017). *Tourism destination evolution.* New York, NY: Routledge.

Butler, R.W. (1980). The concept of tourism area cycle of evolution: Implications for management of resources. *The Canadian Geographer, 24*(1), 5–12.

Calgaro, E., Lloyd, K., & Dominey-Howes, D. (2014). From vulnerability to transformation: A framework for assessing the vulnerability and resilience of tourism destinations. *Journal of Sustainable Tourism, 11*(3), 341–360.

Cochrane, J. (2010). The sphere of tourism resilience. *Tourism Recreation Research, 35*(2), 173–185.

Davoudi, S. (2012). Resilience: A bridging concept or a dead end? *Planning Theory & Practice, 13*(2), 299–307.

Garud, R., & Karnøe, P. (2001). Path creation as a process of mindful deviation. In R. Garud & P. Karnøe (Eds.), *Path dependence and creation* (pp. 1–41). Mahwah, NJ: Lawrence Erlbaum Associates.

Gill, A.M., & Williams, P.W. (2011). Rethinking resort growth: Understanding evolving governance strategies in Whistler, British Columbia. *Journal of Sustainable Tourism, 19*(4–5), 629–648.

Gill, A.M., & Williams, P.W. (2014). Mindful deviation in creating a governance path towards sustainability in resort destinations. *Tourism Geographies, 16*(4), 546–562.

Gunderson, L.H., & Holling, C.S. (2002). *Panarchy: Understanding transformations in human and natural systems,* Washington, DC: Island Press.

Hall, C.M., Prayag, G., & Amore, A. (2018). *Tourism and resilience: Individual, organizational and destination perspectives.* Bristol: Channel View Publications.

Holden, A. (2003). In need of new environmental ethics for tourism. *Annals of Tourism Research, 30*, 94–108.

Holling, C.S. (1973). Resilience and stability of ecological systems. *Annual Review of Ecology and Systematics, 4*(1), 1–23.

Kemp, R., Loorbach, D., & Rotmans, J. (2007). Transition management as a model for managing processes of co-evolution towards sustainable development. *International Journal of Sustainable Development and World Ecology, 14*, 1–15.

Larsen, R.K., Calgaro, E., & Thomalla, F. (2011). Governing resilience building in Thailand's tourism-dependent coastal communities: Conceptualising stakeholder agency in social–ecological systems. *Global Environmental Change, 21*, 481–491.

Lew, A.A. (2014). Scale change and resilience in community tourism planning. *Tourism Geographies, 16*(1), 14–22.

Loorbach, D. (2010). Transition management for sustainable development: A prescriptive, complexity-based governance framework. *Governance: An International Journal of Policy Administration and Institutions, 23*(1), 161–183.

Macbeth, J. (2005). Towards an ethics platform for tourism. *Annals of Tourism Research, 32*, 962–984.

McCool, S., Butler, R., Buckley, R., Weaver, D., & Wheeller, B. (2013). Is concept of sustainability utopian: Ideally perfect but impractical? *Tourism Recreation Research, 38*(2), 213–242.

Martin, R., & Sunley, P. (2015). On the notion of regional economic resilience: Conceptualization and explanation. *Journal of Economic Geography, 15*(1), 1–42.

Moscardo, G., Konovalov, E., Murphy, L., & McGehee, N. (2013). Mobilities, well-being and sustainable tourism. *Journal of Sustainable Tourism, 21*, 532–556.

Pendall, R., Foster, K., & Cowell, M. (2010). Resilience and regions: Building understanding of the metaphor. *Cambridge Journal of Regions, Economy and Society, 3*(1), 71–84.

Simmie, J., & Martin, R. (2010). The economic resilience of regions: Towards an evolutionary approach. *Cambridge Journal of Regions, Economy and Society, 3*(1), 27–43.

Van Assche, K., Beunen, R., & Duineveld, M. (2014). *Evolutionary governance theory: An introduction*. Cham, Switzerland: Springer.

Voss, J.P., Newig, J., Mondstadt, J., & Nolting, B. (2007). Steering for sustainable development and distributed power. *Journal of Environmental Policy & Planning, 9*(3–4), 193–212.

Walker, B., & Salt, D. (2006). *Resilience thinking: Sustaining ecosystems and people in a changing world*. Washington, DC: Island Press.

Index

For Product Safety Concerns and Information please contact our EU
representative GPSR@taylorandfrancis.com Taylor & Francis Verlag GmbH,
Kaufingerstraße 24, 80331 München, Germany

Printed and bound by CPI Group (UK) Ltd, Croydon, CR0 4YY
01/05/2025
01858426-0004